The Royal Family

A PERSONAL PORTRAIT

The Royal Family

A PERSONAL PORTRAIT

by Ralphe M. White and Graham Fisher

DAVID McKAY COMPANY, INC.

New York

THE ROYAL FAMILY: A Personal Portrait

Library of Congress Catalog Card Number: 78-79510

MANUFACTURED IN THE UNITED STATES OF AMERICA

VAN REES PRESS • NEW YORK

CONTENTS

Photographs between 120 and 121

The Royal Family

A PERSONAL PORTRAIT

1. THE QUEEN'S DAY

I

IT is not yet seven o'clock, and in that part of London dominated by Buckingham Palace the morning sun draws mist
from the still quiet streets as it did long ago from the marshy
swamp which once covered the area. At this hour of the day,
the streets which bound the palace—Buckingham Palace Road,
Grosvenor Place and Constitution Hill—are still almost deserted.
Not until nearly eight o'clock will the incoming commuters
start pouring out of nearby Victoria Station and hurry past
the tall black-and-gilt gates of the palace before short-cutting
through Green Park to their shops and offices in Piccadilly and
elsewhere.

The palace gates are not yet open for the day. Beyond the
gilded spikes which top the high railings, the blue-uniformed
bobby standing just inside the forecourt and the scarlet-clad
guardsmen in their sentry boxes are the only signs of life.

But inside, this many-roomed home of England's Queen—
so many rooms that even the Queen's husband, with his navy-
neat passion for accuracy, was content to settle for "more than

600" when he counted them—is shrugging off sleep and stirring for another day. For the past hour, some thirty housemaids in trim white overalls have been cleaning grates, dusting furniture, sweeping carpets with long-handled brushes (vacuum cleaners are not used where the Queen might hear them until later in the day) and otherwise combating the London dust and grime which penetrates palace and tenement alike. In the royal mews at the rear of the palace, hooves ring on the tarmacadam surface as top-hatted coachmen and postillions harness the Cleveland Bays and the famed Windsor Greys to Annie-Get-Your-Gun-type wagonettes for their morning exercise in nearby Hyde Park.

At the sight of a small boy on a bicycle circumnavigating the Victoria memorial at the head of the Mall, the duty bobby swings open the side gates of the palace for the day. (The larger centre gate is opened only for the Queen to drive through in state on occasions of high ceremony.) Whistling, as newsboys do in every country of the world, the youngster wheels across the forecourt to toss a rolled-up bundle of newspapers and magazines onto the red-carpeted steps of the sheltered porch outside the Privy Purse door.

Buckingham Palace has many doors. The Privy Purse door, through which an excited footman darted the night Prince Charles was born to yell "It's a boy!" to the waiting crowd, is perhaps the busiest of them all. Through it each day troop the men and women—secretaries and clerks, typists and telephonists —who run the business side of the Monarchy. The Queen herself usually enters and leaves by the Garden Entrance at the northeast corner of the palace. Prince Philip, when not accompanying his wife, prefers to use what is known as "The King's Door" a name handed down through the reigns of Edward VII, George V, the uncrowned monarch who became the Duke of Windsor, and the Queen's father, King George VI. When the present Queen succeeded to the throne it was suggested that "The King's Door" should be re-named "The Queen's Door." But she would not have it and the old name still remains as a memorial to the father to whom she was so devoted.

[2]

As the newsboy pedals off, a mail-van drives into the courtyard and stops in front of the palace post office on the southeast
side of the building. A succession of bulky hessian sacks marked
with the royal cypher—EIIR—is manhandled through the stone-
built portico for the duty postman, the legend "Buckingham
Palace" gold-embroidered on his breast pocket, to empty and
sort. Not all the mail is for the Queen herself, of course, but
most of it has to do with the complex business of monarchy.
Letters addressed to the Queen go direct to whichever of her
two personal pages—Pickwickian Ernest Bennett or his counterpart, John Taylor, tall and thin—is on duty that particular day.
It is the page's task to sift the Queen's personal mail from that
with which her secretaries and others can deal. He does so
merely by glancing through the envelopes with experienced
eyes. Both Bennett and Taylor have been with the Royal
Family since before the Queen came to the throne and can recognise the handwriting of royal relatives and close personal
friends at a glance.

Over the next hour or so, a miscellaneous succession of
vehicles enters the palace precincts by what is known as "The
Trade Door" (it is actually a wrought-iron gate) in Buckingham Palace Road . . . a butcher's van bringing the day's meat,
bottle-green vans from Windsor, the royal cypher on the door
panels, with flowers, fruit, vegetables and milk fresh from the
royal dairy herd. Every week or so, a lumbering tanker arrives
to pump fuel-oil into the mammoth heating plant, so polished
and burnished you could eat a meal off it, which is tucked away
beneath the palace forecourt. Three times a week, on average,
a truck arrives to dispose of the contents of the shoulder-high
garbage bins, mounted on wheels to make for easier handling.
Twice a week a van calls to collect and deliver the laundry . . .
sheets and pillowcases, tablecloths and table napkins, overalls
and aprons, personal laundry for members of the Queen's staff.
But nothing for the Queen herself. Her personal things are
hand-washed in the wardrobe room on the topmost of the three
main floors of the palace (there are actually five floors if you

include the labyrinthine basement and the attic-like eyries where the residential staff have their sleeping quarters).

Around 250 people are working in the palace at any given time, maids and cleaners, grooms and chauffeurs, footmen and pages, chefs and typists, window cleaners, upholsterers and gardeners. About half of them live in, with beds to be made, rooms to be dusted, meals to be cooked. So there have to be servants who simply wait on other servants, and only a small proportion of the staff in fact have anything to do with the Queen herself.

It is now nearly eight o'clock. In the 43-acre gardens, a royal footman is giving the Queen's corgis their morning run. The footman's made-to-measure scarlet tailcoat is a new design recently introduced by the Queen to replace the navy-blue battle-dress her father devised as a measure of wartime economy... and which remained unchanged for a quarter of a century.

In the basement coffee room—so-called because the royal coffee was ground there up to a generation ago—another footman is making tea in a small pink teapot. Then the teapot is set on an unsophisticated wooden tray, along with a pink cup and saucer, a silver spoon, a small pink jug of milk, and a matching basin of sugar lumps with silver tongs. The footman carries the tray the length of the basement and enters an elevator which takes him up to the second floor where the Queen's private apartment is located. At almost the same time the footman who has been exercising the dogs is on his way up from the garden in a second elevator. The two of them meet in a wide, red-carpeted corridor hung with oil paintings—among them a painting of Elizabeth's coronation ceremony in Westminster Abbey—which leads to the gilt-handled, white-painted door of the royal bedroom.

The tea-tray is deposited on a small round mahogany table just outside the bedroom door. The dogs are left sniffing expectantly at the door. The two footmen retreat. The marble and gilt clock outside the Queen's sitting room, a few yards along the corridor, strikes the hour of eight.

On the dot, like an actress who has been lurking in the wings awaiting her cue, Margaret MacDonald emerges from the nearer

[4]

of the two elevators. A woman of dignified mien, invariably smartly dressed, Miss MacDonald is Elizabeth's personal maid—"The Queen's Dresser." "Bobo," as the Queen calls her, has been loyally at Elizabeth's side for more than forty years ... since the Queen was a baby princess only a few weeks old. As a result, she has achieved a status unique among palace servants—a complex combination of servant, confidante and personal friend. Next to Prince Philip, there is no one who knows the Queen so intimately ... and even he has not known her as long.

The royal corgis scamper excitedly ahead as Bobo picks up the tea-tray, opens the door of the royal bedchamber and walks in.

II

The tea-tray is placed on Philip's side of the double bed above which draperies hang from a gilt crown. He acquired the habit of early-morning tea during his stint in the Navy. The Queen has nothing to drink until breakfast. Bobo crosses to the high windows and draws back the heavy drapes of creamy brocade before going through to the adjoining bathroom to run the Queen's bath and on into the dressing room to lay out the clothes the Queen will be wearing that day. Elsewhere in the royal apartment one of Philip's two valets is drawing his bath and laying out his clothes.

Her task completed, Bobo leaves the dressing room through a door giving directly on to the corridor and goes upstairs to her own suite (bedroom, bathroom and sitting room) immediately adjoining the three long, high-ceilinged "wardrobe rooms" in which the Queen's clothes are stored and maintained. These are Bobo's workrooms. Here are stored the scores of coats, suits, day dresses, evening gowns, kilts and tweeds, riding outfits and raincoats, feminine-styled military uniforms and billowing state gowns, the dozens of hats, shoes, gloves, head-scarves, umbrellas and jewel-handled parasols, handbags in all shapes and sizes in silk and satin, leather and crocodile, which the Queen will wear during the course of an average working year.

By now the rest of the palace is a hive of quiet activity. In the gloomy offices behind the Privy Purse Door downstairs a footman is distributing mail and newspapers against the imminent arrival of clerks and typists and private secretaries. In the royal nursery on the third floor, the children's nanny, cheerful, apple-cheeked Mabel Anderson, is sitting down to breakfast with the youngest of the Queen's four children, five-year-old Prince Edward.

Elsewhere in the palace, royal equerries and whichever of the Queen's Ladies-in-Waiting is living at the palace during her term of duty are sitting down to their breakfast. In the lofty white-walled royal kitchen, the Queen's personal chef, Ronald Aubrey, an amiable giant of a man, is getting ready to cook the royal breakfast on the huge, old-fashioned gas cooker which he swears by.

Unless the day's schedule calls for a particularly early start, the Queen and her husband breakfast always at nine o'clock. By then, the Queen has bathed, dressed and performed the essential feminine functions of brushing her hair and applying her makeup in front of a dressing table on which her silver-gilt hairbrushes, clothes brushes, hand mirror and tortoiseshell combs are set out with almost military precision around the gold-topped, cut-glass containers which hold her cosmetics.

Her hair is light brown and naturally wavy. Whatever the current fashion, she always wears it parted in the centre and clear of the shoulders. Her eyes are blue with just a hint of green, her lashes long and luxuriant. She has the characteristic Windsor nose and a wide, generous mouth. Seen close to, her most striking feature is her flawless peaches-and-cream outdoor-girl complexion.

Except when she is attending a state banquet or some similar public function, her makeup takes no more than a few minutes. She is the type of woman who would rather have the wind and rain on her cheeks than rouge and powder. Normally she relies upon a peach-coloured liquid foundation which she dusts over with peach-coloured powder. A touch of blue-grey mascara enhances her eyes. Another touch of pinky-red lipstick does for her mouth. She seldom uses other than clear, natural nail-varnish and the barest trace of a light, floral perfume.

The Queen is without doubt one of the most-photographed women in the world. Every day, for one reason or another, her picture is seen in newspapers and magazines from Alaska to Australia, from Finland to Fiji. In consequence, there are few people this side of the Iron Curtain to whom her features are not familiar. She is, however, much smaller than she appears in photographs—some 5 feet 3 inches in her stocking feet (though three-inch heels lend her additional height on public occasions). She has slender feet, small, delicate hands, an upright carriage, a crisp, purposeful walk, and a full-bosomed figure to which her clothes rarely do justice. Once in a while she will wear a gown which really becomes her figure ... and the resulting photograph goes round the world.

About her there is an air of regal serenity which you feel nothing can disturb, though in fact two things can and do ... unnecessary noise and unpunctuality on the part of others. She betrays her impatience by twisting her engagement ring, a large square-cut diamond, round and round on her finger. Her father, if he was kept waiting, had the habit of twisting his large gold signet ring with his other hand. The Queen has refined the trick until she can do it merely with quick flicks of the little finger on the same hand.

It may sound corny to say that at heart she is a woman of very simple tastes. Yet it is true. Despite the vastness of her wardrobe, she has little real liking for dressing up and queening it, and is happiest at one of her country homes—Sandringham House on Britain's bleak, windswept eastern coast, or the heathery acres of Balmoral Castle in Scotland—in old, favourite, time-tested clothes: comfortable tweeds and free-swinging kilts, stout, flat-heeled walking brogues, belted raincoats and colourful head-squares.

I recall an occasion at Sandringham when the Queen was going out on a day of cold, blustery rain squalls. She came downstairs wearing her favourite raincoat, thin and rather drab. As I opened the door for her to go out to the waiting car, the outside cold hit her. She hesitated a moment, glancing down at the raincoat.

"I don't think I'll be warm enough in this," she said. "Run upstairs and fetch me something warmer, will you, please?"

I hurried upstairs and told Bobo MacDonald that the Queen wanted a warmer coat. She opened a closet and brought out one of the luxuriant royal minks. I draped it over my arm and went downstairs again.

A look of horror flitted across the Queen's face as she saw the mink. "Oh, no—not that," she said. "I look too much like a film star in mink." Nothing would satisfy her but I must take it back and bring her a tweed coat instead.

As with clothes, so with jewellery. The Queen's personal collection of jewellery (not to be confused with the Crown Jewels) is almost certainly the most valuable in the Western world. Stored in a tall safe hidden behind an innocent-looking white-painted door in Buckingham Palace, carefully catalogued in a series of leather-bound books embossed with her personal cypher, it is a collection which even a mediaeval Eastern potentate might envy ... a shimmering cascade of diamonds and emeralds, rubies, sapphires and pearls. Not even the Queen herself can place an accurate valuation on the scores of tiaras, necklaces, earrings, brooches, bracelets and watches.

Yet for her workaday life around the palace she prefers to cling to a few favourite pieces ... a pearl necklace, a gift from her father, with small matching earrings (her ears were pierced in childhood), a sapphire and diamond brooch handed down from her great-great-grandmother, Queen Victoria, and a gold and platinum wristwatch, whose minute face, only three-sixteenths of an inch in diameter, is said to be the smallest in the world.

The watch is in fact the second of its kind. The first, a childhood gift from the people of France, was lost at Sandringham in circumstances which may seem curious to those who do not know the Queen intimately. She was out with her dogs on one of those long cross-country walks she enjoys so much. She had walked several miles and her way home lay past the corner of a field where farm-workers were threshing corn. Rats scampered in all directions and the countrywoman hidden only skin-deep under the veneer of royalty reacted characteristically. One by one Elizabeth lifted her dogs over the intervening wire-mesh fence to chase the rats.

After about half an hour the Queen retrieved her dogs and set off back home. She had not gone far when she paused to look at her watch . . . only to find it was missing. Hurriedly she retraced her steps, scanning the ground as she went. At the cornfield, when she explained what had happened, the farm-workers suspended their threshing operations to search the stubble around where the Queen had been standing, but dusk fell without a sign of the treasured royal watch. In the days which followed, police, Boy Scouts and village folk from miles around joined in the search. The Army was called in to comb the area with mine detectors. Without result. The Queen's watch has never been found to this day, but the French, with true Gallic gallantry, duly presented her with an exact replica during a subsequent royal visit to France.

That visit to France, incidentally, yielded yet another example of the Queen's modesty in the matter of clothes. One of the functions arranged for her entertainment was an evening boat trip along the Seine. She planned to wear something new and strikingly different from anything she had worn before, a slim-fitting, figure-hugging gown in shimmering silver lamé created for her by fashion designer Norman Hartnell.

For the Queen, so exotic a gown was a revolutionary departure from tradition, but at fittings preceding the trip she seemed happy enough about it. Then, at almost the last moment, she jibbed, and raised her old defence that it would make her look too much like a movie star. Instead, she opted for one of the more traditional gowns she had brought with her, a bulky royal crinoline.

It was left to Bobo to persuade her to wear the Hartnell. No one else—not even Philip—could possibly have done so, for the Queen, once her mind is set on a thing, is a difficult woman to shift. But Bobo finally shifted her . . . with what was tantamount to a stroke of genius. "If you wear a crinoline," she said, "you're going to have difficulty getting up the narrow gangplank onto the boat."

The Queen wanted nothing of that sort. She had already had one slightly embarrassing episode in Paris in wriggling in and out of the official car provided for her, low and small by royal standards, while wearing a voluminous crinoline and a tall tiara. So she settled for the new, slim, shimmering gown . . . and the picture she made that night as she sailed, flood-lit, along the River Seine, was one Cleopatra could not have rivalled.

III

Prince Philip bathes and shaves to the music of a small transistor radio. He switches it on as soon as he gets out of bed, and carries it with him from bedroom to bathroom to dining room, though the music is perhaps less important to him than the news bulletins. He sits down to breakfast in his bathrobe, a tall (6 feet 1 inch), slim-hipped, long-bodied, athletic-looking man with quick, restless movements. The Queen, by contrast, is already dressed for the day when she walks through to breakfast in her private dining room with its walls of pink silk.

With his fiftieth birthday coming up in 1971, Philip is still surprisingly youthful-looking despite the fact that his straight blond hair is receding rapidly, as his father's did before him. He has a tight, uncompromising mouth and the long Mountbatten nose inherited from his mother. Penetrating blue eyes lurk behind the tinted lenses he so frequently wears in public. The short, stubby fingers with which he picks up his knife and fork at breakfast-time belie the artistic sensitivity hidden behind the rugged, sportsmanlike exterior he reveals to the world at large.

The royal couple breakfast side by side at an oval-shaped mahogany table, which can be extended to seat ten on the infrequent occasions when they have relatives or close friends to dinner. For breakfast, they are separated only by a small occasional table on which the day's newspapers are piled, from the mass-selling tabloid *Daily Mirror* to the lofty *Times*, and not forgetting *The Sporting Life* with its closely-printed lists of horse-racing results and runners.

The striking of the quadrangle clock is the signal for the Queen's piper, Pipe-Major Andrew Pitkeathly of the Argyll and Sutherland Highlanders, to strike up on the bagpipes. For the next fifteen minutes, while the royal couple breakfast, Pitkeathly, a magnificent figure in Highland garb, paces back and forth beneath the dining-room window, in accordance with a tradition which dates back to Queen Victoria, skirling a selection of Scottish airs on his pipes.

No servants wait on the Queen and Philip at breakfast . . . nor, for that matter, at dinner if they have no guests. Instead, they serve themselves from covered silver dishes kept warm on an electric hot-plate. Philip pours his own coffee, white for breakfast, black after lunch or dinner, adding his own sugar. The Queen brews her favourite China tea, which she takes with milk but not sugar, in a small silver teapot which she carefully warms first in the English tradition. The electrically operated silver kettle she uses for this purpose, cunningly mounted on a swivel stand to make for easy pouring, was a brainchild of her inventive husband.

They eat from plates edged with gold, and drink from large breakfast cups of like design. Each item of chinaware carries the Queen's EIIR cypher surmounted by a small gold crown. The knives and forks are of solid silver, as are their individual condiment sets. The value of the breakfast silverware alone runs into several thousand dollars. A twin to the Queen's silver teapot, for instance, was valued by experts at £800 (around $1900) when it was shown on a television programme devoted to antiques.

Yet in other respects breakfast is no more elaborate than in millions of ordinary British homes. Indeed, compared with the massive meals wolfed by many industrial workers, the royal breakfast is simple enough, even meagre. There is no initial bowl of porridge or cereal, as in many homes, nor even an American-style glass of orange juice (a habit fast catching on in Britain). Instead, the Queen and her husband start straight in on their main course. Even with this, there is no free range of choice, the meal being pre-set to a menu approved by the Queen the previous day. Eggs abound on the royal breakfast menu. Sometimes they come with bacon, sometimes with sausages, sometimes they are boiled (in which case the royal couple will have two each), sometimes scrambled. Occasionally, by way of a change, there are kippers. Both of them are quite fond of kippers for breakfast and the Queen, as you will have gathered, is extremely partial to eggs, though there was one occasion, I recall, when she got rather more than she had bargained for.

The Queen was paying a state visit to Sweden, and I had gone with her. We were staying at the royal palace in Stockholm, and the night of our arrival I was asked what the Queen would like for breakfast the following morning.

"Eggs," I said. "She loves eggs."

The message was duly relayed to the Swedish royal chef, who presumably decided to ensure that his eggs were exactly the way the Queen would want them. In consequence, there were eggs galore for breakfast the following morning ... boiled eggs, fried eggs, poached eggs, scrambled eggs, omelette.

At Buckingham Palace, as in many less regal homes, breakfast ends with toast and marmalade. The marmalade is thick and chunky. The butter, from the royal farm at Windsor, is served up in dainty pats each embossed with a miniature crown. Sometimes, as a change from marmalade, Philip will opt for honey on his toast, and both honey and marmalade are plonked on the table still in the jars in which they were bought—a striking contrast to the dainty china and elegant silverware surrounding them on the royal breakfast table.

Unlike some past British monarchs, whose main contribution to history seems to have been the size of their appetites, neither the Queen nor her husband is a big eater. Indeed, Prince Philip, considering the amount of energy he burns up in a day of non-stop work and play (which not infrequently runs to eighteen hours), hardly seems to eat enough to keep him going. Food has little appeal for him save as necessary fuel to keep the princely machine ticking over, and I am sure he would be just as happy if he could simply swallow a couple of pills at mealtime and keep right on going.

What little he does eat he is rather inclined to gobble. I remember one morning when the bell rang during breakfast to summon a servant, a rare occurrence. I answered it to find the two of them sitting at the breakfast table with their plates of bacon and eggs already in front of them.

"No toast," snapped Prince Philip, who is apt to be a trifle grumpy early in the morning.

"Sorry, Your Royal Highness," I said apologetically. "I'll fetch it immediately."

I raced to the coffee room, a corridor, two flights of stairs and the length of the Grand Hall away, a total of perhaps one-eighth of a mile. The toast was ready and waiting. I arranged it on a silver tray and raced back. The whole performance could not have taken more than four minutes. But Philip, his bacon and egg finished, was already on his way out of the dining room when I arrived.

"Too late, too late," he snapped.

The royal breakfast is a quiet meal, broken only by music from Philip's radio, the rustle of newspapers, and the occasional growl from Philip if he reads something which is not to his liking. He usually turns first to the tabloid *Daily Mirror*, which, though it may criticise him from time to time, has been reasonably kind to him over the years—unlike the Beaverbrook newspapers, which have seemed to be engaged in a constant feud with him.

Predictably, a sharp attack in one of the morning newspapers does nothing to improve Philip's temper. Though he pretends otherwise, he strongly resents criticism, and his reactions are sometimes volcanic. He will slam the breakfast table with his fist and let rip in a voice which penetrates even the thick doors of the royal apartment.

"Listen to what this bloody fool says," he roars in the rich seagoing language which is a hangover from his Navy days, and proceeds to read out the offending item for his wife's benefit.

The Sporting Life, on which the Queen mainly concentrates, occasions no such outbursts from her.

IV

The Queen, when she first came to the Throne, set herself a number of personal rules to ensure that the time-consuming duties of monarchy should not be permitted to thwart her natural feelings of motherhood. From the outset, she arranged that her children—there were only Charles and Anne then—should be brought down to see her each morning immediately after breakfast. She arranged to see them again at five o'clock, when her working day normally ends, for tea, television and a ninety-minute playtime.

These habits she continued, in turn, with Andrew and Edward when they were born. With Andrew, until he was of an age to start lessons in the nursery schoolroom as a prelude to boarding school, this breakfast-time get-together turned into an informal teaching session involving a small blackboard and easel fitted with a clock face and a counting frame of coloured beads. The Queen would have the blackboard and easel set up alongside the breakfast table, lift Andrew onto her knee and proceed to give him some fifteen minutes of motherly tuition in such childhood subjects as counting, spelling and telling the time . . . a practice which she continued later with Edward, the baby of the family.

The sound of the marble clock in the corridor outside the

royal apartment striking ten o'clock is a signal for the Queen to aise from the breakfast table and go through the white-painted communicating door which leads to her sitting room.

The sitting room also doubles as her study. It is a friendly, cluttered room in which the warm intimacy of family photographs, piled-up magazines, sleeping dogs and, occasionally, children's toys vies with the dignified solemnity of leather-covered dispatch boxes and state papers.

It is a feminine room. There is a glittering chandelier of Waterford glass. A deep, comfortable mushroom-coloured settee and matching armchairs flank the elegant marble fireplace in which logs burn in winter to provide that sense of comfort which central heating lacks. A portrait of the Queen as a young princess hangs on one wall, balancing the handsome gilt-framed mirror suspended above the porcelain cockerels which strut on the marble mantelpiece. Ranged alongside the fireplace is a handsome Hepplewhite cabinet, a joint wedding gift from no fewer than forty-seven members of the Royal Family, in which Elizabeth displays her collection of china and porcelain horses.

Everywhere there are flowers. A vase of long-stemmed carnations jostles with the family photographs, the twin telephones (one fitted with a scrambler device for secret conversations), and the scarlet-crested notepaper on the desk. Other flowers— carnations or roses, freesia or chrysanthemums, perhaps gift orchids from a loyal subject—are dotted here and there about the spacious, high-ceilinged, tall-windowed room.

In the privacy of her sitting room, from now until lunchtime, the Queen tackles an endless spate of letters and documents, sees her Private Secretary, Lieutenant Colonel the Right Honourable Sir Michael Adeane, her two Assistant Private Secretaries, Lieutenant Colonel the Honourable Sir Martin Charteris and Mr. Philip Moore, plans her future schedule, and plugs away at the contents of the leather-bound dispatch boxes which have pursued her inexorably since she first came to the Throne. A change of pace comes with a visit to the Audience Room, farther along the corridor, to receive official visitors, of whom there are seldom less than half a dozen in any one morning.

With Philip out and about on his own busy round of engagements, the Queen usually lunches alone. She does not bother with soup as a starter or dessert to finish. Instead, she contents herself with a main course of meat (lamb is her favourite) and vegetables eaten with a side plate of salad in the American fashion, followed by crackers and cream cheese. A glass of orange squash takes the place of wine, and she seldom has coffee, though it is there on the sideboard should she want it.

Lunch is sometimes followed by a spatter of public engagements in or near London. Monday afternoons are usually kept free for her hairdresser who maintains her hair in an easily managed, centre-parted style which goes equally well with crown or head-scarf. Other afternoons, especially if a royal tour is in prospect—and there are seldom periods of any length when one is not—are taken up with her shoemaker, Edward Rayne, her milliner, French-born Simone Mirman, and her two fashion designers, Norman Hartnell and Hardy Amies. Fresh-faced and broad-shouldered, Hartnell looks more like a country squire or gentleman farmer than a top fashion designer, but behind his ruggedly outdoor appearance lurks a man of almost Old World Victorian charm. Hardy Amies, perhaps better known these days for his mass-produced male fashions than for those he designs so exclusively for the Queen, is gayer, wittier, more of a dandy. But again looks are slightly deceptive, as Resistance fighters in wartime Belgium could testify. Amies made five parachute drops into German-held territory to work and fight with the Resistance.

Hartnell has been designing clothes for the Queen since she was a small girl who fidgeted restlessly during fittings and would dart away to the nearest window at the first hint of horses' hooves in the palace courtyard. Today, in her forties, she is still far more enthusiastic about horses than ever she is about high fashion, though she no longer fidgets during fittings, betraying some slight show of exasperation only if pins are left littering her dressing-room carpet after the designers and fitters have left. This is a rare occurrence—only if someone forgets to go over the carpet with the customary magnet.

Despite her lack of interest in clothes, the Queen's fashion sense has sharpened considerably in recent years under the persuasion of her designers, the influence of Prince Philip, and the prodding coercion of the indefatigable Bobo. As a young princess and even into her early days of monarchy, she was influenced mainly by her mother in matters of fashion . . . and what became the mother did not always become the daughter. The Queen Mother is a flamboyant dresser who can carry off frills and furs, buttons and bows, voluminous crinoline dresses and enormous cartwheel hats with experienced ease. Worn by the Queen, such fashions have sometimes seemed ungainly and at times verged on the faintly ridiculous.

Norman Hartnell, describing his earlier years as a royal designer, has said in his polite, carefully diplomatic fashion, "One did not feel she was interested in clothes. She was happiest, one felt, in country tweeds and very simple things." That still holds true today. But there can be no denying that the Queen, when dressed to impress on some occasion of state, her gown slashed by the blue ribbon of the Garter, one of her twenty or so diamond tiaras winking on her head, a fortune in diamonds and rubies sparkling at her throat, provides a truly dazzling spectacle. Yet she is no fashion setter . . . nor would she wish to be. Indeed, it has been said, and not without a grain of truth, that the only trend she has ever launched has been that of the headscarf.

Over her years of experience as a monarch Elizabeth has formulated her own set of rules governing the clothes she wears. Dresses and coats must allow her to sit as well as stand with dignity, to climb in and out of cars without the slightest risk of embarrassment. Skirts liable to billow in a high wind must be weighted with tiny lead pellets, though there have been odd occasions when a particularly strong wind has regarded the pellets as a distinct challenge to flirt with the royal legs. There

[17]

must be no frills or flounces which might catch on projections as she tours factories and construction sites. Handbags must have straps or handles to slip over the arm, leaving her hands free for handshakes and bouquets. For this reason, clutch handbags and wrap-over coats are definitely out. Colours must be sharp and clear, easily visible at a distance. Gloves must be white—so that every wave of the Queen's hand is glimpsed by the crowds who flock to see her. Hats must be small, off-the-face creations so that the famous features are never hidden. Only at Ascot, at the races, is the rule about hats occasionally broken. For Ascot, which is as much a fashion parade as a race meeting, the Queen sometimes bows to fashion to the extent of wearing an elegant, wide-brimmed hat, ingeniously held in place by two spring clips so that she never has to clutch at it with her hands.

Other afternoons of the Queen's working week are taken up with overseeing the running of the palace. At least once a month, the Queen goes over her household accounts with Lord Tryon, the tall, heavily-built Keeper of the Privy Purse. They are queen-sized accounts, running into thousands of dollars a week. Once a week, on average, she sees the Master of the Household, Brigadier Geoffrey Hardy-Roberts, to discuss problems of staff and housekeeping. From time to time during these sessions, the Queen will send for the "breakages book," which lists any of the valuable china or glass about the palace which may have been broken, chipped, or lost. In fact, breakages are rare and missing items even rarer.

I do recall one occasion when a gold plate went astray after a palace banquet, though the subsequent explanation for its disappearance proved to be innocent enough. Another footman, feeling in need of some refreshment, had taken some left-over ice cream up to his room when he went off duty. Having eaten the ice cream, he popped the plate into a cupboard and promptly forgot all about it until twenty-four hours later when the general turmoil below stairs, as everyone searched frantically for the missing plate, jogged his memory.

V

Just as it has always been the Queen's practice to see her children at breakfast-time each day, so she has had them around her in turn ... Charles and Anne, then Andrew, now Edward ... for the daily ritual of afternoon tea, chatting with them as she nibbles a cucumber sandwich and sips tea from a cup of delicate Chinese porcelain. The Queen's workday may not be entirely over—there will still be the odd document to peruse, the odd letter to sign in the course of the evening—but five o'clock is the signal for the study to revert back to a sitting room, for afternoon tea to arrive on a silver tray, and for five-year-old Edward to join his mother. It also marks the little royal ceremony of "feeding the dogs," a task the Queen insists on carrying out herself despite the dozens of palace servants who could do it as easily.

Promptly at five o'clock a uniformed footman parades along the red-carpeted corridor leading to the royal suite bearing a tray on which reposes freshly cooked meat, biscuit meal and a container of hot, steaming gravy. The tray is set down on a cradle outside the Queen's door while the royal corgis wait in restless anticipation. The Queen emerges from her sitting room and proceeds to dole out the meat, meal and gravy into separate bowls with the aid of a silver fork and spoon. Each corgi has its own feeding bowl, which the Queen carefully sets down on a small mat of white plastic design to protect the richly red carpet.

Teatime also involves the Queen in the ritual of selecting the royal meals for the following day. Suggested menus reach her in a leather-covered book in which the royal chef, Ronald Aubrey, usually lists three choices for each of the following day's meals. The Queen has merely to cross out those dishes she does not want. Mostly she is quite content to settle for one or other of Aubrey's suggestions, though occasionally—very occasionally —she will cross out all three and add some suggestion of her own in her scrawled, almost illegible, handwriting.

Afternoon tea is usually followed—and will be until Edward, too, goes off to school—by a trip to the royal nursery on the floor above for games and stories until Edward's bedtime. If Philip is home, the nursery session is postponed in favour of the heated indoor swimming pool at the northeast corner of the palace in which he has taught each child in turn to swim.

Philip is the sort of father any kid would adore . . . and the royal children are no exception to the rule. More than the Queen, he has a natural, easy ability to come down to the simpler level of childhood without seeming either patronizing or condescending. No matter how many royal duties he undertakes, he always manages to sandwich in time for the children . . . though fatherhood, too, can have its drawbacks, as Philip found out the evening eager, chocolate-coated fingers clutched excitedly at the snowy-white front of the fresh evening shirt he had donned prior to hurrying off to yet another public engagement. There was another occasion when Andrew's small, sturdy fist came into somewhat violent contact with the paternal eye during a bedtime bout of fisticuffs. That evening Philip was obliged to appear at a charity film show sporting something not far removed from the traditional Cockney "shiner."

Over the years, he has been a father to his children in the fullest sense of the word, helping them and guiding them each step of the way—and, if necessary, administering the occasional corrective spanking. Never one to be intimidated by the pomposity of royal surroundings, he has joined gleefully in impromptu football games played amongst the marble busts and valuable antique furnishings in the wide, red-carpeted corridors at Windsor; he has bounded through the royal shrubberies, whooping noisily, as he participated in boisterous games of Cowboys and Indians.

Sometimes, like all fathers, he has been rather inclined to dominate the proceedings. I remember Charles and Anne, when they were younger, emerging from the converted air-raid shelter at Windsor which was then their playroom. Showpiece of this basement playroom was a magnificent tabletop model of Gibraltar with an electrically operated railway on which no fewer than three model trains could be set in motion at one time.

Spying the children's crestfallen looks, their mother asked, "What's wrong? I thought you were going to play with your trains."

"We were," Charles replied, glumly. "But now Papa's taken over."

On a more edifying level, Philip has taught each of his children to swim so that they perform almost like fish in the water. He had taught Charles and Anne how to drive a car long before they were of an age to be permitted on a public highway. He has taught Charles something of the manly arts of shooting, fishing and helmsmanship, as well as his own particularly dashing brand of polo. While Charles was still only a nipper, his father had a miniature polo stick made for him, and the two of them, father and son, would circle each other on bicycles, slamming away at a ball.

These days, the Queen undertakes comparatively few evening engagements. Philip has more, but there are still evenings when there is nothing to keep him away from home. Occasionally, on such evenings, the royal couple will have guests to dinner, perhaps relatives like the Queen Mother; Princess Margaret and Lord Snowdon; Philip's uncle, Earl Mountbatten of Burma; or the Queen's cousin, Princess Alexandra, and her husband, company director Angus Ogilvy; perhaps personal friends like Lord Rupert Nevill and his wife, Anne, an American on her mother's side, or Major and Mrs. David Butter.

If they have guests for dinner, the Queen and her husband will change into evening dress. Elizabeth wears a short evening gown, Philip either a black tuxedo or a green velvet smoking jacket (though in fact he no longer smokes). But if they are on their own, they do not bother to change, though the Queen Mother, just along the road at Clarence House, still clings steadfastly to the old tradition of changing for dinner even when she has only the television set for company.

At Buckingham Palace, when the Queen and Philip are dining

alone, the meal is a curious mixture of old-world royal pomp and modern down-to-earth simplicity. The tall five-stemmed candelabrum in the centre of the table and the four miniature guardsmen which flank it are all fashioned in solid silver. The cutlery and condiment sets are equally of silver. The glassware is gleaming crystal, the plates gold-rimmed, bearing Elizabeth's royal crown and EIIR cypher. But nine evenings out of ten there are no servants in sight (though there is at least one within summons outside the white-painted door of the dining room) and there is nothing exotic or even luxurious about the food to which the Queen and Philip help themselves from the covered silver dishes on the sideboard hot-plate. Such delicacies as caviar, oysters, champagne and out-of-season strawberries are conspicuous only by their absence. Even pheasant is not served out of season, though several hundred brace of birds, shot on various royal estates, are tucked away in cold storage against the certainty of future state banquets.

Instead of such luxuries, the royal couple, skipping any suggestion of a first course, move straight on to a main course of perhaps lamb cutlets, perhaps creamed chicken, perhaps filet steak, served with a side plate of salad and not more than three accompanying vegetables. Neither of them is over-fond of pies, puddings or ice cream, and a further savoury dish—perhaps kidneys rolled in bacon or scrambled egg with anchovies—follows in place of the customary dessert. Fruit—an apple for the Queen, a few grapes for Philip—concludes the meal. Philip usually has a glass of white wine—hock or Moselle—with dinner, though he clings to beer at lunchtime. The Queen will sometimes join him in a glass of wine, but more frequently confines herself to orange squash or a glass of water.

The meal over, Philip rings for coffee. It is brought in by a uniformed page, the only servant to be glimpsed throughout the meal. The Queen has her coffee white without sugar; Philip usually has it black but sweet.

Philip rings again—a double ring this time—as a signal that they are adjourning to the sitting room next door. It is, by then, nine o'clock or a little after. The Queen goes first to her desk to check whether an urgent letter or state paper has arrived during dinner, and usually spends a few minutes dealing with matters left over from her working hours, often a batch of photographs to be signed and sent off as thank-you gifts to people who have hosted her recently. That done, she moves over to the settee by the marble fireplace, kicks off her shoes, and sits with her feet up.

Philip darts nimbly through to his own study, where he has a built-in cocktail cabinet, fixes himself a drink—usually whisky and water—and carries it back to the armchair directly across from his wife. The armchair is his favourite seat for the evening unless, at some point, the two of them decide to watch television. Then he invariably switches to a tapestry-covered stool which gives him a better view of the 23-inch screen.

The royal couple are selective viewers, switching on only occasionally for current-affairs programmes, natural-history programmes, plays they consider worthwhile, or the occasional comedy or variety show. However, both were so keen to see the *Life and Times of Earl Mountbatten of Burma,* when this historic story of Philip's uncle was recently screened in Britain, that the Queen took the (for her) unprecedented step of bringing dinner forward fifteen minutes on Wednesday evenings to ensure that they were through eating in good time for nine o'clock viewing. If there is nothing they wish to see on television, they talk together on family matters, read the evening newspapers, or leaf through the pile of magazines (including *Time, Life* and *Look*) which is kept constantly up-to-date on the long occasional table at the back of the settee.

Sooner or later, the Queen will almost certainly settle down to a crossword puzzle. She is addicted to them and carries a batch of newspapers containing unfinished puzzles between sitting room and bedroom, palace and castle, train and yacht, wherever she goes. Philip, who likes to spend his time to more purpose, will perhaps fetch the draft for some future speech from his study and work on that. The silence of the sitting room is broken only by intermittent conversation as the Queen, stumped for a word, appeals to her husband for help, or Philip, delighted with some phrase he considers particularly telling, insists upon reading it out for his wife's approbation.

Bedtime for the royal couple on these evenings is seldom later than half-past ten. The Queen's bedtime is also a signal to those whose lives revolve around her—the Equerry for the day, the duty page—that they can stand down. Others less immediately involved—footmen and maids, chefs and chauffeurs—have long since been free to lead their personal lives. The days when almost the whole of the palace staff had to be at their posts until the monarch retired for the night are long since over and done with.

But for a small, important handful of royal staffers the day's work is just beginning. In the palace post office, the telephone operator and a telegraph clerk will be on duty throughout the night. A burly police sergeant emerges from the police lodge, enters the palace and takes the elevator up to the second floor. For him a long, lonely vigil lies ahead sitting wakefully on the red velvet settee just outside the door of the royal bedroom.

Night watchmen patrol the rest of the huge palace throughout the night, and police dogs with their handlers prowl the darkened grounds. A scarlet-coated guardsman does sentry-go beneath the Queen's windows while other guardsmen pace their measured tread at the front and back of the palace. In the distance, Big Ben chimes the hour of midnight. The wrought-iron gates of the palace close with a slight clang, but high above the famous balcony, focal point of British emotions on occasions of national sadness or jubilation, the Royal Standard stirs faintly in the night breeze on its 75-foot flagpole . . . a sign that the Queen is in residence and that Britain's age-old monarchy is still a living thing.

2. THE QUEEN'S HOUSEHOLD

I

WHEN I first went to work at Buckingham Palace as a young, raw footman in the fall of 1946 I was completely over-awed by the vastness of the place. I felt sure that I should never be able to find my way around that complex maze of red-carpeted corridors and stairways. But one of the older hands on the palace staff gave me some useful and comforting advice.

"Remember that the palace is built in the form of a square," he said, "and you can't go far wrong. Just follow your nose, my lad, and you're bound to arrive back where you started from."

Like most helpful advice, however, it was only partly true. Seen from the air, Buckingham Palace is indeed built in the form of a hollow square, but viewed from the level of a new and in-experienced footman, the square becomes a cube, an architectural labyrinth. In time I managed to find my way around without difficulty, but the theory of how I did so still eludes me. After fifteen years spent darting and dashing about those corridors and staircases, I still cannot figure out how two people entering the palace at street level, one through the Privy Purse Door in the northeast corner of the building and one by the kitchen door in the opposing southwest corner, can walk steadily towards each other without ever meeting. Somewhere at the back of the palace they pass each other, unseen, on different floors. By the same token, two members of the staff can enter separate elevators in the palace basement. One rides up three floors; the other rides up four. Yet both come out in the servants' quarters on the topmost floor.

No wonder that temporary footmen, hired to help out on the occasion of a state banquet, not infrequently lose their way during the long trek from the lofty kitchens to the State Ballroom, perhaps ending up by mistake in the Grand Hall on the floor below or perhaps wandering bemusedly about the rabbit-warren of staff bedrooms on the topmost floor. No wonder that the Duchess of Devonshire, during the twelve years she held the traditional post of Mistress of the Robes, always insisted on being conducted to her suite each time she visited the palace. No wonder that the present Queen's grandmother, Queen Mary, when she first went to live at the palace, was lost for the best part of an hour after taking a wrong turning.

Successive royal owners have seldom had a kind word to say about their palace home. King Edward VII referred to it disparagingly as "The Sepulchre." George V talked about pulling the place down and going to live at Kensington Palace. Edward VIII (who became the Duke of Windsor) complained of the "dank, musty smell." The Queen's father, George VI, labelled it "an icebox," while the present Queen, when she first went to Buckingham Palace as a small girl, grumbled that she needed a bicycle in order to get around the place properly.

Buckingham Palace is not, of course, the Royal Family's private property. It belongs to the state. Originally known as Buckingham House, it was bought by George III in 1761 from the heirs to the Duke of Buckingham for slightly less than 60,000 dollars. At that time it was generally regarded as the finest mansion in London, and George saw it as a suitable dower house for Queen Charlotte.

It was George IV, a man of big ideas, who first embarked upon the expensive task of converting the mansion into a palace. Parliament authorized him to spend around half-a-million dollars, but by the time he died he had already spent three times that amount and the work was still not done. The final cost ran to something over two million dollars and then William IV liked the place so little that he never lived there. On his death, however, the youthful Victoria moved in with every evidence of delight, though she complained later both about "the state of the palace" and the "total want of accommodation." So a further half-million dollars was spent constructing what is now the front of the palace, a task which necessitated removing the original front arch—London's famed Marble Arch—to its present position at the northern end of Hyde Park.

With the death of her beloved Albert, Queen Victoria lost interest in the palace and retired with her grief to the heathery highlands of Scotland, the granite walls of Windsor, and the monkey-puzzle trees of Osborne. It was left to her son, Edward VII, to modernise the palace, installing electric light in place of gas and providing additional bathrooms (previously, there had been only five bathrooms dotted about the entire three floors of Victoria's new east front). Displaying a curious passion for cleanliness, Edward also provided some of the dressing rooms with as many as three washbasins . . . one for the hands, one for the face, and one for the teeth. By the time George V ascended the throne, the stonework of the new east front was already crumbling. He had it refaced in the Portland stone seen today. George VI, when his turn came, converted the old conservatory into an indoor swimming pool for the benefit of his two small daughters, a move which Prince Philip copied in recent times at Windsor.

Today, installation of central heating has done away with the necessity for employing ten men to go round each day lighting fires in the more important of the palace's six hundred rooms.

Elevators, heated trolleys and electric hot-plates have come to the rescue of servants charged with the task of conveying food from the lofty kitchens to the royal family's private dining room, nearly a quarter of a mile away. But the palace still remains a vast and ungainly place of seemingly endless corridors and notoriously little sunshine, difficult to run and not over-comfortable to live in. Even so, it is, to my mind, more comfortable than either of the Queen's two holiday homes—Sandringham House, which stands on Britain's windswept east coast and bulges at the seams with furnishings dating back through four reigns, or Balmoral Castle, with its Germanic turrets and tartan furnishings, where the glassy eyes of dead stags gaze down unblinkingly from the walls. Of all the royal residences, Windsor Castle, where the Queen has contrived a pleasant private apartment for herself in what is now known as the Queen's Tower, is perhaps the most comfortable, though the castle itself remains a huge, draughty barn of a place with walls more than five feet thick and corridors wide enough to serve as a motorway.

The Queen and her family occupy only one small corner of Buckingham Palace. The royal apartment is on the second floor, its windows looking out over Constitution Hill. It consists of less than a dozen rooms. Communicating doors link the royal bedroom, two dressing rooms (one for Philip), two bathrooms, a dining room and two sitting rooms. One of the sitting rooms also doubles as the Queen's study, and Philip has his own gadget-filled study a few doors along. A smaller suite of rooms on the floor above serves as a nursery for the Queen's youngest child, Prince Edward, and is shared by his brother, Prince Andrew, when he is home from boarding school. Prince Charles, when he is at home, has a bedroom on the same floor but round the corner to the front of the palace. Princess Anne has a bedroom in the same corridor, and the two of them share the same sitting room which the Queen and Princess Margaret shared in earlier years.

The rest of the palace's six hundred rooms form the working headquarters of the monarchy and also serve as a hostel to accommodate many of those who serve the Queen. There are work rooms and state rooms, reception rooms and offices, self-contained apartments and lonely bed-sitters. Indeed, the topmost floor is a positive rabbit-warren of bed-sitting rooms occupied by footmen, housemaids and other servants. The royal chefs live in an annex adjoining the kitchens. Chauffeurs and coachmen, grooms and postillions are housed in flats located above the stables and garages in the royal mews. Gladys Ramsay, the Palace Housekeeper, a brisk, bustling Scotswoman who rules the housemaids and cleaning women with all the efficiency and determination of a regimental sergeant-major, has a private apartment on the ground floor at the front of the palace. Similar apartments serve as homes for Stanley Williams, the palace superintendent, and dignified Robert Smith, the palace steward. Bobo MacDonald, the Queen's dresser, also has an apartment of her own, a bathroom, a large, well-lighted bedroom and a lofty sitting room immediately above the Queen's private suite and looking out across the palace gardens. In the hierarchy of Buckingham Palace, Bobo MacDonald is a very important person. What Bobo wants, Bobo usually gets. When the apartment was first being readied for her, she went along to inspect it. She found workmen in the act of laying new linoleum in the bathroom. Straightway she went to see the Queen. "I prefer carpet in my bathroom," she said. And carpet it was.

In many respects, Buckingham Palace is like a self-contained community of its own, an island isolated from the rest of Britain by tall railings and high walls. It has its own police station, fire station, post office and telephone exchange, even its own amateur football team. Uniformed postmen walk the wide, red-carpeted corridors daily delivering the mail just as they walk the sidewalks of any small town or village. There are stables for horses, garages for cars. The palace has its own gas station and blacksmith's forge, its own workshops for auto, electrical, plumbing and furniture maintenance. There are so many windows that twelve men are employed on the never-ending task of keeping them clear of London's soot and grime. There is a man who comes in weekly for the sole purpose of winding and maintaining the three hundred clocks, many of them valuable antiques. There are over two hundred and fifty telephones dotted throughout the palace; more than four thousand lamps in the chandeliers and other electrical fittings.

For the staff, there is a fully equipped sick bay with a resident nurse and a visiting physician in daily attendance. There is a combination pub and drugstore where members of the staff can buy tea and biscuits, jars of coffee, cans of meat and fruit, candy, chocolate and cigarettes, as well as drink beer or whisky at the cheapest prices in London. There are a swimming pool and a movie theatre, though these are really for the personal use of the Queen, her family and friends. Occasionally, however, senior officials will be invited to take a dip in the pool, and all levels of the staff are invited to fill the spare seats in the movie theatre on those rare occasions when the Queen puts on a film show as an after-dinner divertissement for her personal guests.

There is, in addition to all this, a whole range of state and semi-state apartments which take up nearly one-half of the interior space of the palace and come to life only on official occasions. These include the seldom-used Throne Room, a magnificent chamber some sixty feet long, its walls adorned with high-relief friezes depicting the Wars of the Roses. The Brussels carpet, window drapes and the draped canopy above the handsome throne are a rich crimson. The State Dining Room is an equally regal chamber, even longer at seventy-four feet, to which the lavish use of gold has given an effect of shimmering brilliance.

The ground-floor Belgian Suite, so-called after King Leopold of the Belgians, who so often occupied it on visits to London, is an apartment in itself. Its reception room (known as the Eighteenth Century Room), its sitting room (the Regency Room), its Orleans Bedroom with its heavy mahogany furnishings, and its Spanish Dressing Room are usually placed at the disposal of overseas monarchs and presidents paying a state call on the Queen. Then there is the Bow Room, where the Queen usually receives luncheon guests; the 1844 Room (so named because it was occupied in that year by the visiting Tsar Nicholas of Russia); the 1855 Room, similarly named after a visit by the Emperor Napoleon III; the Green, Blue, and White Drawing Rooms; and the Royal Closet, smallest of the state rooms, with its secret doorway. It is in the Royal Closet that the Queen and her entourage assemble on state occasions; the touch of a spring causes one of the ebony china cabinets in the adjoining White Drawing Room to swing back for the Queen to make a surprise and effective entrance.

II

The busiest part of Buckingham Palace is the series of ground-floor rooms immediately behind the Privy Purse Door. Through this door each day come and go the small, devoted band of men and women who keep the machine of monarchy ticking like a well-oiled clock. Through it, with a few notable exceptions such as the prime minister, come and go all those who have business of one sort or another with the monarch. It is extensively used, too, by a third category, those who still like to maintain the quaint old social custom of "calling."

In a small anteroom inside the Privy Purse Door is housed the massive, leather-covered, gold-embossed Visitors' Book. Anyone who can muster up sufficient courage is free to walk in and sign merely by announcing his intention to the policeman on duty at the main gate—provided only that the Queen is actually in residence. It is, after all, a book for the signatures of those who have "called" on the Queen, even if they do not actually get to see her, and consequently it goes wherever she goes—to Windsor at weekends, to Balmoral in summer. At royal garden parties a considerable queue of people shuffle their way slowly across the palace forecourt in order to sign. And at times when national emotion runs high the queue seems neverending. When the Queen's father died, the "callers" reached right across the palace forecourt, out into the street beyond, round the corner and continued for a full two hundred yards along Buckingham Palace

Road. But however many or few people sign the Visitors' Book in the course of a day, it is unfailingly carried up to the Queen's sitting room around half-past six each evening and placed on her desk so that she can see who the "callers" have been that day.

Beyond the anteroom which houses the Visitors' Book, lying right and left of the seemingly endless corridor which plunges deep into the palace entrails, are a succession of gloomy offices, stuffed with dark, heavy, antiquely valuable oak and mahogany furniture. This is the working headquarters of the monarchy. Here, with a few notable exceptions, the senior members of the Queen's Household bend to their labours—the Queen's Private Secretary, her two Assistant Private Secretaries, the Keeper of the Privy Purse. The exceptions are the Lord Chamberlain, who still functions from nearby St. James's Palace, and the Master of the Household, who, along with his clerks and assistants, occupies almost a complete wing on the second floor of the palace.

The structure of the Queen's Household is extremely complex and, to the outsider, completely baffling, an intricate mixture of ancient tradition and modern necessity. On paper, the latest list of Members of the Queen's Household available at this writing runs to a staggering total of 383 names, ranging from the Lord Chamberlain through Gold Sticks and Aides de Camp, Ladies of the Bedchamber and Lords in Waiting, Chaplains and Physicians, Gentlemen Ushers, Gentlemen at Arms and Extra Equerries, down to a gentleman rejoicing in the quaintly Old World title of President of the Council and Silver Stick for Scotland.

For all practical purposes, some four-fifths of the names in the list can be speedily discounted. They are the holders of purely historic and traditional posts and are called upon today to perform only occasional and ceremonial duties. The Master of the Horse, for instance, once commanded the monarch's troops in battle while the Lord Steward, in earlier days, had the task of rooting out those who planned treason against the person of the sovereign. Today neither of them has any true executive function, though both attend upon the Queen on state occasions; the Master of the Horse rides immediately behind her while she reviews her troops during the annual ceremony of Trooping the Colour. Similarly with the Yeomen of the Guard and the Corps of Gentlemen at Arms. The Yeomen of the Guard, as their name implies, served originally as royal bodyguards; among other things, they acted as food-tasters against the possibility of poisoning. Today they parade to "guard" the Queen only on state occasions, picturesquely attired in their Tudor outfits of royal scarlet and the Elizabethan ruff which came along later. The Gentlemen at Arms, who did indeed defend the Palace of Westminster during the Wyatt rebellion of 1533, are now called upon to form a guard of honour only for occasions such as the coronation, when they parade in ceremony with their traditional halberds (long-handled battle axes). Much the same applies to many others in the long, long list—the ten Gentlemen Ushers, the twelve Extra Gentlemen Ushers, the twenty-eight Extra Equerries, the extent of whose duties may be gauged from the fact that one of them is Group Captain Peter Townsend, who has not set foot inside Buckingham Palace since the ending of his much-publicised romance with Princess Margaret.

Of the 383 names currently listed as Members of the Queen's Household, only about sixty (the number varies slightly from time to time) work for her on a regular day-by-day basis. On the other hand, many others who work for her are not included in the list. Royal servants, such as pages and footmen, do not rank as Members of the Household. They are "the staff" and a clear-cut line is drawn between staff and Household. Indeed, there is a further division even among members of the staff, those of senior rank being addressed as "Mr." ("Mrs." in the case of women, whether married or single), while those rating less seniority are addressed merely by their surnames with no polite prefix. The Queen herself, incidentally, addresses those few who serve her in a personal capacity by their first names.

Buckingham Palace, in fact, is as sharply hierarchical as any military establishment. Nowhere is this more clearly seen than in the traditional and elaborate catering arrangements. There are five separate dining rooms available to those who work at Buckingham Palace. In descending order of rank, they are the Household Dining Room, the Officials' Dining Room, the Clerks' Dining Room, the Steward's Room and the Servants' Hall.

The Master of the Household, his Deputy, the Queen's Private Secretary and Assistant Private Secretaries, the Keeper of the Privy Purse and his Deputy, Equerries and Ladies-in-Waiting have their meals in the Household Dining Room, sitting together at a large polished mahogany table. The Master of the Household sits at the head of the table, though yielding pride of place to the Lord Chamberlain on those rare occasions when he comes over from St. James's Palace. They lunch and dine in the grand manner with pages and footmen waiting on them at table. The food they eat is prepared by the royal chef in the royal kitchen and there is wine for those who want it, unlike the Officials' and Clerks' Dining Rooms, where there is beer, and the Steward's Room and Servants' Hall, where there is only water.

Food for the Officials' Room is prepared in the staff kitchen. Here sit the Chief Accountant, the Establishment Officer, the Comptroller of Supply and his Deputy, the Chief Clerk and the Palace Superintendent, with waitresses in dainty white caps and aprons to wait on table as they do in the Clerks' Dining Room where clerks and typists and junior accountants have their meals.

The Queen's two personal pages, the Sergeant Footman, the Queen's assistant dresser and the maids of the Ladies-in-Waiting eat in the Steward's Room along with the Royal Steward (who sits at the head of the table) and the Palace Housekeeper, and are waited on by young trainee footmen. No one waits on those who eat in the Servants' Hall, where footmen, housemaids, chauffeurs and the like serve themselves from a long, cafeteria-type hot-plate and make up their own foursomes to sit at individual tables.

Inevitably, this sort of segregation has its anomalies. In Britain, a children's governess would be highly indignant if ever she were classed as a servant. So Lavinia Keppel, whose job it is to give Prince Edward his pre-school education, eats in the Household Dining Room, though in fact she does not rank as a Member of the Queen's Household. Bobo MacDonald, on the other hand, the Queen's Dresser and easily the most influential servant in Buckingham Palace, was originally allocated to the Steward's Room for her meals. But following a serious illness a few years ago she mentioned to the Queen that the food served there did not suit her. Since then, her meals have been specially prepared in the royal kitchen and served in her private apartment.

The structure of Britain's monarchy is not unlike a pyramid with the Queen at the apex. On the next level come five key men whose combined responsibility it is to mastermind all facets of her public and official life. They are the Lord Chamberlain, the Private Secretary, the Master of the Household, the Keeper of the Privy Purse and the Crown Equerry. Each has his own small staff of clerks and assistants and masterminds a separate sector of the Queen's life, though inevitably their departments tend to overlap in certain areas.

If anyone expected the Queen, in keeping with the spirit of a new Elizabethan age, to make a clean sweep at Buckingham Palace as soon as she ascended the throne, he was due for disappointment. Indeed, one of the most often-heard criticisms of Britain's monarchy over the next few years was that the Queen continued to select her top brass more for their social status than for their administrative or intellectual ability—scions of the Peerage, products of Eton, the Royal Military College at Sandhurst and the Brigade of Guards . . . what Lord Altrincham, in a trenchant look at the monarchy, referred to as "people of the tweedy sort."

Not until the last few years was any significant change apparent. The first sign came with the retirement in 1966 of Sir Edward Ford, one of the Queen's two Assistant Private Secretaries. To replace him, the Queen settled upon a third-generation civil servant in his mid-forties, Mr. Philip Moore, who moved over to Buckingham Palace from the Ministry of Defence, where he had been chief of public relations. When Sir Mark Milbank retired as Master of the Queen's Household shortly after, he too was replaced by a new-style courtier in the person of Brigadier Geoffrey Hardy-Roberts, who had served as Chief Administrative Officer with the 2nd Army from D-Day onwards, and subsequently held the post of secretary-superintendent at one of London's largest hospitals.

Initially, however, aware that she had much to learn about her new duties, the Queen was well content to take over her father's top brass ... his Private Secretary, Sir Alan Lascelles, who taught her much; his two Assistant Private Secretaries, Sir Edward Ford and Sir Michael Adeane; his Press Secretary, Commander (later Sir) Richard Colville. To the two Assistant Private Secretaries she added a third, Sir Martin Charteris, who had been her own Private Secretary when she was still a princess.

Similarly, she retained her father's Master of the Household, Sir Piers Legh; the Keeper of her father's Privy Purse, Sir Ulick Alexander; his Assistant Treasurer, Lord Tryon (destined to succeed Alexander when he retired); and his equerries, Sir Harold Campbell, Lieutenant Commander Peter Ashmore, and a 38-year-old ex-R.A.F. fighter ace, Group Captain Peter Townsend. Lieutenant General Sir Frederick ("Boy") Browning, wartime commander of Britain's airborne troops, who had been her Comptroller at Clarence House, now moved over to work as Treasurer to Prince Philip. Philip's old naval buddy and wartime comrade-in-arms, Lieutenant Commander Michael Parker, continued in office as his Private Secretary until his somewhat unexpected resignation some years later when his matrimonial problems resulted in tall headlines.

Of all these, it was Commander Richard Colville, the Press Secretary, who was to find himself occupying the hottest seat at the palace during these early years of Elizabeth's reign. Rightly or wrongly, the advent of a new Queen was interpreted in some literary quarters as a signal that the old regal curtain draped between monarch and public should be finally torn down. Commander Colville, son of Admiral Sir Stanley Colville, a close friend of George V, did not see it that way. A courtier of the old school, he saw his job as that of maintaining royal privacy and upholding royal dignity and not of providing information for press and public. As a result, there were those who labelled him uncooperative. The editor of one Sunday tabloid remarked that he had come to accept that Colville's policy "is to ensure that an absolute minimum is published about anything of interest concerning the Royal Family. In our experience they have always performed this function with unfailing and melancholy efficiency."

To such attacks, Colville's answer was that the Queen had a right to a private life and he intended to see that she got it. In fairness, too, his task was made no easier by the fact that he had too little direct contact with the Queen herself. Often he had to rely upon members of her staff to supply answers to questions posed by journalists, and on several occasions during the course of royal tours, he asked me to find out for him what the Queen would be wearing at a particular function. I did so by asking Bobo.

Apart from Martin Charteris, who moved over with her from Clarence House, the only newcomer the Queen introduced into the palace hierarchy at the beginning was Major (later Sir) Mark Milbank, who was to be her Master of the Household for some twelve years following the retirement of Sir Piers Legh. Peter Townsend might have got the job—he already held the post of Deputy—but he preferred to go along with the Queen Mother and Princess Margaret as their Comptroller at Clarence House. So Milbank, like Charteris a product of Eton and Sandhurst, and a man with an impeccable pedigree (he was to succeed his father as a hereditary baronet in 1964) was brought in instead.

But if the new young Queen made no very startling innovations, there were occasions when she was quick to reveal that she had a mind of her own. I was on duty outside her room one day soon after her accession, when Sir Alan Lascelles had occasion to go in and see her. He emerged again a few minutes later, looking white-faced and shaken. "And they said the King was dead," he muttered audibly as he walked back along the corridor, a remark suggesting that the young Queen, for once, had displayed something of her father's will and obstinacy.

Head of the Queen's Household is the Lord Chamberlain, a post held since 1963 by Lord Cobbold, formerly governor of the Bank of England. Symbol of his position as the Queen's chief servant is the gold key he wears at his hip when attending her on state occasions. He has another symbol of office seen less frequently—a white staff or wand. Twenty-two years older than the Queen he serves, Cobbold is unlikely to witness her funeral. But his successor as Lord Chamberlain, as his last act of service, will break his white wand in two at the Queen's graveside and cast the fragments into the royal vault.

The Lord Chamberlain supervises a large and varied assortment of royal functions. In effect, he is master of ceremonies at royal investitures, palace garden parties, royal weddings and that annual combination of horse racing and high fashion known as Royal Ascot. He is responsible for all royal ceremony, with three important exceptions. The coronation of the Sovereign, the state opening of Parliament and the funeral of the Sovereign remain the traditional responsibility of England's premier peer, the boyish-faced Duke of Norfolk, in his hereditary role of Earl Marshal. But for all other royal occasions it is Cobbold who advises the Queen whom to invite (and whom to leave out), sends out the necessary formal invitations, decides the order of precedence, and rules on the question of correct and incorrect attire. It was on Cobbold's instructions that women wearing trouser-suits found themselves barred from the royal enclosure at Ascot in the summer of 1967 (for some curious reason, those wearing miniskirts were admitted), though the Queen herself, that same month, did not bat an eyelid when Lady Chichester turned up at Greenwich wearing a brilliantly scarlet trouser-suit to watch her sailor-husband receive the accolade of knighthood following his adventurous single-handed voyage round the oceans of the world.

Cobbold's other duties are wide-ranging in the extreme. Acting for the Queen, he appoints royal physicians, royal chaplains and the Poet Laureate. He oversees the royal chapels, the royal library, the royal collection of art and antiques, even the royal swans. He issues royal warrants and the highly-prized "By appointment" tag which goes with them to those who supply the Queen with everything from her luxurious Rolls-Royces to cans of beans and bottles of sauce.

To gain one of these coveted royal warrants, a trader must supply goods to the Queen for a minimum period of three years. Each warrant is essentially personal, issued to the individual trader or the head of the firm. If the trader dies, or the business changes hands, the warrant lapses and any new owner taking over the business must win his own laurels by a further three years of loyal and discreet service. In the same way, each warrant is strictly limited to the particular wares or form of service being provided. A manufacturer of food products, for instance, may receive a royal warrant on account of the jars of pickles he supplies to Buckingham Palace. From then on, he can display the royal arms outside his business premises, on his transport, on his notepaper, and on his pickle jars, but not on any other products— perhaps bottles of ketchup—which he may also happen to produce. He can also use the royal arms in his advertising, provided that he does so with discretion, dignity and good taste. Any warrant-holder so foolish as to advertise "The Queen Loves Our Scrumptious Oaties" would soon find his warrant withdrawn and his name struck from the royal shopping list.

Despite such limitations, a royal warrant remains not only a highly-prized and eagerly-sought honour, but also a first-rate advertisement in its own right. The Royal Warrant Holders' Association, with its headquarters not far from the side entrance to Buckingham Palace, devotes a not inconsiderable part of its energies to nailing down firms who from time to time try to trick the public into thinking they supply the Queen when in fact they do not. Such instances are rare in Britain, more frequent overseas, though even then the long arm of the association can usually intervene successfully. It did so in Greece when a distiller began marketing whisky with Britain's royal arms on the bottles, and again in Germany where a manufacturer did likewise with packets of knitting needles.

The present-day list of royal warrant-holders is a good deal more orderly than it was years ago. The Queen's great-grand-father, Edward VII, had merely to take a passing fancy to some-one's cigars or meat pies for another name to be added to the list. On one occasion the King was backstage at a London theatre when he was given a muffin to munch. "This is jolly good," he mumbled as melted butter trickled into his beard, and the name of Mrs. Forscutt, who ran a boarding house for theatricals, was straightway added to a list of royal warrant-holders which al-ready included strongman Eugene Sandow, the King's physical training instructor.

The present Queen has granted some 623 warrants. Philip has his own list of 54 and there are a further 174 issued by the Queen Mother. The Queen's list covers almost every conceivable royal requirement, from electric lamps to motor vehicles, from agricul-tural machinery to dog food. It includes not only fashion de-signers, shoemakers and photographers, but also the owners of small, tucked-away village stores around Sandringham and Bal-moral, as well as a racehorse plater in Nottingham, a reed thatcher near Norwick, bagpipe makers in Glasgow, a farrier in Newbury, a heraldic painter on the outskirts of London, and the breeder of the Cleveland Bays which draw the royal coaches. Philip's list includes a boatbuilder in Hamble, a gunmaker in London, a supplier of polo sticks in Aldershot, a yacht refitter on the Isle of Wight, and a kiltmaker in Edinburgh. The Queen has also granted warrants to a handful of firms overseas...a silversmith in Calcutta, another in Australia, a whisky firm in Ontario, several French champagne growers, and a firm in Copenhagen which distills cherry brandy.

IV

The position of Private Secretary to the Queen is theoretically subordinate to that of the Lord Chamberlain; in practice, it is the most powerful position at Buckingham Palace. It is a role which calls for intelligence, political judgement, discretion, tact, commonsense and good manners in the highest degree, and all these qualities are currently brought together in the person of Lieutenant Colonel the Right Honourable Sir Michael Adeane, Knight Grand Cross of the Royal Victorian Order, Knight Commander of the Most Honourable Order of the Bath, a short, compact man whose balding head, pink complexion and neatly clipped moustache combine to give him the outward appearance of a successful stockbroker or bank manager. In his late fifties, he has been serving the royal family in one way or another since the tender age of thirteen, when he was appointed page of honour to King George V.

It was Adeane's grandfather, Lord Stamfordham, who, as Private Secretary to Queen Victoria and later to George V, elevated the post into the high and unique status it possesses today. Before Stamfordham, the monarch's Private Secretary was a mere scribbler of letters, a fetcher and carrier of messages. Stamfordham changed it from a walking-on role to a star part in its own right... with such success that George V was to say of him, "He taught me to be a king."

Today, his grandson handles the official correspondence between Queen and Government, schedules her engagements, deals with her private papers, and drafts her speeches for her. He is helped in this mammoth task by two Assistant Private Secretaries, Mr. Philip Moore and Lieutenant Colonel the Honourable Sir Martin Charteris, who was Elizabeth's Private Secretary when she was still princess.

Adeane is the first Member of the Household to see the Queen each morning. Scorning the elevator, he climbs the red-carpeted stairs from his ground-floor office to her private apartment with a wickerwork basket of papers tucked neatly under one arm. Government papers reach the palace in the traditional "Boxes" which have plagued Britain's monarchs for generations. Rectangular in shape, covered in black, red, or green leather, with the two words "The Queen" embossed in gold on the lid, they were collected right up until fairly recent times by a horse-drawn barouche, driven by a top-hatted coachman, which clip-clopped its way twice daily from the palace mews to Whitehall and Downing Street. But changing times have forced the replacement of this picturesque conveyance by a speedier, if less colourful, royal car.

It is one of Adeane's tasks to sift the contents of the Boxes on arrival at the palace, sorting the important from the trivial, the urgent from the less urgent, so that the various documents are placed before the Queen in order of merit for her perusal and signature. Her abbreviated, hastily scribbled "App" (for "Approved"), followed by the initials E.R. (for Elizabeth Regina), has the effect of turning each document into an official state paper.

But this, along with the drafting of speeches and the planning of schedules, is only the tip of the iceberg. It is, as Sir Alan Lascelles pointed out in 1947, very much a twenty-four-hour-a-day job . . . as is the Queen's own equally indefinable job. "We serve," Sir Alan told a parliamentary Select Committee, "one of the very few men in this world who never gets a holiday and who, unlike the rest of us, can look forward to no period of retirement at the end of his service, for his service never ends."

Those words are as true today of Adeane and the Queen as they were of Lascelles and her father. Adeane sees Elizabeth at least once every day, sometimes twice or more. He accompanies her on all state visits and on the more important royal tours. When she weekends at Windsor, so does Adeane. When she vacations at Balmoral, so does Adeane. With rare exceptions, he is always within call and on call. To enable him to be so with a minimum of personal inconvenience, the Queen provides him with a rent-free grace-and-favour house at St. James's Palace, another at Balmoral, and a rent-free apartment in one of the massive, gray-stone towers at Windsor.

Adeane, during his years of office, has helped to steer the royal family through more than one delicate situation. He was at the heart of the furore which blew up over Princess Margaret's attachment to Peter Townsend. With Prince Philip away in the Antarctic, it was left to Adeane to handle the unpleasant publicity a few years ago of a rumoured "rift" between royal husband and wife.

Others before him have had equally grave royal crises to resolve, and the delicate way in which men like Adeane must sometimes go about their duties was never more clearly revealed than in those critical days before the World War II invasion of Europe. That old war-horse, Winston Churchill, for all that he was prime minister of Britain, was determined to be where the action was on D-Day. When word of this trickled through to him, the Queen's father, King George VI, said that if Churchill was sailing with the invasion fleet, then so was he. In the small circle in which this news was known there was consternation. That two men so important to Britain—the prime minister and the monarch—should hazard their lives at the same time was a possibility too alarming to contemplate. But both were headstrong men, not easily dissuaded from anything on which they had set their minds. It was left to Adeane's predecessor, Sir Alan Lascelles, to turn the key of dissuasion.

He sought out the King. What advice, he asked him, would he be expected to offer the King's daughter concerning her choice of a new prime minister in the event that neither Churchill nor the King returned from their D-Day expedition?

The point was well made, and the King took it. He decided not to sail with the invasion fleet himself, and applied a spot of regal blackmail to Churchill with the object of dissuading him also. If he, as King and head of Britain's armed forces, could not go, then what right had his prime minister to so do? he demanded of Churchill. And monarch and minister stayed behind, however reluctantly, when the D-Day fleet set sail.

It was another Private Secretary, Sir Alexander Hardinge, who wrote the now famous letter to King Edward VIII, warning him of what would almost certainly happen if he persisted in his attachment to Mrs. Simpson. The depth of emotion Hardinge must have felt comes through clearly in the last, touching paragraph:

"If Your Majesty will permit me to say so, there is only one step which holds out any prospect of avoiding this dangerous situation—and that is for Mrs. Simpson to go abroad without further delay—and I would beg Your Majesty to give this proposal your earnest consideration before the position becomes irretrievable."

V

If Sir Michael Adeane holds the most influential post at Buckingham Palace, then that held by Brigadier Geoffrey Hardy-Roberts, Master of the Queen's Household, is perhaps the most complex. Hardy-Roberts is the Queen's major-domo, the man responsible for the day-to-day running of her five homes—Buckingham Palace, Windsor Castle, Balmoral Castle, Sandringham House, and the seldom-used Palace of Holyroodhouse in Edinburgh. It is an organisational task to which he is well fitted following duties as Chief Administrative Officer with the 2nd Army from D-Day onwards and subsequently as secretary-superintendent of one of London's largest hospitals. Of the palace staff of over 250, more than half come under his command. They are tidily grouped into various departments, each headed by a subordinate Member of the Household who serves in the capacity of a lieutenant to the brigadier.

Chief of these is Stanley Williams, who, as Palace Superintendent, is responsible for the fabric and furnishings of Buckingham Palace. Windsor Castle has its own superintendent, Stanley Lucking. It is Williams' job at the palace—and Lucking's at Windsor—to see that any frayed patches in the miles of red carpeting are instantly repaired, any worn curtains at the scores of high windows are repaired or replaced (though he must have the Queen's consent to replacement), that the valuable antique furnishings are properly maintained, the windows cleaned, tables polished, clocks wound, the central heating, plumbing, elevators, chandeliers, and other light fittings kept in working order, and to ensure that instant fresh air (in spray form) is available to freshen the rooms of the royal apartment following a visit by any cigar-smoking guest or relative such as Philip's uncle, Earl Mountbatten of Burma.

Neither the Queen nor Philip smokes. The Queen has never smoked. Philip smoked cigarettes and occasionally a pipe up to the time he married. He had his last cigarette at a rather hectic stag party on the eve of his wedding. Today, like many other reformed smokers, he is a clean-air addict and cannot tolerate the smell of stale tobacco smoke. As soon as cigarette or cigar-smoking friends have departed, he is ordering windows to be opened and rooms purified with air-fresheners. It is one of Stanley Williams's tasks to see that this is done.

To help him in the mammoth task of maintaining the palace fixtures and furnishings, Williams has the assistance of three expert upholsterers and carpet-layers, four electricians, two plumbers, one french polisher, three or four carpenters, a boilerman to oversee the oil-fired central heating installation, twelve odd-job men to clean the windows and move the furniture around, and one man who does nothing else but burnish the scores of iron grates and steel fire-irons which still adorn so many of the rooms.

His feminine counterpart, Gladys Ramsay, the Palace House-keeper, organises the two dozen housemaids who are responsible for such chores as dusting and bed-making, as well as the dozen or so buxom charwomen who arrive promptly at seven o'clock each morning to tackle the heavy scrubbing and cleaning. Also under her supervision is the vast linen room in the basement at the rear of the palace, where white-painted cupboards groan under the weight of thousands of sheets, pillowcases, towels, dusters, tablecloths and table napkins. So huge and heavy are some of the tablecloths used for state banquets that it takes two strong men to manhandle them on to the wheeled trolley which transports them from the linen room to the State Ballroom.

Yet another of the brigadier's lieutenants is Robert Smith, the Palace Steward. Under Smith comes the quaintly named Page of the Chambers, James Walton (who also serves as his deputy), the four Pages of the Back Stairs (who attend personally upon the Queen and Prince Philip), six others known as the Pages of the Presence, the Yeoman of the Glass and Silver, the Yeoman of the Gold, the Yeoman of the Cellars, a fluctuating number of footmen, usually twelve, four under-butlers, an equal number of pantry assistants, the boys—they are always known as "boys," though some have long since left boyhood behind—who wait on table in the Steward's Room, and a couple of coal porters.

The Comptroller of Supply, who has charge of a vast storeroom well-stocked with everything from dog biscuits to frozen pheasant, from candles (in case of an electricity breakdown) to the Queen's favourite chocolate mints, does not come under the Master of the Household but under the Keeper of the Privy Purse, whose responsibility it is to keep the Queen's finances straight. Also under the Keeper of the Privy Purse come the vast, echoing kitchens where royal chef Ronald Aubrey presides over four assistant chefs, an equal number of staff chefs and three kitchen hands who keep the copper pots and pans sparkling bright by the old-fashioned but surprisingly effective method of scouring them with a mixture of sand and vinegar.

Like any other employer of labour in present-day Britain, the Queen has her staff problems, though the Master of the Household serves as a buffer between her and the harsh realities of the workaday world. The faults are not all on the royal side. Despite strenuous efforts by Prince Philip to streamline and update the running of Buckingham Palace, traditionalism and stubborn resistance to change remain stumbling blocks to efficiency.

In many respects, things have changed little at the palace since Queen Victoria's day. Victoria once summoned her Master of the Household and asked for a fire to be lit in the palace dining room. She was calmly informed that it was not the responsibility of the Master of the Household. It was the Lord Steward's job to see that the fire was laid and the Lord Chamberlain's duty to ensure that it was lit.

Times may have changed, but not all that much. Even today,

a royal servant will not tackle a task he feels is outside his duties or beneath his dignity. No palace footman would ever accept an order to clean silver. That is a job for one of the under-butlers. Protocol is strict among the staff. Not long ago there was a palace chauffeur who huffily handed in his resignation because a junior chauffeur was dispatched to collect Prince Charles from a railway station. No palace footman would dream of answering the Queen's bell if she should ring. That is a job for her personal page. If the page is absent, the footman on duty simply goes in search of him while the Queen sits waiting.

It was this sort of thing that turned the Queen's intended "quiet weekends" at Windsor into a cavalcade. When the Queen and Prince Philip first conceived the idea of weekending away from London, they planned to take with them only the Queen's Dresser, Philip's valet, a page, a footman and a chef. In no time at all, a kitchen assistant was going along to prepare the vegetables and clean the pots and pans, a maid was added to make the coffee and an under-butler to lay the table. In consequence, another chef had to be included to cook for this growing staff, and one of the "boys" from the servants' hall to wait on the other servants at mealtimes. All this, in turn, meant another chauffeur to transport the extra hands to Windsor and back, with the result that a quiet weekend at Windsor today involves never less than fourteen servants and sometimes more.

Changing social attitudes in Britain have not helped the palace staff problem. Older members of the staff may still rate the honour and glory of working for the Queen as more important than mere money and consequently stay on at the palace for years— Robert Smith, the Palace Steward, has been in royal service for more than a quarter of a century, while an elderly housemaid who retired not long ago had been at the palace so long she could remember preparing the mashed potatoes the Queen's grandfather, King George V, liked to accompany his early-morning pot of tea.

But the younger generation of Britons rank money ahead of honour and glory, and the wages at Buckingham Palace, if no lower than those paid for domestic work elsewhere in Britain, are certainly no higher. A starting footman these days can expect to receive around £9 a week (equivalent to a little short of $22 since the devaluation of the pound), in addition to his keep and accommodation, which would be worth roughly a further £9 a week in present-day London. Senior footmen and pages who have been at the palace for some years are paid around £20 ($48) a week. A further difficulty in recruiting stems from the fact that the pace of life elsewhere in Britain, and especially in London, has quickened in recent years, while the palace way of life remains firmly rooted in an earlier era. Consequently, young newcomers to the staff find it dull and constrained, and they tend to remain only a short time before moving on in search of new and more exciting jobs. The result of all this is that the Royal Steward not infrequently has difficulty in filling his quota of footmen, while the Palace Housekeeper, Gladys Ramsay, has to fall back on girls from Germany, France, and Switzerland to augment her staff of housemaids.

Even so, their troubles are relatively small in comparison with the difficulty Lieutenant Colonel John Miller, the Crown Equerry, experienced at one time in maintaining staff and peace among the garages and stables which make up the royal mews. Colonel Miller, a former officer in the Welsh Guards, is a military man of the old school, a stickler for discipline. Such ideas do not go down well in present-day Britain, and in the first year and a half following his appointment to the post of Crown Equerry in 1961 no fewer than eighteen members of the staff of the mews handed in their resignations. Those who remained petitioned their Civil Service Union that they were being subjected to "excessive regimentation." Among those who resigned was Bill Chivers, the head chauffeur, who had been at Buckingham Palace for some seventeen years. The Queen, when she heard the news, sent for Chivers herself. She was successful on that occasion in persuading him to change his mind, but only a few months later he tendered his resignation a second time, and this time he stuck to his guns.

Responsible for keeping the Queen's accounts in order, paying her bills, advising what charities she might patronise, and overseeing the financial administration of her private estates at Balmoral and Sandringham, is Brigadier the Lord Tryon, a tall, greying man with the cool, calculating mind the job requires. The household accounts with which he deals are staggering by any normal standards. The royal grocery bill alone can easily run to something like £1,000 in an average week. Repairs and replacements of carpets, curtains, tablecloths, and furnishings may go as high as £1,500 in a single month. Wines and spirits for royal banquets make an annual dent of around £6,000 in the royal housekeeping money. Where does it all come from?

The Queen has two sources of income—public and private. The public part of her income totals £475,000 a year. It is called the Civil List—the word "Civil" underlining the fact that Britain's monarchs no longer pay and control the armed forces as they did once.

The Civil List, as it exists today, is the result of a bargain hammered out between Parliament and Sovereign between the restoration of the monarchy in 1660 and the accession of the young Queen Victoria in 1837. An arrangement resulted under which the revenues of what are known as the Crown Estates are surrendered to Parliament by the monarch in exchange for a fixed annual income.

Under the British constitution, each successive monarch still inherits these vast and valuable Crown Estates, though left-wing Socialists would argue that inheritance today is no more than polite fiction. However that may be, the Crown Estates include thousands of acres of land in England, Scotland, and Wales, along with miles of foreshore around Britain's coast. But the really valuable holdings are in the very heart of London. Much of Mayfair, Piccadilly, and Whitehall—including stores, theatres, restaurants and at least one hotel—stand on land which constitutionally belongs to the Queen. Much of Regent Street and Lower

Regent Street along with Carlton House Terrace belong to her, too. So does certain property in the financial heart of London—the City—along with holdings in the suburbs of London, at Windsor and Ascot and elsewhere in southern England.

All this is "inherited" by each succeeding monarch in turn and promptly surrendered to Parliament in exchange for the Civil List. During the financial year which ended on March 31, 1967, total receipts from the Crown Estates were in excess of £5 million and, even after meeting expenses, surplus revenue to the tune of £3,600,000 was handed over to the national exchequer. In return, Parliament gives the Queen an annual tax-free allowance of £475,000 which, on the face of it, sounds like a very good parliamentary bargain in return for some £3½ million. But, of course, it is not quite so simple as that; nor does it end there.

Leaving aside the socialistic debating point as to whether the Crown Estates should really belong to the Queen in this day and age, the Civil List, because it is free of tax, represents a considerably larger gross figure, even allowing for what would be deductible expenses in any ordinary business. And whether by accident or design, much of what the monarchy costs Britain is shrouded in statistical mystery, with the Civil List forming only part of the overall total. Some of the running costs of royal palaces, for instance, are billed to the Ministry of Works. Royal telephone and telegram charges are debited to the Post Office. The aircraft and helicopters constituting the Queen's Flight are a charge on the Air Estates, while the cost of running the royal yacht *Britannia* borne by the Naval Department.

In addition to what she gets from Parliament, the Queen has a further substantial income from another royal estate, the Duchy of Lancaster, which has been handed down to her from the distant days of Henry IV and is not included in the Crown Estates succeeding monarchs surrender to Parliament. Financial details of royal estates are not made public, but a parliamentary Select Committee set up to look into the question of royal finances in 1952, the year of the Queen's accession, revealed that revenues from the Duchy of Lancaster were averaging around £90,000 a year at that time. Presumably, like everything else in Britain, they have gone up since.

Separate parliamentary allowances are also paid to Prince Philip (£40,000 annually), the Queen Mother (£70,000), the Duke of Gloucester (£35,000) and Princess Margaret (£15,000 since marriage). In 1952, when the House of Commons debated the new Civil List for the new Elizabethan reign, one Socialist Member of Parliament castigated the proposals as "the largest wage-claim of the century" while another condemned the royal palaces as "white elephants." However, amendments designed to cut the Civil List by a quarter of a million pounds a year, to reduce Philip to an annual £10,000 budget, and to delete the provision under which Margaret was to get an increase of £9,000 a year on marriage were all defeated.

The annual total of £475,000 paid to the Queen in the form of the Civil List breaks down under six main headings. There is what is officially styled "Her Majesty's Privy Purse." This is, in effect, the Queen's personal spending money, though clothes for royal tours inevitably take a big chunk out of it. The amount paid under this heading is £60,000. There are the salaries of the Queen's Household— £185,000—and the expenses of the Household, a further £121,000. Royal alms and bounty account for a comparatively small £13,000. The fifth heading is a supplementary provision of £25,000 to provide for other members of the Royal Family who carry out public duties but for whom no separate financial provision is made. With provision already made for Prince Philip, the Queen Mother, the Gloucesters and Princess Margaret, this £25,000 is presumably shared out between the Duke and Duchess of Kent and Princess Alexandra. The remaining £70,000 was originally approved by Parliament as a hedge against inflation, and rising costs have doubtless long since overtaken it.

In fact, the Queen today is receiving only £5,000 a year more than her grandfather and great-grandfather received, though the value of the pound is perhaps only one-fifth of what it was then.

And with Britain's cost of living rising steadily, it may be that she is already being forced to rob Peter to pay Paul, as her father did before her. The report of the Select Committee which probed the whole question of royal finances at the time of the Queen's accession revealed that George VI, over the last five years of his reign, had been forced to dip into his Privy Purse, the personal part of the Civil List, to the tune of £190,000 in order to meet deficits in Household accounts. It was because of this that Parliament, in 1952, approved an increase of £20,000 a year for Household salaries and expenses, mainly in order that "about 100 officials of the Household and senior members of the staff who had for several years accepted remuneration lower than appropriate to their duties might have their salaries increased to an appropriate level." However, this increase was offset in part by the Queen's offer to have her Privy Purse allowance cut by £17,000.

Separate financial provisions are also agreed on between the Queen and Parliament for the maintenance of her eldest son, Charles, Prince of Wales and heir to the Throne. Just as the monarch inherits the Crown Estates on succession to the Throne, so the monarch's eldest son traditionally inherits the Duchy of Cornwall, a royal estate created by Edward III back in the fourteenth century to ensure that the Black Prince should live in suitable style. Curiously enough, most of this estate is not in the county of Cornwall at all. It consists of farms, villages, mines, quarries and oyster-beds scattered throughout half a dozen different west-of-England counties as well as in the Isles of Scilly off Britain's westernmost tip. But as with the Crown Estates proper, the most valuable portion is in London, some 40 acres of offices and apartment blocks in the vicinity of the famous Oval cricket ground.

As a result of the deal made between Queen and Parliament in 1952, Prince Charles received one-ninth of the Duchy revenues up to his eighteenth birthday in 1966. The remaining eight-ninths went into the national exchequer to help offset the cost of the Civil List. Between his eighteenth and twenty-first birthdays, Charles, in addition to his one-ninth, receives a flat sum of £30,000 a year, which almost certainly means that already he gets more than his father. And one of his birthday presents when he celebrates his coming-of-age in November, 1969, will be the entire revenues of the Duchy—estimated in these days of rising rents to be worth rather more than £200,000 a year.

The Queen is, of course, an enormously wealthy woman in her own right, though any attempt at computing the actual size of her private fortune can never be more than an educated guess, since the private side of her finances is even more shrouded in mystery than the public side. She has inherited the accumulated cash of generations of monarchs before her, free of death duty. So while crippling death-duties have decimated the fortunes of other once-wealthy British families, the fortune of the royal family has gone on increasing. Details of royal wills, like the finances of royal estates, are never made public, but fragments of the jigsaw can be seen here and there. Old Queen Victoria is known to have left at least £2 million when she died. Queen Mary, the Queen's grandmother, left a further £400,000. Much of the Queen's inherited capital is invested in real estate and railroad stocks, including, it is said, large blocks of stock in U.S. companies.

It is almost impossible to disentangle her personal fortune from her official inheritance. While Buckingham Palace and Windsor Castle belong to the state, Sandringham House with its 17,000 fertile acres and Balmoral Castle with 80,000 acres of heathery moors are part of the Queen's private inheritance. As sovereign, she inherited the royal art collection, handed down from the days of Henry VIII and steadily added to by successive monarchs. It includes works by most of the great masters—Rubens and Rembrandt, Van Dyck and Canaletto, Titian, Reynolds and Gainsborough—and was valued at £15 million as far back as 1958. Rising art values have probably doubled that since then. In addition, the royal collection of gold plate weighs around five tons and includes table centres so massive it takes four strong men to lift them into place for state banquets. Her collection of furniture and antiques is catalogued in no fewer than 75 volumes. Her stamp collection runs to over 330 albums. It was started by her grandfather, George V, who assiduously devoted three afternoons a week to collating and cataloguing the collection. Added to by her father, it was valued at £1 million in his day and is certainly worth at least 25 percent more at present-day values. The same applies to her library which runs to more than 100,000 volumes, including illuminated books dating from mediaeval times and finely illustrated volumes of natural history, which would fetch up to £10,000 each on the open market.

The Crown Jewels, like Buckingham Palace and Windsor Castle, belong to the state, but the Queen's magnificent personal jewel collection remains one of the most valuable in the world. Many of the items are inherited, including more than twenty tiaras and diadems handed down to her by Queen Mary, her grandmother, Queen Alexandra, her great-grandmother, and Queen Victoria, her great-great-grandmother, many with matching necklaces and earrings.

One, which the Queen calls "Granny's tiara" because it was made for Queen Mary from oddments of jewellery, consists of 19 large drop pearls suspended in scrolls of diamonds. Another— the Russian fringe or "Sunray" tiara—is a graduated circle of solid diamond bars dating from the days of George III, which can be worn either on the head as a tiara or round the throat as a collar. Another tiara, once the property of the Grand Duchess Vladimir of Russia, consists of intertwined diamond scrolls in which can be suspended either drop pearls or the pear-shaped emerald drops given to Queen Mary's mother by the Duchess of Cambridge, who won them in a German state lottery. Other emeralds forming part of that nineteenth-century lottery prize are today in one of the Queen's many necklaces. But of all the Queen's many diadems and tiaras, her favourite, because of its lightness—"You can't dance comfortably in anything heavier," she says—is the dainty confection of diamond rosebuds and fluer-de-lis which caused former U.S. President Harry Truman

toria should be included as well, but finally decided it was not necessary). She was the King's first granddaughter, and her birth merited a 21-gun salute in Hyde Park.

While others may have wished that the child had been a boy, her parents certainly did not. Her mother had always said that she wanted a girl first, and her father was only too happy that his wife's wish had been granted. However, when another child was on the way some four years later, both parents were convinced that it would be a boy. When it turned out to be another girl, they were so unprepared that at first they had no idea what to call her. After considerable hassling they opted for Margaret Rose.

Elizabeth, at birth, was third in the line of succession. Between her and the Throne stood the handsome, perennially boyish figure of her Uncle David, the Prince of Wales, and his younger brother, her father, the Duke of York. The line of succession could be lengthened if her uncle married and had children, or even by the birth of a son to her father. At the time, neither possibility seemed remote. But four years later, with the Prince of Wales still showing no inclination towards marriage—his first meeting with Mrs. Simpson was still some months in the future—and the birth not of a son but of another daughter to the Yorks, Queen Mary glimpsed at least the possibility that her small, fair-haired, rosy-cheeked granddaughter might one day ascend the Throne and began to plan accordingly. It has been said that Elizabeth's apprenticeship in monarchy began at the age of ten, when her father succeeded so dramatically and unexpectedly to the Throne. In fact, it began at least five years earlier, and possibly even before that. Queen Mary was a remarkably far-sighted woman, and what she had once put her hand to, she never relinquished.

For some twenty years, Queen Mary of the straight back and regal countenance painstakingly coached her granddaughter towards the high office of monarchy. Elizabeth was only a few weeks past her fifth birthday, with her uncle and father still squarely between her and the Throne, when her grandmother suggested she be taken to see the colourful annual ceremony of Trooping the Colour. She rode in a carriage with her parents and Queen Mary, and it was her grandmother who showed her how to lift her hand in regal acknowledgement of the cheers of the crowd.

Queen Mary had very firm and perhaps somewhat old-fashioned ideas of how royalty should conduct itself. Royalty, she insisted, should be regal and aloof—she herself would never speak on the telephone, because she considered it an unregal instrument—but at the same time gracious and gentle. When the young Elizabeth, accompanying Queen Mary to one of London's many tournaments and exhibitions, gleefully demanded, "Have all these people come to see me?" her grandmother considered that she had fallen below royalty's high standards and promptly took her home again.

Her mother, too, was concerned that Elizabeth should never commit the sin of ungraciousness. Constantly she reminded her, "Royalty is no excuse for bad manners," and on one occasion, hearing the child address a clock-winder by his surname, she took her to one side, pointed out the error of her ways and sent her back to apologise. "I'm sorry I didn't 'mister' you," the small Elizabeth told the clock-winder contritely.

The lesson stuck and has been passed on, in turn, to her own children. The present generation of royal youngsters, during my years at Buckingham Palace, were always told to employ the prefix "Mister" when addressing senior members of their mother's staff. The Queen was equally insistent that they should say "please" when they wanted something, "thank you" when they got it. So firm was her training that her children, by ordinary, everyday standards, were almost excessively polite, even saying "Thank you" to their pet corgis when they obediently fetched a ball or a stick.

Her grandmother, her mother, her father—these were the main personalities influencing Elizabeth's early years. But there was, almost from birth, an additional, non-royal influence in the person of Bobo MacDonald, who is now, and has been for many

[60]

years, the Queen's personal maid, her closest friend and, Philip apart, perhaps her only real confidante.

Margaret MacDonald was born the daughter of a railroad worker in a small, isolated Scottish village. Her home was a tiny, three-roomed cottage. Her first job was as assistant chambermaid in a small hotel a few miles from her home, at a lowly six shillings a week. From the hotel she moved in due course to the Scottish home of the Marchioness of Linlithgow, and it was the Marchioness who recommended her to the Duchess of York as a suitable nurserymaid for the new baby, Elizabeth.

The baby already had a nanny in the person of Mrs. Clara Cooper Knight. But Mrs. Knight, previously nanny to the Bowes-Lyon children at Glamis, was a nanny of the old school, quite above such menial tasks as kindling the nursery fire or washing the baby's diapers. Margaret was hired for a few shillings a week to perform such chores for her. She was only twenty then, a petite and attractive redhead, whose natural Scottish shyness could still not prevent her being the belle of the ball when she was invited, along with others of the Duke of York's small staff, to royal servants' balls at Buckingham Palace and Balmoral. There was many a tall and handsome footman who had his eye on wee Maggie MacDonald in the late 1920s. But her first loyalty, then as now, was to Elizabeth, and she has never married. Her greatest pleasure, in those days, was when she was permitted to take over from Mrs. Knight and give the baby Elizabeth her bedtime bath. There was one period when Mrs. Knight was ill with influenza and Margaret had to take over entirely. Her joy knew no bounds as she bathed the baby and fed her and took her for outings in the horse-drawn carriage which grandfather George V sent round from the royal mews at Buckingham Palace. With the birth of another baby, Princess Margaret, to occupy Nanny Knight's attention, Margaret MacDonald had virtually sole charge of the young Elizabeth. Hide-and-seek was a favourite game for the two of them among the sooty shrubs in Hamilton Gardens at the rear of 145 Piccadilly, the new home into which the Yorks had recently moved.

Margaret MacDonald would hide. The baby Elizabeth would toddle in search of her. If the search failed, as it usually did, Margaret would spring from her hiding-place, crying "Boo." Elizabeth would clap her small, pudgy hands together in excitement. "Boo-boo," she would cry back.

From then on Margaret MacDonald was always "Bobo"—to Elizabeth, to Margaret when she was old enough to talk, to the children's parents and, indeed, to all the Royal Family.

Over the years she has been beside the Queen at all the important moments of her life. Carefully preserved among the royal archives at Windsor, written in red pencil in a schoolroom exercise book, is Elizabeth's own account of how she was awakened by the sound of martial music on the morning of her father's coronation, how she leapt out of bed and ran to the window and how the doting Bobo carefully wrapped an eiderdown round her young shoulders to keep her warm.

Similarly, it was Bobo who came to the rescue when a nervous teenage princess was due to make her first public speech.

"My mouth feels so dry," she said, apprehensively. "I'm sure I'll never get a word out."

Bobo suggested that she suck a small piece of barley sugar to keep her mouth moist and calm her young nerves. The trick worked. Today, a quarter of a century later, a small silver cannister, with the royal crest embossed on the lid, travels with the Queen wherever she goes. It is Bobo who ensures that the cannister is kept filled with barley sugar so that Elizabeth can pop a piece into her mouth if ever the old nervous dryness returns. The Queen also finds barley sugar a useful counter to possible travel-sickness and she was still noticeably sucking a piece on one occasion when she walked towards the reception committee waiting to accord her an official welcome to Canada.

To Elizabeth, Bobo has been like a second mother. Indeed, it was to Bobo rather than her mother that she first confided her love for Philip, and it was with almost motherly joy that Bobo helped her to dress on her wedding morning. The wedding dress is still carefully preserved in the wardrobe-workroom on the third floor of Buckingham Palace where Bobo today reigns supreme as "the Queen's Dresser" and I well remember, during my years at the palace, how she would bring it out of storage from time to time and drape it over a dressmaker's dummy to air and freshen.

Other royal servants take it turn and turn about to accompany the Queen on her overseas trips. Bobo goes on every one. She was with her in Kenya that historic morning when a princess climbed down from a tree to discover that she was Queen. Like everyone else, she curtsied to the princess who was now the Queen. "Oh, no, Bobo," Elizabeth cried, protestingly. "*You* don't have to do that."

II

Another person of not inconsiderable influence was to enter the life of the future queen just ahead of her sixth birthday. This was Marion Crawford, another young Scotswoman, 22 at the time, her hair close-cropped in rather boyish fashion which was to arouse the curiosity of the young Elizabeth. "Crawfie," as she was soon known to all around, had been engaged as governess to undertake the child's formal training, a task in which she was left to act pretty much on her own initiative. The Duchess, though she had already started teaching her daughter to read, seemed to have no very clear idea of what else she should be taught. The Duke was hardly more forthcoming, and was seemingly quite content to leave the curriculum to Miss Crawford. The child's grandfather had only one idea to offer, though he was pretty firm about that. Gruffly the King demanded that she should be taught "to write a decent hand—a hand with some character in it."

Queen Mary, as might be expected, was more explicit, and it was with her that Miss Crawford finally drew up the curriculum. It was hardly the sort of regimen to produce a classics expert or a mathematical genius. From half-past nine until eleven o'clock on five mornings of the week, in easy, half-hour bursts,

Elizabeth tackled arithmetic, history, geography, English grammar, English literature, writing and composition, poetry, and Bible study. Left to her own devices, Miss Crawford would have included more arithmetic, but Queen Mary thought her granddaughter was unlikely to need it. Indeed, she urged the inclusion of more history—to give the girl a proper sense of dynasty—and the learning of poetry as an aid to memory-training. Later, when French was added, it was the Queen who arranged for an additional French tutor so that there was no break when Miss Crawford was on holiday. The hour between eleven and twelve was devoted to outdoor walks and games in Hamilton Gardens and the remaining hour till lunchtime was given over to reading. Afternoons were divided between singing, drawing, music and dancing lessons, with Monday afternoons specifically earmarked for "educational visit with Queen Mary."

The young Elizabeth tackled her lessons conscientiously, if without marked enthusiasm. Then as now, she was patient and painstaking, placid and serious. She showed early that she had inherited her grandmother's bent for detail. Even the coffee crystals which she infinitely preferred to candy had to be sorted into neat piles according to size before being eaten. (Margaret, by contrast, simply stuffed hers into her mouth in handfuls.) Shoes had to be straight at bedtime and clothes tidy. The slightest deviation would find Elizabeth hopping in and out of bed like mad in the interest of tidiness. Christmas presents had to be compiled into neat lists immediately after being opened. Only occasionally did Elizabeth rebel or indulge in childish horseplay (once, bored with writing out French verbs, she protested by the simple expedient of up-ending her silver inkpot and tipping the contents all over her hair and face).

But there was one lesson which never bored, never palled. This was her weekly riding lesson. Elizabeth was then—and is now—horse mad. Miss Crawford's first glimpse of her was of a small figure in a nightdress, the cords of her dressing gown tied to the bedposts, busily engaged in driving an imaginary coach and four "twice round the park." Had she never succeeded to the Throne, Elizabeth would almost certainly have matured into a very horsey, tweedy young matron, perfectly content to live quietly in the country surrounded by her children, her horses and her dogs.

There was, in childhood, never any difficulty over what to give her for Christmas. A toy horse or a book about horses and she was your friend for life. At one time, she and Margaret had a collection of more than thirty toy horses stabled on the landing of their Piccadilly home, brushing and grooming them each night, lavishing upon them the same care and attention other girls devote to dolls. When they moved to Buckingham Palace, their toy horses moved with them and were still there, neatly "stabled" along the nursery corridor, on the eve of Elizabeth's marriage to Prince Philip.

Elizabeth had her first riding lessons at Windsor when the Royal Family went there for weekends. Her first mount was a diminutive Shetland pony, a gift from her gruff old grandfather, George V. She was taught by a groom named Owen, who soon could do no wrong in her eyes. She credited him with the gift of omniscience and was constantly quoting him to her parents as the authority on all manner of subjects. Her habit of beginning sentences with "Owen says..." so irritated her father that in time the occasion came, as it was bound to, when he answered one of her childhood questions with "Why ask me? Ask Owen."

Compared with the sort of life her own children lead today, Elizabeth's upbringing was cloistered in the extreme. An occasional foray with her governess into Hyde Park or Kensington Gardens was real adventure. Once a year she and Margaret went to the theatre with their parents. Twice a year, just ahead of Christmas, they went to the shops—to Harrods with their mother, to Woolworth's with their governess. Needless to say, Elizabeth's carefully saved shilling-a-week pocket-money went further at Woolworth's.

Slowly, inexorably, her young life was moving towards its ultimate destiny. With the death of her grandfather, that bearded father-figure, King George V, she became second in succession to the Throne. As such, young as she was—she was only ten at the time—she was rigged out in a black coat and a black velvet hat to attend the lying-in-state and the ritualistic funeral which followed, her small face hidden behind the emotionless royal mask she was already learning to wear in public. "I have been trained since childhood never to show my feelings in public," she was to confide in a friend, years later. In fact, she learned the lesson almost too well, and in the years ahead, as she graduated more and more into the royal round of public chores, her mother, who is seldom seen without a smile on her own face, was continually impressing upon her that she should smile more. When Elizabeth, as a young princess, recently married, toured Canada for the first time, her mother was so concerned at the ultra-serious features her daughter revealed in so many newspaper photographs, that she telephoned her to ask, "Are you sure you're smiling enough?"

It was considered unseemly for Elizabeth to continue with her dancing lessons during the six months of court mourning which followed her grandfather's death. But there was apparently no breach of protocol in the swimming lessons which were substituted. The instructress at the Bath Club in nearby Brook Street went into a dither when she learned that Elizabeth and Margaret were to be amongst her pupils. She queried whether the pool should be closed to other pupils while the two princesses were there, and whether she should learn to curtsey. She was informed that neither innovation was necessary.

For all her initial dither, she proved an excellent instructress, and before their period of instruction with her was through both Elizabeth and Margaret could swim well enough to gain their life-saving certificates.

Elizabeth's favourite relative at this time was her Uncle David, who was now King Edward VIII. Preoccupied with his new duties as monarch, he now called less often at the York home in Piccadilly. Previously, he had been always in and out, frequently joining the family for tea and the young princesses in their bedtime games. He was, even if Elizabeth was too young at the time to realise the fact, a lonely and unhappy man who longed to have the same close-knit family ties as his brother.

The new King was, of course, preoccupied in another direction also. The storm-clouds of the coming abdication were already gathering the day he drove over to Royal Lodge, the York home at Windsor, in a shiny new American station-wagon, accompanied by a handsomely attractive woman in smart clothes and sparkling jewels who spoke with an American accent and in a forthright manner. "Who is she?" the young Elizabeth wanted to know. It was, of course, Mrs. Simpson.

The four grown-ups, the King and his companion, Elizabeth's father and mother, walked in the gardens for a time, chatting together in a desultory fashion. Then they went back into the house for tea with the children. While the grown-ups drank their tea, Elizabeth sat and sipped her orange juice, completely unaware that events were in train which would bring her within a single heartbeat of the throne.

But young though she was, she came to understand much of what was happening in the weeks that followed. Perhaps, indeed, she understood a great deal more than her parents realised at the time, as, unseen at the top of the staircase in 145 Piccadilly, she watched the frantic comings-and-goings of Stanley Baldwin, Britain's pipe-smoking prime minister, and others concerned with preserving the fabric of monarchy as it came within an inch of cracking. How nearly the monarchy failed to survive the struggle between King and Parliament, few realised. But certainly Elizabeth's father was alive to the danger. "If I have to take over," he remarked at one point, "I shall do my best to clear up the inevitable mess—if the whole fabric does not crumble under the shock and strain of it all."

It seems somehow appropriate that the young Elizabeth should have been starting her history lesson at ten o'clock that historic morning of December 10, 1936, as her Uncle David sat down at Windsor to sign the Instrument of Abdication which was to turn him from King Edward VIII into the Duke of Windsor.

As the princess sipped her orange juice during the break for "elevenses" which followed, she was, though she did not know it, now Heiress Presumptive to the Throne ("Presumptive" because it was still not beyond the bounds of possibility that her parents might have a son, who would automatically take precedence over her in the line of succession).

III

Though she was kept at her lessons that historic day—arithmetic, history and poetry in the morning, followed by music in the afternoon—the princess cannot have been unaware of the great changes going on around her. She doubtless caught a glimpse of her grandmother, Queen Mary, when she came to pay allegiance to the younger son who was now the new monarch. She must have heard the crowds which gathered outside 145 Piccadilly to cheer the untrained, uncertain man who had stepped, however hesitatingly, into his brother's shoes. Certainly by evening, when she glimpsed a letter addressed to "Her Majesty the Queen" lying on the side table in the hall, she knew sufficient about what was going on to remark, "That's Mummy now." Her mother at the time was ill in bed with one of the heavy, influenza-type colds to which she has more than once succumbed at times of strong emotion, and it was left to the governess, Marion Crawford, to explain things to Elizabeth more fully. If the princess felt much, she showed little, and only one small part of what she was told produced any real reaction in her. When told that the family, now that her father was King, would be moving to Buckingham Palace, Elizabeth, her young roots securely entrenched in the cosy intimacy of her Piccadilly home, was immediately perturbed. "You mean forever?" she queried, her eyes wide with dismay. And later, after the move had taken place, she uttered a childhood sigh for a tunnel from the palace to 145 Piccadilly so that she could slip back there to sleep at night.

Two days after the momentous events of December 10 came

the formal ceremony of proclamation. Queen Mary, her eyes still trained firmly on the future, had her two small grand-daughters visit her at Marlborough House, where they could look down on the ancient ceremony taking place in the Friary Court of St. James's Palace. They were back at 145 Piccadilly when their father returned. As he came in they bobbed him a curtsey as their governess had instructed them. For a moment he was clearly taken aback. Then he grabbed them into his arms and kissed them both.

Years later, when Elizabeth had become Queen in her turn, Charles and Anne were given similar instruction by their nanny, Helen Lightbody. I was outside the door of the Queen's room when nanny and children came along from the nursery. Charles was not yet five at the time, and Anne was some sixteen months younger. "Now remember," Nanny Lightbody instructed them, "Mummy is now the Queen. You, Charles, must bow to her. And you must curtsey, Anne."

She opened the door for them to go in. The two children paused in the doorway and did as they had been told. But the Queen wanted no such new formality creeping into her relationship with her children, and never again during my years at the palace did I see Charles bow to his mother, or Anne curtsey to her.

It is not part of the purpose of this book to deal with the reign of King George VI, except as it shaped Elizabeth for future sovereignty. But it would be remiss not to mention the great strength of character this frail and largely untrained man brought to the duties which he inherited so suddenly and reluctantly. The result was to leave the throne not weaker, but stronger than it had ever been. And there can be no more fitting tribute to him than that paid by his daughter when she unveiled a memorial to him, some three years after succeeding him on the throne.

"Much," she said, "was asked of my father in personal sacrifice and endeavor, often in the face of illness. His courage in overcoming it endeared him to everybody. He shirked no task, however difficult, and to the end he never faltered in his duty to his peoples. Throughout all the strains of his public life he remained a man of warm and friendly sympathies ... a man who by the simple qualities of loyalty, resolution and service won for himself such a place in the affection of all of us that when he died millions mourned for him as for a true and trusted friend."

With the move to Buckingham Palace, the pace of Elizabeth's training quickened. Aware of his own deficiencies in this connection—until he was actually King he had never seen the contents of one of those interminable "Boxes"—her father now took a hand in her training himself. Within weeks, she was standing beside her parents at the head of the Grand Staircase in Buckingham Palace to receive guests and accompany them through the state rooms. Her reading lessons were broadened to include appropriate volumes, including the youthful journal of her great-great-grandmother, Queen Victoria. She accompanied her father to Greenwich as he opened the National Maritime Museum. She was again at his side at Windsor for a march-past of Boy Scouts from many countries. Following each of these occasions her father would have her with him in his study while he explained some new aspect of monarchy to her, and these periods of explanation and discussion between father and daughter were perhaps as instructive to him as they were to her. As the time of her father's coronation drew near, she was taught a short speech in French with which to welcome President LeBrun of France. Again the time when she would have to undergo the same ceremony in turn, her father had a picture book specially devised for her explaining the significance of the coronation. Not to be outdone, Queen Mary produced from her vast collection of historical bygones a Victorian peepshow in which the coronation procession of George IV unfolded slowly over a total of ninety feet. Her father went over all the details of the coronation with her, and she was taken to Westminster Abbey to watch the final rehearsal.

In all this, childhood was not entirely forgotten, though her father had less time than previously to join her and Margaret in their girlish games. Exploring their vast new palace-home provided an additional adventurous pastime, as it did again, years later, for Charles and Anne. But if the palace was big, so was the garden—much more spacious and well-kept than the small, sooty garden at the rear of 145 Piccadilly. There was a summer-house which became an outdoor schoolroom in good weather, and even a lake where wild duck nested and raised their young only a few yards from the rumbling traffic of Grosvenor Place. It was, curiously enough, the quieter, more sedate Elizabeth rather than the tomboyish Margaret who overbalanced one day while looking for a duck's nest and fell into the lake, from which she scrambled out dripping with green slime. It is curious how history, in small things, so often repeats itself. Years later it was to be the quiet, serious Charles instead of the more boisterous Anne who fell into the sheep-dip at Windsor, emerging in tears, covered from head to foot in pinky-red dye.

On the morning of King George's coronation, Bobo helped Elizabeth to dress in an outfit which had been specially made for her, a lace frock, a diminutive train, an ermine-trimmed cloak, silver slippers and a small, lightweight coronet. Her sister, Princess Margaret, had the same outfit except for the train, an omission which caused some small degree of childish resentment.

Elizabeth, for her part, was worried that Margaret might disgrace the family by falling asleep in the middle of the long ceremony. "You're very young for a coronation," she told her with all the dignity of her eleven years. However, Margaret did not fall asleep. On the contrary, she remained sufficiently awake to cause rather too much noise at one stage of the proceedings. "I had to nudge her," Elizabeth said, slightly indignantly, when they returned home.

As though she could see into the future, she was always worrying, even then, that Margaret might do or say something to impair regal dignity. "If you see someone wearing a funny hat, you are not to point," she cautioned her when the two of them attended their first royal garden party, adding, "And you mustn't be in too much of a hurry to get to the tea table."

Elizabeth's own training for future monarchy proceeded with ever-growing momentum. She knew by heart the stirring speech her illustrious ancestor, Elizabeth I, had delivered to her soldiers at Tilbury, with its immortal line: "I know I have but the body of a weak and feeble woman, but I have the heart of a King—and of a King of England." Latin was added to her curriculum; tennis was introduced to ensure that she got sufficient exercise. The thought of sending her to school never seems to have occurred to her parents. Had it done so, Queen Mary, with her rigidly old-fashioned views on the fitness and unfitness of things, would doubtless have disapproved. However, she did go later to Eton College for private lessons in constitutional history from the Pickwickian vice provost, Sir Henry Marten, who interspersed instruction with a habit of chewing his handkerchief while gazing soulfully at the ceiling. But scholarly and remote though he seemed, he did not forget that his solitary girl pupil was only a child of twelve. Educational novelties helped to capture and hold her attention—an umbrella which converted into a world globe, a chess-like game of coloured counters which traced her lineage down the centuries.

Tirelessly, Queen Mary played her part in her granddaughter's training. Diligently she set aside Monday afternoons to collect Elizabeth and take her on educational excursions to places of interest—to Westminster Abbey and the Tower of London, to the British Museum and the Science Museum, to Hampton Court and the Bank of England, to the postal sorting office in Mount Pleasant and to the Royal Mint where they saw coinage for the new reign coming off the presses, to the National Gallery and the Wallace Collection. It was during the course of these outings that Elizabeth acquired her knowledgeable interest in art and antiques. Queen Mary found her an apt pupil. Only one thing about her granddaughter disappointed the old queen. Elizabeth was no good at needlework. Her grandmother was an expert needlewoman, and the chair on which the Queen today sits at her desk is a fine example of the delicate petit-point work Queen Mary could still do into old age. But Elizabeth, though she tried assiduously, could never capture the knack.

There were other, less formal, outings to the Horse Show and the Military Tournament. There was a brief ride on the top of a double-decker bus—her first and only experience of that mode of transport. She was accompanied on that occasion by her governess. Queen Mary would never have lowered her regal dignity to the extent of clambering on to a bus. Again with her governess, there was a trip on the London Underground and tea in a Y.W.C.A. canteen. Elizabeth bought her own ticket for the Underground and stood in a serve-yourself queue to collect her own tray of tea. Overcome by the excitement of the occasion, she marched off without her teapot. "If you want it, you must come back and get it," the woman in charge called after her, unaware that she was addressing her future queen.

The young Elizabeth had her portrait painted and her bust sculpted. A special company of Girl Guides was formed at Buckingham Palace to give her some sort of contact, however flimsy, with other girls of her own age. She watched her father open Parliament, accompanied her parents on a state visit to Scotland. But when President Roosevelt suggested that the two princesses should accompany their parents on a tour of Canada and the United States—"I shall try to have one or two Roosevelts of approximately the same age to play with them," he wrote to King George VI—Elizabeth's father demurred. "They are much too young for such a strenuous trip," he wrote back.

However, a less strenuous trip was in the offing—a visit to the Royal Naval College at Dartmouth, where the King had once been a cadet. No one at that time, with Elizabeth still only a girl of thirteen, could possibly have foreseen what long-term consequences that was to have. The fair-haired boy she met on that trip was described by her governess as "rather like a Viking, with a sharp face and piercing blue eyes." His name, of course, was Philip.

IV

When World War II broke out, Elizabeth was a girl of thirteen. Initially, at least, the war made little difference to the tempo of her young life. Her parents returned posthaste from Scotland to London, leaving her and Margaret in comparative safety at Birkhall, a Georgian house—small by royal standards—on the Balmoral Castle estate, which is now used by the Queen Mother. Lessons continued as usual under the direction of her governess, Marion Crawford, though constitutional history became a sort of correspondence course conducted by remote control from Eton. Elizabeth played her small part in the war effort by handing round tea and cakes at a weekly knitting and sewing party in the schoolroom organised to provide comforts for the troops. Her own knitting, like her needlework, was too slow and inferior to enable her to do anything more constructive. Old Laurel and Hardy and Charlie Chaplin movies provided occasional entertainment.

From Scotland, as the "phoney" war in Europe ran its plodding course, she was moved south to Royal Lodge at Windsor, where lessons with Sir Henry Marten were resumed and she followed the progress of the war with the aid of a large map and paper flags.

Suddenly, the "phoney" war became grim reality as the German panzers and dive-bombers swept across Europe. Elizabeth and Margaret were hurriedly transferred from Royal Lodge to the safer confines of the immensely thick-walled Lancaster Tower at Windsor Castle, with the walls sandbagged for extra protection, the chandeliers taken down and glass-fronted cupboards turned to face the wall. A company of Grenadiers acted as her special guards. She was sent to Windsor Castle originally "just for the rest of the week." She stayed there for five years. It was suggested at one time that she should be sent from Britain to Canada for greater safety. Her mother would not hear of it. "The princesses could not possibly go without me," she said. "I cannot go without the King. And the King will never go."

At Windsor, Elizabeth helped to collect scrap metal to build aircraft for the Battle of Britain, knitted a few shapeless socks as "comforts" for the troops, took part in gas-mask drills and fire-fighting drills. In her scrawling schoolgirl hand she wrote newsy letters of comfort and encouragement to members of the royal staff serving overseas with the British forces. To her other lessons was now added instruction in statecraft. She would join her father in his study and they would sit together as he perused the contents of his "Boxes."

For her, as for other youngsters, war hastened the process of growing up, and at fourteen she was considered old enough to make her first broadcast. She helped to draft the script and spent hours rehearsing what she was going to say. Even so, last-minute nerves played tricks with her phrasing. "All we children at home are full of cheerfulness and courage," she told her listeners. "We are trying to do all we can to help our gallant sailors, soldiers and airmen, and we are trying, too, to bear our share of the danger and sadness of war. We know that in the end all will be well." Her grandmother, Queen Mary, who was spending the war years with the Duke and Duchess of Beaufort in Gloucestershire, listened to the broadcast with tears of pride glistening in her eyes.

To earmark her sixteenth birthday, Elizabeth was given her first official appointment, honorary colonel in the Grenadier Guards. Her birthday was celebrated with a march-past of units of the regiment at Windsor, where she took the salute in a pleated skirt and woollen jacket. Ever since, the Grenadiers have held a special place in her affections, and years later, when two guardsmen were caught pilfering from Buckingham Palace, she reacted indignantly to a suggestion that they might be Grenadiers. "Certainly not," she retorted. "Grenadiers would never do such a thing." Another highlight of her sixteenth birthday was a much-publicised trip to the local labour exchange in Windsor, where she registered for war work as required by Britain's National Service Act. But despite her own pleas, work itself never actually came her way. Her father felt, perhaps rightly, that she was training for something much more important, and that such training should not be interrupted.

The King who never wanted a crown saw clearly the long, lonely years which lay ahead for his elder daughter when she, in turn, ascended the pinnacle of monarchy. "Poor Lilibet," he said on one occasion. "She will be alone and lonely all her life. No matter who she has by her side, only she can make the final decisions." This, of course, is true to a very large extent. Prince Philip, for all that he is her husband, is debarred from advising her on political or constitutional matters.

At seventeen, her training was already nearing fruition, and her father urged Parliament to allow her to serve as one of the Counsellors of State who acted for the King during his war-time absences from Britain. He wanted her, he said, to have "every opportunity of gaining experience in the duties which would fall upon her in the event of her acceding to the Throne." Hitherto, no one under the age of twenty-one could be appointed as a Counsellor of State. But Parliament saw the point and the Regency Act was amended so that Elizabeth could serve from her eighteenth birthday.

There was a public clamour in certain quarters, particularly among the Welsh, for her eighteenth birthday to be marked in more fitting fashion . . . by creating her Princess of Wales. Her father declined. In his view, the title "Princess of Wales" was one reserved for the wife of the Prince of Wales, even if there was at that time no Prince of Wales. However, to get about on her growing round of royal duties, he gave her her own car, a Daimler. She was also given her first Lady-in-Waiting (who served as her secretary) and accepted her first presidency, that of the National Society for the Prevention of Cruelty to Children. She dined with the Commonwealth prime ministers at Buckingham Palace, visited a number of air bases, including at least one American air base in Britain, launched the battleship *Vanguard*, and deputised for her father while he was away visiting allied troops in Italy.

By now firmly in love with Philip, her dearest wish was to

join one of the Services, so that she could feel she was sharing the risks and hardships he was undergoing in the Navy. Reluctantly her father gave way, and shortly before her nineteenth birthday she was granted an honorary commission as second subaltern in the Auxiliary Territorial Service. She duly donned her new khaki uniform—much to Margaret's envy—but there were no risks and few hardships. Her company commander even drove to Windsor to collect her and escort her to No. 1 Mechanical Transport Training Centre at Camberley, where she was to undergo a course in driving and auto engineering. Britain's newspapers, waxing enthusiastic over the idea that the heiress to the Throne was just like the girl next door, announced that she would share quarters with other junior officers and sleep in a camp bed. In fact, she returned to Windsor each night for dinner and continued to sleep in her own bed.

In this respect, at least, Britain's royalty has made big strides since Elizabeth came to the Throne ... though the moving spirit is almost certainly that of Philip rather than the Queen herself. Left to her own devices, the Queen would surely have raised her children as she herself was raised. After all, she knew no other way. But Philip did. At Gordonstoun and in the Navy he made his own way in a wider, more rugged world, and on his insistence, his children are having to do the same. There is still a fair degree of featherbedding, of course. They do not experience all the knocks and buffets of life which come the way of ordinary youngsters, but they experience many more than ever their mother did ... and their horizons are doubtless the wider for it.

Nevertheless, in those end-of-war years, it was still a considerable innovation for the heiress to the Throne to drive army trucks, change flat tires, scramble down into repair pits and work away at oily benches. If it did nothing else, Elizabeth's brief cushioned spell in the Services at least opened her eyes to some of the things that go on in the name of royalty. After her unit had been the subject of a royal inspection carried out by her aunt, the Princess Royal, she commented, "You've no idea what a business it has been . . . spit and polish all day long. Now I know what happens when Papa and Mummy go anywhere." There was, later, another royal inspection, this time by the King and Queen. Her father, every bit as much a practical joker as Philip was later to prove himself, surreptitiously removed the distributor arm from the vehicle on which his daughter was working. "What, not got it going yet?" he inquired, straight-faced, as she tried vainly to start the sabotaged vehicle.

Her brief spell in the Services also gave Elizabeth a new outlook on some aspects of life. When one of her Ladies-in-Waiting—she now had three to cope with mounting royal duties and growing correspondence—turned up for work at Buckingham Palace wearing a head-scarf instead of a hat, her mother was horrified. "She can't come here like that," she said. "She *must* wear a hat. You must speak to her." But Elizabeth only laughed. "Don't be old-fashioned, Mummy," she replied.

As she neared the age of twenty, the pace of Elizabeth's duties increased. She toured the counties of Northern Ireland and launched a new aircraft carrier. She took the salute at the passing-out parade at the Royal Military College, reviewed Army cadets at a parade in Hyde Park. She journeyed to Wales to inspect Girl Guides, to Scotland with her parents to attend an end-of-war thanksgiving service in St. Giles' Cathedral, Edinburgh. Her schedule was formidable enough to daunt the heart of an ordinary girl. But Elizabeth, trained to it from childhood, said only, "I must do it. It's my job." Sometimes, perhaps, she took the job too seriously, as at one parade when she pointed out an unpolished brass buckle worn by a young officer-cadet. Word got back to her father, and he cautioned her that royal justice should be tampered always with mercy.

It was around this time that I started work at Buckingham Palace as a junior footman. I saw Princess Elizabeth occasionally. My first impression of her was of a reserved, regally upright, still rather leggy young woman with a loud, carrying voice, dressed in sensible, fashionless clothes . . . pleated skirts, woollen twin-sets, boxy jackets, thick, unflattering stockings and flat, no-nonsense shoes. The love and respect she had for her father were obvious in the way she looked at him. He looked back at her with mingled affection, admiration and pride. Between the two of them there was a kind of telepathic communication, and more than once I intercepted a brief, flickering exchange of glances between them almost as though they were talking to each other without words.

Even then, punctuality was her watchword. She was never a minute late. In this, as in so many other things, she was her father's daughter. The desk in her third-floor sitting room was set out as neatly and tidily as clothes and shoes had been in childhood, the virgin blotter flanked by neat lines of pens and pencils drawn up like troops on parade. (By contrast, her desk today is crammed and cluttered, a royal battlefield with time as her constant enemy.)

Work and correspondence were mounting fast. She became president of the Student Nurses' Association, the Life Saving Society, the Red Cross. Speeches, handshakes and bouquets became part of her everyday life. But again and again in public life she showed that she was her mother's daughter as well as her father's. In Ireland, presented with a pair of finely-embroidered sheets, she asked to meet the elderly widow who had done the needlework. "Your poor eyes must ache," she told her, sympathetically. In South Africa, she was inspecting Basuto Girl Guides when she noticed a small group carefully segregated from all the rest. She was told they were lepers. She insisted on going over and speaking to them.

By contrast, in private at least, Elizabeth could be imperiously indignant if ever she thought she was being accorded insufficient respect. There was an occasion when, new and nervous, I addressed her simply as "Your Highness" (instead of "Your Royal Highness"). She said not a word, but she froze me with an icy stare of offended regality.

There was another occasion, at dinner, when a servant dropped a knife so that it struck the King on the back of the neck. A few minutes later, the King, turning his head sharply, struck it on

[79]

a silver meat dish I was offering to him. "They're bloody well trying to kill me tonight!" he roared good-humouredly. But there was nothing good-humoured in the icy glance directed at me by his elder daughter. Like Queen Victoria, she was not amused.

In this respect, the Queen has not changed with the years. Today, if she is offended, she still says nothing. But her glare speaks volumes. Even Prince Philip has been shocked into silence by one of those regally imperious looks. He was once regaling a family dinner party with a story of something that had happened to the Queen at a banquet the previous night, when suddenly he looked up to find his wife focusing him with a regal stare of offended dignity. Hurriedly he changed the subject.

The South African tour Princess Elizabeth made with her parents coincided with her coming-of-age. The gifts poured in, mostly diamonds . . . a casket of diamonds in East London, another in Cape Town, two superb blue-white diamonds from De Beers . . . and it was in South Africa, on her twenty-first birthday, April 20, 1947, that she made her memorable broadcast of dedication:

"I declare before you all that my whole life, whether it be long or short, shall be devoted to your service and the service of the great Imperial Commonwealth to which we all belong."

If the words were not her own, the sentiments assuredly were. Reading through a draft of the speech, which had been prepared by her father's Private Secretary, she was so stirred by emotion that she actually cried.

V

After Elizabeth's marriage to Philip, her father, despite his own own uncertain and failing health, did his best to limit the number of royal chores which fell on her shoulders. "There will be enough for her to do later on," he said, though not even he could gauge how soon that would be.

In company with Philip, she essayed a state visit to Paris. It was, for both of them, a nerve-wracking ordeal. Philip, for all that he is generally credited with complete freedom from nerves, became so wrought up in the course of the visit that he went down briefly with jaundice. Elizabeth felt faint during a wreath-laying ceremony at the Arc de Triomphe and had to summon up all her reserves of steely will to see things through. However, her faintness had less to do with nerves than with the fact that she was, by now, expecting her first baby. Time and again during the years since, she has demonstrated the strength of her regal willpower. Shortly after the birth of Charles she embarked on an official visit to the Channel Isles. The sea trip was a rough one, and Elizabeth had not yet developed the sea-legs she was to find later. Indeed, she was so seasick on that occasion as to require medical treatment. Yet she obstinately refused to cancel a part of her itinerary which involved a further sea crossing to the tiny island of Sark. Pale but determined, she crammed down a couple of pills and made the trip. So rough was the sea on that occasion that she had to try three times before she could jump from the heaving deck of the torpedo boat to the waiting quayside.

As her father's health declined, the extent of her own work increased. With Philip, she carried out a series of tours of provincial Britain, including another trip to Ireland. She deputised for her father at the annual ceremony of Trooping the Colour which marks the monarch's official birthday. The King, convalescent following major surgery to restore a defective blood supply in his right foot, watched her proudly from an open carriage. Elizabeth looked every inch a future queen as she rode side-saddle on to Horse Guards' Parade to take the salute, and perhaps only her father, who had drilled and inspected her before permitting her to ride at his side on a previous occasion, knew how nervous she really was as she took over the leading role for the first time.

Between flying visits to Malta to be with Philip, who had resumed his naval career, Elizabeth continued her work as a princess and her training as a future monarch. She helped entertain President Auriol of France on his state visit to London. She sat in the House of Commons to hear a debate on Britain's economic situation, and listened to part of a murder trial in the criminal courts at the Old Bailey. Taking time out for the birth of Princess Anne and further flying visits to Philip in Malta, she attended the £12-million Festival of Britain on the south bank of the Thames, helped out with entertaining the King and Queen of Denmark, deputised for her sick father during a state visit by the King of Norway, and, after another year had run its course with the King's health showing no real improvement, she again took the salute on Horse Guards' Parade.

She hopped from one provincial city to another in a growing welter of engagements, her own and her father's, and, in such spare time as she could command, planned ahead for her coming tour of Canada and the United States. She planned to go by sea, but at the last moment, with her father undergoing further surgery, she postponed her departure and finally made the trip by air two weeks later. With her when she left London she took a large sealed envelope which she was under strict instructions to open only in the event of the King's death. It contained all she needed to know for her own accession to the throne. For the King, time was running out, and the changeover of monarchy, when it came, must be swift and smooth. Few daughters can have undertaken so much with their minds so burdened emotionally.

If the Canadian visit did not get off to a good start, herein lies the answer. She was worried about her father; Philip was worried about her. If, in consequence, she was sometimes stiff and unsmiling and Philip occasionally grumpy—"This is a waste of time," he growled at an Ottawa reception when he found himself shaking hands with the same people all over again—it was surely understandable. There was another brief display of royal tantrums in Vancouver when Elizabeth was unexpectedly asked to receive an Indian princess. Philip felt his wife had done enough already. "The Indian princess stuff is out," he snapped. But Elizabeth intervened to countermand his instruction.

Yet, despite her personal worries and even if sometimes un-smiling, again and again she displayed those deft human touches. In a hospital a crippled boy hoping to take a photograph of her found his flashgun out of action when she arrived at his bed. She told him to get it fixed and she would be back. She kept her promise, and a delighted youngster got his picture.

Daily she telephoned London to check on the King's health. News of a seeming improvement buoyed her spirits, and a square-dance which cropped up unexpectedly in her schedule found her sending the indispensable Bobo out shopping for a suitable skirt and blouse from a nearby department store.

That Canadian tour was hectic. In thirty-five whirlwind days Elizabeth and her husband travelled 16,000 miles, shook more than that number of hands—she was clocked as shaking 3000 hands in little more than two hours at a reception in Toronto—and visited every Canadian province, including Newfoundland, stopping off at more than seventy places. A single day in Ottawa found her attending no fewer than thirteen different functions, in addition to an official luncheon and a state banquet, at both of which she made speeches.

Bad weather dogged one part of the tour and it was the in-ventive Philip who conceived the idea of a plastic bubble to cover the royal car so that his wife, while protected from the weather, could still be seen by the crowds. It was turned out in double-quick time by workers in a Toronto aircraft plant. Eliza-beth met the Dionne quints, saw her first ice hockey game, at-tended the Calgary Stampede warmly wrapped in an electric blanket, toured hospitals and paper mills, and visited McGill University, where 7000 students greeted her with a raucous yell of "Yea Yea Betty Windsor Rah Rah Rah." (She was in fact at that time, following her marriage to Philip, not Betty Windsor, but Elizabeth Mountbatten.) By contrast with those hectic weeks in Canada, her two-day side trip to Washington, where President Truman called her "a fairytale princess," was almost a rest cure. "As one father to another," the President wrote later to Britain's sick King, "we can be very proud of our daughters."

[83]

Back home in England, George VI was pleased and proud with everything he heard and read about his daughter's tour. To signify his pleasure he appointed Elizabeth and Philip to his Privy Council. He also felt less perturbed about his physicians' firm refusal to let him undertake his long-planned tour of Australia and New Zealand. If he could not go himself, then the princess should go for him. She had proved herself well capable of it.

There is little doubt that as autumn turned into winter, as 1951 gave way to 1952, and as Elizabeth and Philip busied themselves with preparations for the coming tour and finally flew out, the King himself sensed that his end was near. Once, in an unguarded moment, I saw him looking at the daughter to whom he was always so close, and whom he had trained so conscientiously and painstakingly to succeed him. In the King's eyes, as he looked at her, was the old mixture of love and pride. But there was something else also ... an infinite sadness.

Perhaps, as he stood in the biting wind at London Airport to wave her goodbye on that last day of January, he guessed that he would never see her again.

But no one else who was there that day realised how short the intended tour was to be ... or guessed that when they saw her next she would be not Princess but Queen, the office towards which her father and grandmother had coached her ever since she was a small girl of five.

4. *THE BEGINNING OF A REIGN*

I

IT was February 6, 1952. I was in my green-carpeted bed-sitting room on the top floor of Buckingham Palace. Although it was nine o'clock in the morning, I was not long out of bed. I was off duty that day, and, in any event, with the King and Queen still at Sandringham and Princess Elizabeth and Prince Philip in Kenya, en route for Australia, there was comparatively little work for anyone to do at the palace.

For my part, I was glad of the respite. I had been at Sandring-ham with the Royal Family over Christmas—and Christmas, with its family parties and other festivities, means long hours and extra work for those in royal service. Not that anyone really minded. Christmas was then, and is now, a period of royal life which servants enjoy almost as much as the Royal Family themselves.

King George VI, in particular, always made the most of Christmas and the opportunity it afforded for him to get away, however briefly, from the public life he had never sought. "Christmas is the one time of the year I really enjoy," he re-marked on one occasion. "I have my family around me and can forget for a little while that I am King."

I remember all too vividly that last Christmas he spent at Sandringham, happy in the warmth of family love and affection which surrounded him, striving hard not to let others see how desperately sick he was. He was never a robustly healthy man. Major surgery for thrombosis and, later, cancer had undermined his frail physique still further. But nothing could ever dim his conscientiousness in kingship or his capacity for enjoying family life. And that year, almost as though he had forebodings of the future, he seemed to drive himself to enjoy Christmas as never before.

When carol singers paid their customary call at Sandringham, he had them invited as usual into the vast "Saloon," cluttered with furniture handed down through successive generations, where three-foot logs hissed and crackled in the huge, open fireplace. But while others of the family joined in singing the favourite, familiar carols, he could only sit and listen. His Christmas Day broadcast, usually delivered "live" from Sandringham, had been pre-recorded a few words at a time. The result was an illusion of wellbeing and regained health which actuality did not bear out. The King was so exhausted he was forced to sit when he distributed Christmas gifts to his staff in the high-ceilinged ballroom with its tall Christmas tree sparkling with tinsel and fairy lights.

Worn out in body, but a man of indomitable spirit. In the days and weeks following Christmas he was out pheasant-shooting nearly every day in the crisp, cold winter air. But he no longer tramped for miles, dog at heel and gun tucked smartly under one arm, as he had done once. Instead, his valet, Tom Jerram, carried his gun for him, and the King travelled from beat to beat in a Land Rover specially fitted with electrically heated gloves to restore circulation in his thin, blue hands.

He still tackled the contents of his Boxes as industriously as ever. But instead of joining the family for afternoon tea in the drawing room, as he had always done previously, he now retired to a small ground-floor suite which had been fitted out with a bed and rested there until it was time for dinner.

A royal tour of Australia and New Zealand, postponed once on account of the King's health, had been re-scheduled, but his health was clearly not up to it. His physicians favoured a quiet convalescent cruise to the warm sunshine of South Africa, and to this he agreed once he had ascertained that Elizabeth and the Duke of Edinburgh would undertake the scheduled tour in his place.

As a farewell treat for Elizabeth, the King took the whole family to see the American musical, *South Pacific*. It was essentially his type of show—robust and full-blooded, with plenty of belly laughs—and he thoroughly enjoyed it. But next day, January 31, at London Airport, his hair disarrayed by the chill wind as he said goodbye to his daughter and her husband, he again looked the desperately sick man he undoubtedly was. To Bobo MacDonald, who was travelling with Princess Elizabeth, he said quietly during those moments of intimate farewell aboard the aircraft, "Look after Lilibet for me."

When the King returned to Sandringham, I did not go with him. To give us a break, the King always arranged for a change of staff at roughly the halfway point of any long stay at either Sandringham or Balmoral—a practice which the Queen continues today. James MacDonald (no relation to Bobo) took over from Tom Jerram as the King's valet . . . and it was MacDonald who made the tragic discovery of the King's death when he took him his morning tea on February 6.

Of this I knew nothing as I dressed in my room at Buckingham Palace. It was an hour or so later, in the footmen's room, that word first reached me. And even that, at first, was no more than an unconfirmed rumour which another footman had heard from the newspaper vendor on the corner of Buckingham Palace Road.

"Have you heard?" he said, rushing white-faced into the room. "The King's dead."

"He can't be," I said. "We live here and we'd be the first to know."

Despite my outward disbelief, I experienced an acute inward

sense of shock. I had been at Buckingham Palace for six years. As a comparatively junior footman, in those days, I had little immediate contact with the King. To me, he was a slightly remote and rather awe-inspiring figure. Yet a figure capable of inspiring real devotion in those who worked for him, and a sense of deep attachment in millions to whom he was only a picture in the newspapers or a voice on the radio at Christmas. Sick though we knew him to be, his death seemed unthinkable.

We switched on the radio, but got only a static hum. Subsequent investigation revealed that other sets throughout the palace were equally silent. The silence itself confirmed the rumour.

Then, at fifteen minutes past eleven, the radio was silent no longer and rumour was finally fact. In the footmen's room we looked at each other with ashen faces. "We'll never have a better Guv'nor," said one of the others... a phrase I was to hear in varying forms a dozen times during the next few hours. As I came out of the footmen's room, one of the housemaids was coming along the corridor towards me; tears were streaming unashamedly down her cheeks.

II

It is a traditional part of the British constitution that the Throne is never vacant. Elizabeth, though she herself was completely unaware of it, became Queen at the very moment of her father's death. It is not possible, however, to pinpoint the exact moment when she followed him to the Throne. The King died in his sleep. At midnight he was still awake and moving about his room. At half-past seven the following morning, when James MacDonald took him his tea, he was dead.

At some indeterminate point between midnight and half-past seven, Her Royal Highness the Princess Elizabeth, Duchess of Edinburgh, became Her Most Excellent Majesty Elizabeth the Second, Queen of the United Kingdom of Great Britain and Northern Ireland and of her other Realms and Territories, Head of the Commonwealth, Defender of the Faith, Sovereign of the

British Orders of Knighthood. She was without doubt the first monarch in British history to succeed to the Throne while perched thirty feet up in the branches of a tree.

The tree was a wild fig located in the depths of the Aberdare Forest in Kenya, and the new Queen's presence in its branches was due to her desire to make a home movie of the big game of the area before flying on to Mombasa.

Her treetop vigil over, she was back at the Sagana Royal Lodge, busily catching up with arrears of correspondence, when radio confirmation of the King's death was finally received. Until then, the rumoured news had been carefully kept from her, though everyone else already knew of it. Now it had to be broken to her as gently as possible. There was only one possible person for so personal a task—Philip, her husband.

The daughter may have wept in the privacy of her bedroom when news of her father's death was given to her, but the Queen who emerged from the bedroom some time later was thoroughly composed. Her first duty as Queen, in response to an urgent telephone call from London over the single line to the Lodge, was to decide her own official name. Her father, when he succeeded to the Throne, switched his name from Albert to George —though he continued to be called "Bertie" in the family circle— in order to form a link with his father and perhaps paper over any cracks the monarchy may have sustained from the abdication of his elder brother. The new Queen had no such necessity, and her reply was characteristic.

"My own name, of course . . . what else?"

Crisp and clear-cut though her decision was, it was to cause some small confusion during the months which followed. With both the new Queen and her mother residing at Buckingham Palace, correspondence addressed to "Queen Elizabeth" and intended for the mother was not infrequently delivered to Queen Elizabeth II and opened by the daughter. It was difficult at first to think of the Princess as "the Queen" and the woman we had always known as Queen as "the Queen Mother."

The accession of a new monarch is not something to be accomplished without attendant pomp and ceremony. Even while the new Queen was driving along the red-dust roads of Kenya on the first stage of her long journey home, the Accession Council, meeting in solemn conclave at St. James's Palace, declared Elizabeth to be her father's true and rightful successor. That evening members of both Houses of Parliament took an oath of allegiance to the new Queen. And that night the ceremony of "The Keys" within the grim, grey walls of the Tower of London had a new litany. The answer to the centuries-old challenge of "Who goes there?" was now "Queen Elizabeth's keys." But public proclamation of the new Queen's accession was postponed until she had returned to her realm.

The Queen arrived at London Airport the following afternoon suitably dressed in black mourning, an item of wardrobe which members of the Royal Family include in their baggage wherever they go. She was met by her uncle, the red-faced Duke of Gloucester; her husband's uncle, Earl Mountbatten of Burma; Lord Woolton, President of the Privy Council; Winston Churchill, her prime minister; and Clement Attlee, leader of the Labour opposition in the House of Commons. These last two greeted her not in their political guise, but in their historic role as members of her Privy Council. Churchill, a man whose emotions always ran close to the surface, was unashamedly in tears as he took her hand.

Her mother was still at Sandringham, where the King had died, but her grandmother, Queen Mary, was waiting at Clarence House to greet her. As a child, Elizabeth had been brought up to curtsey whenever she entered her grandmother's presence. But now positions were reversed, and it was the grandmother, at eighty-four, who curtsied to the granddaughter at twenty-five who was now the Sovereign. Yet she could not, I have been told, entirely resist a typical comment on the new monarch's clothes. "Much too short for mourning," she said.

Also awaiting her arrival at Clarence House (which was to continue as her home until the changeover to Buckingham Palace could be arranged) was the first of the Boxes. She had previously dealt with them, briefly and intermittently, as one of the Counsellors of State appointed to act for her father while he was undergoing surgery. But now the Boxes were hers in her own right and would be until the end of her reign, though the name lettered in gold on the leather-covered lid of that first one was still "The King." There had not yet been time to make the change.

Another early duty—and a sad one—was to receive the Duke of Norfolk, hereditary Earl Marshal of England, and the Earl of Clarendon, Lord Chamberlain and senior official of the Royal Household, and "command" them to make arrangements for her father's funeral, though these in fact were already in hand. Considering her deep affection for her father, and how heart-broken she must have been at his death, her composure was truly remarkable. There was no chink in the iron mask royalty must wear always in public. Before leaving Kenya she had signed and distributed photographs to those who had looked after her during her brief stay ... to house servants, chauffeurs, policemen. She had personally drafted the telegrams which went out to Australia, New Zealand and elsewhere regretting the inevitable postponement of her promised trip. At London Airport she had paused briefly to thank members of the aircrew who had flown her back.

The following morning she walked through the connecting door from Clarence House to St. James's Palace to make her formal Declaration of Accession. Her husband went with her, but once inside the precincts of St. James's Palace, custom required that he leave her side and take his place among the other 174 members of the Privy Council. The new Queen was now entirely on her own, a young woman of twenty-five about to undergo one of the most nerve-wracking experiences of her life.

No one except the few who have actually undergone it can possibly realise the intense degree of nervous tension that goes with such a moment. The Duke of Windsor has recalled how his own installation as Prince of Wales had him half-fainting with nerves. Of course, he was only sixteen at the time. But his father was in his forties when he made his Declaration of Accession upon succeeding to the Throne, and he noted in his diary that it was "the most trying ordeal I have ever had to go through."

The Queen was pale and set-faced as she read the words of the Declaration, but her voice was clear and controlled and she did not falter, even at the passages which referred to her "revered and beloved" father, though those closest to her thought they detected a misting of the eyes. She replaced the Declaration on the table at which she stood, signed two copies of the Oath for the Security of the Church in Scotland, and withdrew to the privacy of the Throne Room, where her husband and uncle, unobtrusively withdrawing from the main body of Privy Counsellors, were quickly at her side.

As Big Ben struck the hour of eleven, trumpets shrilled a fanfare. The sergeants-at-arms, carrying their ornate maces, heralds magnificently garbed in scarlet and blue and gold, and the Earl Marshal, a resplendent figure weighed down with gold braid, emerged onto the Tudor balcony of St. James's Palace. The new Queen, unseen behind the lace curtains of an upstairs window at Clarence House, had an angled view of the ancient ceremony as the parchment scroll was unrolled and the sonorous, rolling phrases of the proclamation were read out, informing the populace that "the Lords Spiritual and Temporal of this Realm, being here assisted with these of His late Majesty's Privy Council, with representatives of other Members of the Commonwealth, with other Principal Gentlemen of Quality, with the Lord Mayor, Aldermen and Citizens of London, do now hereby with one voice and consent of tongue and heart proclaim that the High and Mighty Princess Elizabeth Alexandra Mary is now, by the Death of our late Sovereign of Happy Memory, become Queen Elizabeth the Second, by the Grace of God, Queen of this Realm and all Her other Realms and Territories. . . ."

III

Until the changeover to Buckingham Palace could be conveniently arranged, the new Queen continued to live and work at Clarence House, a few hundred yards away along the Mall. As a result, my first real glimpse of her as Sovereign was aboard the funeral train which conveyed her father's coffin to its last resting place at Windsor. I had seen her often enough about Buckingham Palace when she was still Princess Elizabeth—a quiet, serious, composed young woman, old for her years, certainly not given to girlish giggles and high jinks. Even so, my impression as I watched her, black garbed and heavily veiled, was that the accession had somehow wrought in her a metamorphosis. Even under the impact of personal grief she was composed, dignified, and firm, and the power which held her emotions in check was surely a formidable one. Others may have thought of the new monarch as a mere girl, inexperienced and malleable. Watching her that day, I had no such illusions. This was indeed a *Queen.*

In the years which followed, watching her in public and in private, in all sorts of countries and under all sorts of conditions, I had cause to change that first quick assessment, but only fractionally. There was then and is now much about Queen Elizabeth II that is reminiscent of her grandmother, the stiff-backed, regally imperious Queen Mary. True, the Queen can and does unbend occasionally as her grandmother never did, but inside her always is a firm, unfaltering belief in herself and in the position she occupies.

Princess Margaret, by contrast, is a more temperamental person, less strong-willed—haughty, rather than regal. She could not sustain her composure as her sister did. No longer did she sing and whistle the hit tunes from the latest shows. No longer did she charge about like a long-legged teenager. Instead, she withdrew inside herself, spending long hours walking alone in Buckingham Palace gardens with only her pet Sealyhams, Johnny and Pippin, for company.

The Queen Mother, grief-stricken though she was, was more composed than her younger daughter, though the radiant smile no longer came as readily or as frequently. They ate together, the mother and the daughter, but their meals for months to come were eaten with downcast eyes and silent lips, as often as not with the television set blaring out to avoid the necessity for conversation.

Temporarily at least, Clarence House, where the Queen still lived, became the focal point of monarchy. It was there that the High Commissioners of the Commonwealth and representatives of other countries went to offer their condolences. It was there that members of the Government made their way, as the new Queen held a series of official audiences to ease her into the manifold intricacies of monarchy.

She was fortunate, as a young and inexperienced monarch, to have the help and counsel of the top royal officials who had served her father ... his Private Secretary and Assistant Private Secretaries, his Keeper of the Privy Purse, and his Master of the Household. Buckingham Palace, she found, was a much larger and more complex establishment than Clarence House. That it continued to tick over so efficiently was due in no small measure to the Master of the Household, Sir Piers Legh, who ruled it, if not with a rod of iron, at least with one of mild steel.

There was little change in either the organisation of the monarchy or the running of Buckingham Palace. But one change, at least, was important on a personal level. This was the Queen's decision in Council—which means a decision taken on the advice of and in the presence of members of her Privy Council—to revert to her maiden name of Windsor. Her grandfather, George V, when he renounced his original German dynastic name of Saxe-Coburg and Gotha during World War I, had been guilty of a small oversight in declaring that "from this day forth the name of Windsor shall be borne by my Royal House and Family." He had overlooked the possibility that he might one day be succeeded on the throne by a married woman.

Elizabeth, when she married, complied with ordinary matrimonial custom and took her husband's (adopted) name of Mountbatten. She was still a Mountbatten when she succeeded to the Throne, and for the first two months of her sovereignty she reigned as a Mountbatten.

But on April 9, 1952, by her Order in Council, she announced her "Will and Pleasure that I and My children shall be styled and known as the House and Family of Windsor and that My descendants, other than female descendants who marry and their descendants, shall bear the name of Windsor."

I have been told—and see no reason to disbelieve it—that the Queen took this decision largely on the insistence of her prime minister, Winston Churchill, a man to whom lineage and dynasties, ceremony and tradition, were the very fibre of national greatness. In those days, as a young and untried Queen, she was somewhat in awe of Churchill; he was perhaps the only man who could have influenced her to make the decision to discard her married name.

It can hardly have brought joy to the heart of Philip's uncle, Earl Mountbatten of Burma. His proud claim is that he can trace his family tree back forty-four generations. But Mountbatten's disappointment was no doubt assuaged eight years later when the Queen, then awaiting the birth of her third child, made a further Order in Council:

"And whereas I have given further consideration to the position of those of My descendants who will enjoy neither the style, title nor attribute of Royal Highness nor the titular dignity of Prince and for whom therefore a surname will be necessary:

"Now therefore I declare my Will and Pleasure that, while I and My children shall continue to be styled and known as the House and Family of Windsor, My descendants other than descendants enjoying the style, title or attribute of Royal Highness and the titular dignity of Prince or Princess and female descendants who marry and their descendants shall bear the name of Mountbatten-Windsor."

Stripped of its Old World phrasing and boiled down to its essentials, this means that certain of the Queen's great-grandchildren—those descended through her two younger children, Andrew and Edward—will one day bear the double-barrelled name of Mountbatten-Windsor as visible proof of the lineal link between the royal Windsors and the proud Mountbattens.

If the Queen's reversion to the name of Windsor was at all wounding to her husband's manhood, there were other decrees early in her reign which were doubtless pleasing to him. Philip's position has always been an anomalous one, and never more so than when his wife first succeeded to the Throne. He was the Queen's husband, a Royal Highness and the Duke of Edinburgh. But the British constitution makes no allowance for the husband of a Queen, and Philip was not a Prince (though the world outside Buckingham Palace persisted in referring to him as "Prince Philip"). In fact, he was not elevated to the "style and titular dignity" of a Prince until February, 1957. But long before that—in October, 1952, some eight months after her accession—the Queen assured a constitutional place for him by a royal warrant which assigned to him "Place, Pre-eminence and Precedence next to Her Majesty." Thus, though Philip himself could never succeed to the Throne, he ranked in protocol above his son, who could.

The following year he was named Regent to act for his son in the event that the Queen should die and Prince Charles should succeed to the Throne while still a minor. Until then, Princess Margaret, at that time next in line to the Throne after Charles and Anne, had been the nominated Regent. So Philip, for all that he complained in those early days that he felt "like a lodger" at Buckingham Palace, secured the first toehold which was to lead to the highly influential position he occupies today.

IV

Neither the Queen nor Philip had any real desire to move from Clarence House. It was small enough to be homey, large enough to be royal. But it was not large enough to accommodate all the staff and activity that went with the monarchy. So the Queen took advantage of the traditional six weeks when she resided at Windsor Castle to have her things moved over in her absence.

To avoid any suggestion that she was pushing her mother out, she and Philip moved initially into the ground-floor Belgian Suite at the rear of the palace, leaving the Queen Mother in the royal suite upstairs. Princess Margaret, who had continued to use the old royal nursery long after nursery days were over, obligingly moved to another suite at the front of the palace so that the nursery could revert to its former use. Prince Charles, already revealing something of his father's inquisitive nature at three and a half, and Princess Anne, a two-year-old toddler with a golden topknot, moved in along with their nannies, Helen Lightbody and Mabel Anderson.

With their coming the palace came suddenly to life again. The Grand Hall, with its marble columns and statues, became an improvised trotting track for a pedal-operated horse and cart propelled by a small tousle-haired boy in blue shorts and a white shirt. The long red-carpeted corridors became racetracks for the royal corgis with the Queen, her hair disarrayed, serving as starter while the children tore off ahead as the hares. The Queen was a mother as well as a monarch, and even the prime minister, calling each Tuesday to keep her informed on political matters, came an hour later so as to leave her free to help bathe the children and get them to bed.

At Clarence House, Elizabeth had been able to make do with comparatively few servants. As Queen she needed many more. The Pickwickian-looking Ernest Bennett, who had been her butler, now became one of her two pages. Maurice Watts, who had been one of her father's pages, shared duty with Bennett. Her footman, Joe Pearce, moved over from Clarence House with her. But because the hours of duty were so long, extending sometimes from seven o'clock in the morning until ten or half-past ten at night, he needed a relief. Three of us who were already at the palace were given a trial, and I got the job. The indispensable Bobo returned to the palace as the Queen's Dresser, and Elizabeth MacGregor, who had been housekeeper at Clarence House, became her assistant.

Prince Philip brought his valet, John Dean, and also took over one of the late King's valets, James MacDonald. Philip also inherited one of the King's pages, Stanley Childs, and appointed William Holloway, who had been under-butler in the Clarence House menage, as his other page.

Almost the first thing Maurice Watts asked the Queen when he became her page was how she wanted things run, now that she was mistress of the palace.

Her reply was precise and definite. "I want everything to continue exactly as it did for my father," she said.

And that was the way things were to be, with the rest of us taking our cue from Watts. At Clarence House, members of the Household staff had been accustomed merely to tap on the sitting room door and then walk straight in. But the Princess was now the Queen and protocol must be satisfied, as "Boy" Browning quickly discovered following the move to Buckingham Palace. He tapped on the Queen's door and was on the point of walking in when Maurice Watts checked him. "You must wait to be announced," said Watts. "Nobody can simply walk in on the Queen."

Those first eighteen months after she succeeded to the Throne were the busiest the Queen had ever known. She had to adapt herself to long hours of desk work, dealing with official correspondence, perusing state documents, signing papers and letters. She received hundreds of official visitors.

At one investiture she was taken unwell, but she insisted on seeing things through before going to her room and taking to her bed. An authoritative medical journal, *The Lancet,* sounded a warning against allowing her to do too much. So did the Select Committee set up by Parliament to go into the question of a new Civil List. Said the Committee's report, "In spite of the assistance of a devoted staff and notwithstanding constant attempts to lighten the burden, the burden of Her Majesty's duties is still formidable and likely to remain so." It mentioned the increasing number of official visitors she had to receive, and the continually increasing number of public functions she was required to attend, adding, "Moreover, with increasing facilities for air travel, it is to be expected that the Sovereign will pay more frequent visits to the other countries of the Commonwealth and Empire. The relations between the Sovereign and the Commonwealth are certain to mean a considerable extension in the demands made on Her Majesty and the Royal Family as a whole." Over the years the report's prophesy has turned out to be only too accurate.

But whatever others may have thought, to those of us who saw her regularly about the palace she looked well and vital most of the time. It was as though she thrived on the hard work of monarchy. It is a curious thing about the Queen, but to this day she looks more tired when she has little to do—when relaxing at Balmoral or Sandringham—than ever she does when she is working full out. On a royal tour, necessitating an early rise, non-stop days of travel, receptions, speeches, banquets and hand-shaking, and frequent changes of wardrobe so that she presents a new royal picture at each fresh stopping place, she will end up at midnight or after still looking full of beans, and get up the next morning full of zest and ready to go again.

Despite all else she had to do in so many different directions, the Queen still made time for her children. She saw them, if only briefly, at breakfast-time each day, and again for at least one and a half hours each evening. Whenever her work permitted, she would also take the elevator up to the nursery floor at lunchtime to check on how they were coming along. Of course she did not wash and dress them in the morning, cook their meals, wash and iron their clothes, or tackle any of the hundred and one other tasks ordinary mothers take for granted in the upbringing of their children. Time would not permit her to do so, even if she had the inclination. But she did give Charles his earliest lessons in reading and writing and taught him to tell the time. Of an evening, she would help to bathe the children, sit with them in the nursery while they ate their suppers, and read them a bed-time story before going downstairs again for her own dinner.

With so much to do and so much still to learn, inevitably the Queen was compelled to take some short cuts. There was, for instance, a world-wide demand for photographs and portraits of the new monarch. The Queen posed for as many artists as possible, but obviously she could not afford all the sittings they requested, and many a royal portrait was finished from a dress-maker's dummy decked out in the Queen's clothes. Yet when it was suggested that she cut down the time spent signing official photographs by rubber-stamping them, she declined firmly. Without her actual signature, she said, the photographs would lack personal significance.

So busy was she that she could not even afford the time necessary to sit for a painting she wanted for herself—an informal family group of herself, her husband, the children and the pet corgis to serve as a personal memento of this important period in her life. So she posed only for the features—and Bobo sat in for her while the artist worked away at the rest of the body. In the same way, I was roped in to serve as a stand-in for Prince Philip, sitting on a tapestry-covered stool in the Queen's sitting room while one of the royal corgis rested her head on my knee . . . and the artist captured us both on canvas.

V

Preparations for the Coronation made additional work in many directions, much of it falling upon the Queen. The actual ceremony on June 2, 1953, lasted only some two and a half hours, but the planning went on a full twelve months beforehand. The Queen, by her own wish, was consulted and brought in on things at each step of the way, and there was much she insisted upon doing for herself. For instance, in selecting the design for a new postage stamp to mark the Coronation, she studied and finally eliminated seventy-four alternative designs. Philip helped, as he did in settling designs for the new coinage.

Inevitably there were upsets and alarums along the way. Her choice of a royal cypher—EIIR—upset not a few Scots who insisted that where Scotland was concerned she was Elizabeth the First. The initial plan not to televise the ceremony created a furore of such proportions that the Queen herself intervened to reverse the decision. One reason for the proposed ban was to ease the strain on the Queen, likely to be considerable in any event. Elizabeth quickly made it clear that no such easement was required. A suggestion that part of the Coronation ceremony should be eliminated for the same reason brought a prompt query from her:

"Did my father do it?"

"Yes, Your Majesty," the Archbishop of Canterbury was obliged to concede.

"Then," said the Queen, "I will, too."

Work on the fabulous gown she would wear for the Coronation started in October when fashion designer Norman Hartnell prepared the first hand-painted designs for her consideration. Studying them, the Queen's initial reaction was that the proposed gown, basically white and silver, was too much like her wedding gown. Hartnell reminded her that her ancestor, Queen Victoria, had been crowned in a white gown. But the Queen had done her homework and had a ready answer. "Queen Victoria," she said, "was unmarried when she was crowned." She suggested that the gown should be embroidered with symbolic designs in pearl, crystal and diamante—England's rose, Scotland's thistle, the Irish shamrock, the leek of Wales, Canada's maple leaf, the Australian wattle, the New Zealand fern, and others. And this was the form the dress finally took. At Christmas, Hartnell and his assistants came to Sandringham for the first fitting. The Queen obliged enthusiastically. Her wedding dress apart, the Coronation gown is perhaps the only item she has ever worn over which she has displayed real excitement.

Back at Buckingham Palace after the Christmas recess at Sandringham, the pace of preparation quickened. The two hundred-odd boxes stored in the palace basement since pre-war days were hauled out and opened up to reveal the traditional state liveries—breeches of scarlet velvet, scarlet and gold coats, black velvet jockey caps. Replacements were ordered for the pink silk stockings which had deteriorated during the long years of storage. New gold aiglettes displaying the controversial EIIR cypher were made to go on the liveries. Feet were measured for the handmade black pumps with their big gold buckles which would complete the outfits. To break in these new shoes and to familiarise ourselves with the processional route, several of us on the royal staff painstakingly trudged over it half a dozen times before the big day, first removing the gold buckles so as to avoid looking conspicuous. It was a mistake. Not until we tramped the same route on Coronation Day did we realise how those buckles would move with the movement of the foot, skinning and cutting sensitive insteps. For me, Coronation Day is memorable for its acute discomfort.

The huge state coach, four tons of history dating from the days of George IV, was hauled out of its resting place in the royal mews and fitted with rubber tyres to make for a more comfortable ride. So that the new Queen should be clearly seen by the crowds, concealed electric lights (operated from a battery tucked away under one of the seats) were installed in the coach, along with concealed rests to take the weight of the orb and sceptre the Queen must appear to be holding as she rode through the streets of London.

The mounting excitement attendant upon all these preparations was checked by the death of the Queen's grandmother, Queen Mary. The ageing Queen had been as enthused as anyone over the prospect of the coming Coronation, and only a few months before her death she went with her granddaughter to inspect the coronation gown worn by that earlier queen, Victoria. But, sadly, she did not live to see her granddaughter crowned, though legend has it that she saw her with the crown on her head. Just before Queen Mary died, so the legend runs, the crown was taken secretly from its resting place in the Tower of London to her home at Marlborough House. And in the old Queen's bedroom, briefly and secretly, the new Queen donned the great crown so that her grandmother could see her wearing it.

Such is the legend . . . for whatever legends are worth. I can neither vouch for it nor deny it. I can add only that what legend says happened was in line with the characters of the two persons concerned.

I myself saw the new Queen with the crown on her head some time before the actual Coronation. In fact, both the crowns the Queen would wear on Coronation Day were brought over to Buckingham Palace well beforehand so that the Queen could try them on for size. There was the great seven-pound Crown of St. Edward—it derives its name from one supposedly worn by Edward the Confessor, though the present model was in fact made for Charles II—which the Queen would be wearing briefly during the actual Coronation ceremony, and the lighter Imperial State Crown, made originally for Queen Victoria, which she would wear for the subsequent processional drive through London. Characteristically, the Queen was not content merely to try them on. She wanted to be sure she would be completely comfortable in them, that no shadow of discomfort would mar her features as they endured the penetrating scrutiny of the television cameras.

About two weeks before the Coronation I went into the Queen's sitting room to collect the corgis for their afternoon walk in the palace grounds. The Queen was sitting at her desk, writing busily. On her head, glinting in the light from the big bay window, was the crown.

I could not prevent surprise from showing in my face. The Queen looked up at that moment, caught my surprised glance, and gave me a little half-smile of shy embarrassment.

Eager that she herself should be perfect in her part on the great day, the Queen went along to Westminster Abbey ahead of the Coronation to practise her descent from the throne, a tricky manoeuvre. Back home at Buckingham Palace, with bed-sheet pinned to her shoulders to represent her robe, she practised getting in and out of the state coach—in this case a number of gilt-framed chairs. She had rehearsed it once when a sudden thought struck her.

"We've forgotten His Royal Highness," she said. "He'll be sitting beside me, won't he?"

And once again I was pressed into service as a stand-in for Prince Philip, sitting briefly beside the Queen on one of the gilt chairs which formed the make-believe coach.

As the days slid away with gathering momentum, the palace filled with guests. Several were Prince Philip's relatives. For him, the Coronation offered the opportunity of a family reunion. Because they were married to German princelings he had seen little enough of his sisters in recent years. They had been invited neither to his wedding nor to the christening of Prince Charles. But with wartime enmity showing the first signs of fading, Philip's eldest sister, Princess Margarita of Hohenlohe-Langenburg, was invited to London to be one of the godmothers at Anne's christening. Now, for the Coronation, his three surviving sisters—Princess Margarita, Princess Theodora of Baden, and Princess Sophie of Hanover—were all invited along with their husbands and several of their children. Philip's ageing mother was there, too, her nun's robes making a small patch of sombre grey among the glitter and colour that was Westminster Abbey on Coronation Day.

VI

Coronation morning . . . with the rain coming down in a steady drizzle which was to turn into a downpour later. In the inner quadrangle of Buckingham Palace the huge, lumbering state coach with its 18th-century painted panels drew up under the two-storied portico of the Grand Entrance. I stood beside it in my state livery of scarlet and gold, my hair plastered to the traditional whiteness with an unpleasant mixture of flour and starch, soap and water.

From my position beside the coach I could see the whole width of the Grand Hall with its coupled columns of Carrara marble and the broad flight of matching marble steps beyond. The Yeomen of the Guard, in their Tudor tunics and Elizabethan ruffs, formed a guard of honour from the steps to the entrance. Beyond them, tightly massed, were as many of the palace servants as could possibly get there—housemaids in their white aprons and lace caps, chefs in check trousers, gardeners, plumbers and electricians in their Sunday-best suits of blue serge or grey worsted...along with the staffs from Windsor, Balmoral, and Sandringham with their relatives and friends. The Queen had invited them all along for a sneak preview.

A mass gasp followed by an almost tangible hush told me that the Queen was coming. She appeared at the top of the marble steps, escorted by her husband wearing the full-dress uniform of an Admiral of the Fleet. Not that anyone really noticed Philip. All eyes were focused on the Queen, a smiling, radiant, self-possessed figure, the pearls, crystal and diamante which encrusted her Coronation gown glittering and winking in the soft glow of hidden lights, her heavy Parliamentary robe of crimson velvet draped over one arm, and on her head, glistening to match her dress, the pearl and diamond diadem handed down from her great-great-grandmother, Queen Victoria.

I can honestly say that the Queen has never looked more beautiful—nor have I ever seen a more beautiful woman—than she was that Coronation morning. The emotions of the moment brought an unexpected lump to my throat as I handed her into the state coach. Then I stood aside to let Prince Philip climb in after her, tucked away the folding steps, and closed the massive, gold-embossed door.

Postillions in high, highly-polished leather boots, white breeches, and tunics of scarlet and gold stood by the heads of the eight Windsor Greys harnessed to the great weight of the coach. Other postillions straddled the backs of one horse in each pair. There was no coachman. The Queen's great-grandfather, Edward VII, had the coachman's box removed so that he was better seen by the public. Beyond the coach, rain glistened on the steel breastplates and helmets of the mounted troops forming the Queen's escort. Swords jingled and restless hooves clattered. And outside the quadrangle, beyond the archways which linked it with the outer forecourt, was the distant roar of the crowd.

The Duke of Beaufort, resplendent in a plumed hat in his traditional role of Master of the Horse, cantered up to the coach, saluted and asked the Queen, "Have we your permission to proceed, Ma'am?"

The Queen nodded her assent.

Beaufort gave an unseen signal, the Windsor Greys strained forward, the body of the coach swayed back and forth on its leather-covered braces like a ship in a slight swell, the wheels gained momentum, and we were off ... through the archway, across the forecourt, picking up a second mounted escort on the way, and out through the tall, wrought-iron gates. The murmur of the crowd became a sudden sharp thunderclap of sound, and I knew why the old-timers on the royal staff had advised us to pack our ears with cottonwool. (I ignored their advice and four days later my ears were still ringing.)

Round the Victoria Memorial and off along the Mall. A golden topknot bobbing at a nursery window showed where Princess Anne was watching her mother's departure. She was too young to go to the Abbey, but her brother, Charles, was being rigged out in white silk trousers and a frilled shirt to take his place among the spectators.

Massed schoolchildren packed the Victoria Embankment. As the coach turned the corner, they all yelled together as though motivated by a single switch—a great welter of sound which sent startled starlings soaring skywards from the grime-encrusted stonework around. I turned my head at that moment and glimpsed the Queen through the open window of the coach. She was still smiling, still giving her gentle royal wave, but her eyes were suddenly filled with tears.

The bells of the Abbey and those of neighbouring St. Margaret's peeled a welcome as the coach arrived at its destination. Momentarily the rain had ceased. I opened the coach door, let down the steps for Prince Philip to skip nimbly down. He stood by, helping his wife out while I and the Sergeant-Footman, Charles Oulton, who had entered the coach by the far door, manipulated the heavy crimson robe and handed it over to the six waiting maids-of-honour. Then, her husband beside her, the

Queen walked under the silk canopy screening the entrance to the Abbey and forward to the solemn ceremony of Coronation.

The Queen emerged from Westminster Abbey nearly three hours later looking serene and unruffled, regal and as self-composed as ever. The crimson Parliamentary robe had been replaced by the longer, weightier and more ornate Coronation robe of rich purple. On her head, in place of the pearl and diamond diadem in which she had arrived at the Abbey, was the Imperial State Crown. Balanced on her outstretched left palm was the glistening globe of the Sovereign's Orb; in her right hand was the Sovereign's Sceptre with its great diamond of 530 carats. With the help of the Sergeant-Footman, her maids-of-honour taking the weight of the ornate robe, skilfully she accomplished the tricky feat of climbing back into the coach while still holding the orb and sceptre. With Oulton filling one doorway of the coach, myself crowding the other, she was unseen by the watching crowd as she placed the orb on the specially-constructed rest and slid the sceptre into the concealed brackets on the other side. Oulton and I draped the robe around her and across the coach so that the huge gold crown and EIIR cypher which adorned it looked back at her from the facing seat.

For the first time that day she showed the slightest trace of pent-up tension.

"I shall be seasick if I have to stare at that all the time," she said. "Cover it up, please."

Quickly we rearranged the robe so that the crown and cypher were lost in the folds of rich purple.

It was raining again, heavier than ever, as the procession moved off from the Abbey, back-tracking its way along Whitehall and into Pall Mall in order to make a circuit of Piccadilly, Hyde Park and Oxford Street. By the time Buckingham Palace loomed into view again beyond the spans of Admiralty Arch, those of us who were on foot were in a sorry state. Our shoes were full of water and the heavy state livery was rendered all the heavier by the amount of rain it had absorbed. Rain had washed the pink from our stockings and the white from our hair. Legs and backs ached with the unaccustomed marching, and ears throbbed with the sound of bands and the roar of the crowd.

Buckingham Palace, when we finally reached it, was like an oasis of quiet in a sea of sound. The Queen must have been every bit as exhausted as we were, but nothing could dim the radiance of her smile. Straight out onto the palace balcony she went to acknowledge the cheers of the crowd packed tight around the Victoria Memorial and all the way along the Mall, the first of several such appearances she was to make that evening.

I saw her again as she went along to the Throne Room after making her first appearance on the balcony. She had taken off her crown. It was swinging from her hand as she walked along the corridor, and she looked as happy as I have ever seen her.

I bowed as she drew level. She greeted me with a remark of down-to-earth solicitousness.

"How do your feet feel?"

I was so taken aback at the unexpectedness of the query that I could manage only a stammering, "Not too bad, Your Majesty."

In fact, they felt terrible.

5. *LOVE AND MARRIAGE*

I

FROM time to time real life comes up with a coincidence so strange that no Hollywood script-writer would ever have dared to invent it. On the day Queen Elizabeth II was born, while the still unnamed princess was lying in her crib at 17 Bruton Street in London, her paternal grandparents, bearded King George V and straight-backed Queen Mary, were sitting down to lunch at Windsor Castle with three guests. The King's guests were the Dowager Marchioness of Milford Haven and her two daughters, the Crown Princess of Sweden and Princess Alice of Greece ... respectively the grandmother, aunt and mother of a blue-eyed, flaxen-haired four-year-old boy, His Royal Highness Prince Philip of Greece, a descendant of the royal house of Schleswig-Holstein-Sonderburg-Glucksberg, grandson of King George I of Greece, great-great-grandson of both Queen Victoria and King Christian IX of Denmark.

During my years at Buckingham Palace I saw Prince Philip's mother many times. I recall her as a small, upright, Victorian figure, somberly clad in the grey habit of a nun, who passed her time playing endless games of solitaire and relied upon her ability to lip-read in order to interpret what was said to her. Just as Queen Mary always considered the telephone an instrument lacking true regality, so Princess Alice of Greece regarded the deaf-aid.

Her life, though dogged by misfortune, was marked by extraordinary willpower. Her deafness was with her at birth. Speech training for the deaf in those days was virtually unknown. Yet at the time I knew her she could express herself fluently in English, French or German. Presumably, though I never heard her, she can speak Greek equally well, for much of her early married life was spent in Greece.

Those years were uneasy ones. Twice she and her husband, the youngest son of the Greek King, were forced into exile. The second time they were snatched to safety by a British cruiser, with Philip, a youngster of eighteen months, cradled in a cot improvised from an old wooden box. Philip grew up to a life of exile in Paris, at that time a city of exiles. His early schooling was at an American kindergarten in the suburb of St. Cloud, where he learned to box and swim and began to talk English with a pronounced American accent. Money was not plentiful. His parents were not exactly poverty-stricken, but neither were they especially affluent. When Philip wanted a bicycle, he had to save up his pocket money. And there was a day of pelting rain when he had to stay behind at school until the downpour eased because he had no raincoat.

Relatives helped out from time to time, notably Princess Alice's younger brother, the second Marquess of Milford Haven —"Uncle George," who took the boy under his wing when he outgrew kindergarten and was sent to England for the next stage of his schooling. It was "Uncle George" who paid the bills during his years at Cheam preparatory school. It was "Uncle George" who had the boy to stay with him at Lynden Manor in Berkshire when Philip's parents drifted apart and the boy was left with no home of his own. Sometimes, by way of a change during school vacations, Philip would stay with his grandmother, the Dowager Marchioness of Milford Haven, at her apartment in Kensington Palace. Broadlands, the Hampshire home of "Uncle Dickie"—now Earl Mountbatten of Burma—was another holiday refuge, and in the years to come Philip was to be taken more and more under the wing of "Uncle Dickie." Though he adored his two daughters, Mountbatten was disappointed that he never had a son. Philip filled the vacancy.

But this was still in the future when Philip, at the age of twelve, was sent to Germany for the next stage of his education. His four elder sisters had all married German princelings. One of them, Theodora, married Prince Berthold, the son of the Margrave of Baden, in whose castle at Salem on the shores of Lake Constance, was housed the now famous character-building school founded by the visionary Dr. Kurt Hahn.

When Philip first went there in 1933, Salem was already regarded as one of the best schools in Europe. For this reason, the Nazis wanted it under their influence and control. Kurt Hahn barred their way, so he was arrested, and released only on condition that he leave the country. He headed for Britain, where the principles responsible for Salem were directed towards founding a similar establishment at Gordonstoun on the shores of Scotland's Moray Firth.

Philip at Salem was, as now, a high-spirited individual . . . and youthful high spirits took the form of mocking the Nazi salute. Mockery of the Nazis was deadly dangerous in the Germany of the 1930s, and Philip's sisters concluded that it would be safer for him, and for themselves, if he left the country. So he was transferred to Gordonstoun, by no means the large, well-organised establishment it is today, but then a smaller, more close-knit educational community, where boys and masters shared not only lessons, but also the work of constructing and converting the school buildings. Philip, during his time at Gordonstoun, helped with the work of turning old stables into an extra dormitory as well as laying the bricks for a pig-sty.

Philip revelled in the rugged outdoor life he found at Gordonstoun. He went out to the fishing grounds in the small boats belonging to local fishermen. He helped crew the school schooner on an adventurous—by schoolboy standards—trip across the North Sea to Norway. He represented Gordonstoun in the Scottish athletic championships. He captained the school at cricket and hockey. It was a very different life from that which a girl called Lilibet was leading in the more rarefied confines of Buckingham Palace. Yet these two young people were moving steadfastly, if unknowingly, towards their first meeting.

Philip was seventeen when he moved from Gordonstoun to the Royal Naval College at Dartmouth with the intention of following "Uncle Dickie" into the Navy. He had been there only a few months when, amidst considerable spit and polish on the part of college cadets, the royal yacht *Victoria and Albert* dropped anchor at the mouth of the River Dart. King George VI was paying his first visit to the college since he himself had been a cadet there some twenty-six years earlier. He came ashore accompanied by his wife and two daughters, Elizabeth, a straight-faced, rather leggy 13-year-old, and Margaret, a plump little giggler some four years younger.

At almost the last moment, part of the programme for the royal visit had to be hurriedly rearranged when it was realised that a feverish epidemic of either mumps or measles was scything its way through the ranks of the younger cadets. Frightened that the King's daughters might become infected, the college physician opined that it would be better if they were not jammed into the college chapel along with a crowd of cadets who, though seemingly healthy, might well be sickening for something. What to do with the girls while their parents were attending the chapel service?

Accidentally or otherwise, Philip had been selected to act as messenger for the Captain of the College, Admiral Sir Frederick Dalrymple-Hamilton, during the royal visit. By another coincidence—or was it?—his Uncle Dickie, Lord Louis Mountbatten, was amongst those accompanying the King, and it was Mountbatten who suggested that his nephew escort the young princesses around.

Possibly Mountbatten, far-sighted though he has often shown himself to be in other directions, had no motive other than helpfulness in a difficult situation. But wittingly or unwittingly, his suggestion was responsible for lighting a fuse which was to cause bonfires to blaze on village greens eight years later in celebration of a royal wedding.

Not that there was anything at all romantic about that first meeting of Elizabeth and Philip. At 13 and 18, they were too young and too far apart in years for romance. So they munched ginger biscuits and drank lemonade. Elizabeth was not only shy by nature, but quite unaccustomed to the company of boys. In consequence she said hardly a word. Margaret, as usual, did more of the talking, and most of Philip's teasing conversation was directed at her.

For his part, Philip, brought up in the exclusively masculine, almost monastic surroundings of Cheam and Salem, Gordonstoun and Dartmouth, was at something of a loss as to how to entertain two small girls. He suggested a game of croquet, which he rounded off with an exuberant leap over a nearby tennis net. He says today that he has no recollection of leaping the tennis net, but others remember it.

When the two princesses went back to the royal yacht for lunch, Philip went with them. In the afternoon he showed them round the college and its grounds. That evening, along with other cadet captains, he was invited aboard the yacht to dine with the King. But Elizabeth was not present. At thirteen she was still considered too young to join her parents for dinner.

The following day, whether by accident or design, Elizabeth and Philip were thrown into each other's company again. They had lunch together and afternoon tea. Then, the royal visit over, the *Victoria and Albert* set sail with an escort of more than one hundred small boats manned by the college cadets.

One by one, as the royal yacht steamed out into the Channel, the escorting small craft fell behind and turned back. But one or two still carried on. Fearing for their safety, the King ordered a signal to be flown for them to turn back. All did so—

save one. Philip, alone, continued to strain on the oars in the small cockleshell of a craft he was rowing. If Elizabeth was enthused at this display of daring-do, her father was furious. He castigated Philip as "that damned young fool." Finally, after considerable bawling through a loud-hailer from the deck of the yacht, Philip too was prevailed upon to turn back. But the episode had imprinted itself indelibly upon the impressionable mind of the 13-year-old girl destined to be Queen Elizabeth II.

As always, her beloved Bobo, Margaret MacDonald, was never far away, and it was to her, later, that the young Elizabeth confided that she had met her Prince Charming ... "so tall, blond and good-looking." Ever since she was a small girl, Elizabeth had talked of the Prince Charming she hoped one day to marry. Her ideal was not tall, dark and handsome in the storybook tradition. She visualised someone tall, *blond* and handsome. Philip, when she met him that first day at Dartmouth, filled the bill remarkably well.

II

Six weeks later Britain was at war, and by the following January Philip was a midshipman aboard the battleship *Ramillies*. Other ships followed ... the *Kent*, the *Shropshire*, the battleship *Valiant*. The *Valiant* formed part of the British battle squadron which intercepted the Italian fleet in the Mediterranean, and Philip received a Mention in Despatches (from Britain) and the War Cross (from his native Greece) for his part in the subsequent action in which the *Valiant* sank two Italian cruisers, *Zara* and *Fiume*.

Like many another young man, Philip matured quickly under the impact of war. Boyish good looks hardened into more masculine appeal, and wherever he went he was a head-turner and a heart-breaker. Tall and athletic-looking, with the profile of a Greek god coupled to a quick wit and a readiness to have a go at anything from water-skiing to table tennis, it could hardly have been otherwise. But Philip, though he flirted charmingly enough during spells of shore leave, remained seemingly uninvolved.

Behind the scenes, however, he was conducting a sort of correspondence courtship with Elizabeth. They exchanged Christmas cards. By the summer of 1941 he was writing her colourful and amusing letters from Cape Town. That October he spent part of his leave at Windsor, where he regaled the royal family with witty tales of his seagoing adventures. The King liked him. They had in common the same down-to-earth, slapstick sense of humour.

The King, as subsequent events showed, was far from thinking of Philip as a prospective son-in-law at this stage. After all, Elizabeth, that autumn of 1941, was still only a girl of fifteen. But others were looking further ahead. The published diaries of the late Sir Henry Channon have revealed that as early as January, 1941, Philip's aunt, Princess Nicholas of Greece, expressed the hope that her handsome young nephew would marry Elizabeth and become Britain's Prince Consort.

For Christmas, 1942, Elizabeth sent Philip a photograph of herself signed "Lilibet," the affectionate diminutive only members of her family employed. Philip in return sent her a photograph of himself in the naval uniform of a sub-lieutenant (though he had in fact been promoted to first lieutenant a month or so earlier), standing smartly to attention and delivering a crisp salute. Elizabeth thought it too easily recognisable to have standing around where others could see it, so Philip sent her another in which his features were partly disguised by the blond Viking beard he was cultivating assiduously. Today, as Queen, Elizabeth still treasures these first two photographs Philip ever gave her, and has them facing her across the flat-topped desk where she plugs away at the contents of her "Boxes."

There has never been any man in the Queen's life other than Philip. The wartime years, during which she grew from girlhood to womanhood, coupled with the restrictions of her unique position, never permitted her the romantic experiments of an ordinary girl. For her there was never any question of petting in the rear seat of a parked car, or lingering kisses in the shadow of the back porch. The closest she came to enjoying any other male companionship was during the all-too-rare parties held at wartime Windsor. But the young Guards officers who danced with her on these occasions were all too conscious of the fact that she was the King's daughter. They held her carefully at arms' length and kept their conversation on the same distant footing. She, for her part, was too shy and serious by nature to offer them the encouragement which might have thawed the social ice. Margaret, less shy, more impetuous, fared rather better when her time came in the years immediately following the war.

Christmas, 1943, and Philip was again at Windsor while he waited for his destroyer to be re-fitted. One evening Philip sat with the King and Queen in the forefront of an invited audience, consisting mainly of members of the royal staff, to watch a stage version of the ancient fairy tale of Aladdin and His Wonderful Lamp. Margaret acted the part of the princess, and Elizabeth, wearing silk tights which revealed a pair of shapely legs, played the title role of Aladdin. Some may have noticed a special sparkle about Elizabeth as she strutted the stage that night. Indeed, it did not go unnoticed by her father, and later he dropped a jesting remark about Philip. He was amused and intrigued to see his daughter blush scarlet.

There were, of course, many other young women—to say nothing of their mothers—who visualised Philip as their own possible future consort. But Philip at twenty-two was already well experienced at playing the game of hard-to-get. If he took a girl to a dance, as he did sometimes, he usually found some good excuse for not seeing her home afterwards. If a girl baited her hook for further dates, he fell back on the old, old naval excuse ... "Sorry, I have to rejoin my ship."

The tale is told of one young lady who telephoned him in the hope that he would ask her out again. But whoever took the call said that Philip had left to rejoin his ship. Only after she had replaced the telephone did it occur to the young lady that the voice which had answered her had sounded suspiciously like Philip's own.

III

With the end of the war, Philip became an increasingly frequent visitor to both Buckingham Palace and Royal Lodge at Windsor. Royal Lodge, a secluded, pink-tinted royal "cottage" —a country mansion by more conventional standards—had been given to King George VI by his father when he was still Duke of York. He conceived much the same sort of passion for the place that the Duke of Windsor had for Fort Belvedere, and even after he came to the Throne he continued to use it as a weekend retreat in preference to Windsor Castle.

It was almost the ideal spot for a "secret" courtship. At weekends Philip would drive there from the naval base at Corsham in Wiltshire, where he was now an instructor at a training school for petty officers. Courtship took the customary course common to young people in love. Philip would take Elizabeth for drives in his well-worn little black-and-green M.G. sports car. Sometimes they played croquet together on the lawn at the rear of the house. If the weather was warm enough, they would take a dip in the green-tiled pool adjoining the rose garden. They would go horse-riding together in Windsor Great Park, and of an evening would take long, leisurely walks with the royal family's frolicsome pet corgis. Margaret, not realising at first what was going on between them, frequently clamoured to accompany them on these evening strolls. Later, as understanding dawned, she contrived to leave them alone as much as possible.

Philip, on these weekend visits, stayed overnight at Uncle Dickie's residence in Chester Street. On Sunday evenings, while Elizabeth and Margaret returned to the palace in one of the royal cars, he would shoot on ahead in his nippy little M.G. to be awaiting their return. Sometimes he would stay to have supper with them in the chintzy little third-floor apartment

[117]

which had once been their nursery, before driving the 98 miles back to Corsham. Then, as now, he was a fast driver (on one occasion he is said to have covered the distance in 100 minutes flat—no mean performance on narrow, winding country roads), and one night he skidded and overturned his car. He escaped with no more than a few bruises and got a lift from a passing driver, but, fearing that the incident might get into the papers, he put in a call to London to tell the story himself. Elizabeth, overhearing the call, was considerably upset, and insisted on speaking to Philip personally to assure herself that he was unhurt.

During the brief period before the royal romance became public property, the young couple, while they could not go out and about as freely or as frequently as any ordinary sweethearts, did occasionally have a night on the town. Sometimes they went dancing at the Bagatelle Club. One evening they saw the American musical *Oklahoma!*, which had just opened its London run. The words and music of one of the hit tunes from the show, "People Will Say We're in Love," struck a responsive chord in Elizabeth, and for weeks afterwards, in the privacy of her room, she played a recording of the song over and over again until it was all but worn out.

But the Royal Family had not yet acquired their later skill at keeping romantic secrets, and inevitably there was gossip in the newspapers. Cries of *"Where's Philip?"* greeted Elizabeth during a visit to one factory. Well-meant though they were, such greetings upset her, and she returned to Buckingham Palace almost in tears. For a time after that, though she determinedly carried on with her public engagements, she was much more nervous about them. "Poor Lilibet," Margaret sympathised with her. "Nothing of your own—not even your love affair."

When Philip joined the Royal Family at Balmoral in the late summer of 1946, and again at Sandringham at Christmas, the cat was well and truly out of the royal bag. The newspapers interpreted these visits as Philip's trial-by-ordeal ... a close-up scrutiny to ensure that he would make a fit husband for the future Queen.

At Balmoral, Philip was given a ground-floor bedroom with tartan floor-carpet, tartan-covered furnishings, and faded wallpaper bearing the royal cypher of Queen Victoria. In the narrow corridors of the castle, the glassy eyes of long-dead stags surveyed him from the walls as he passed by. Hot water for shaving was brought to his room each morning by a footman. The brass jug containing the water was towel-wrapped to keep it warm.

Life in the Royal Navy no doubt accounted for the slenderness of his wardrobe. His solitary naval valise contained no spare shoes, no pyjamas, no slippers. His only walking shoes were too worn to endure the toughness of the heathery moors, and the royal footman assigned to act as his valet promptly whipped them over to the local cobbler in nearby Crathie to be repaired. His tuxedo had been borrowed from his always obliging uncle, Earl Mountbatten. He lacked the traditional tweed knickerbockers, and went grouse-shooting with the King in his customary casual wear, flannel trousers and a tweed sports jacket—and carrying a borrowed gun.

The newspapers, in their assumption that Philip was already as good as betrothed to Elizabeth, were inclined to run ahead of events and ignore a number of complications. Not the least of these was that Philip, though he had been brought up mainly in Britain from the age of nine and had served throughout the war in the British Navy, was technically still a citizen of Greece. Philip also desired naturalisation for another reason. With the war over, he wanted a permanent commission in the Royal Navy, and this was granted only to British subjects.

But for Philip, even naturalisation was more complicated than for any ordinary person. Because he was still a prince of the royal house of Greece—despite the fact that he had lived in exile since the tender age of eighteen months—the permission of the King of Greece had to be obtained first. Then the British government, despite considerable urging on the part of Philip's Uncle Dickie, insisted again and again on postponing the question of naturalisation because of the tricky political relationship between Britain and Greece.

Even when this situation had finally cleared, two outstanding problems yet remained: What name was Philip to take as a naturalised Briton, and what title was he to be given once he was no longer Prince Philip of Greece? The question of name was perhaps not too difficult. Philip thought at first of calling himself "Oldcastle," an anglicisation of the Danish royal name of Oldenburg. To Uncle Dickie's delight, however, this was finally discarded in favour of his mother's maiden name, Mountbatten, the anglicised version of the German Battenberg.

The question of a title imposed rather more difficulty. Elizabeth's father was willing to grant him the style and title of "His Royal Highness Prince Philip." Philip, however, had never found his title anything more than an embarrassment. Addressed as "Prince Philip" at school, he had flown into a paddy. "Call me Philip—just plain Philip," he stormed. Addressed as "Your Royal Highness" in Navy days, he had flushed pink. He could not see that replacing his Greek title with a British one would be anything less of an embarrassment. So he thanked the King for his offer, but politely insisted that he wished to be simply "Lieutenant Philip Mountbatten."

The King was impressed by this democratic attitude, but not so impressed that he was yet prepared to consent to marriage between Elizabeth and Philip. "I simply cannot believe that Lilibet has really fallen in love with the first young man she ever met," he said. Yet though the King withheld his formal consent, between Elizabeth and Philip there was a tacit understanding that they were unofficially engaged.

Philip's naturalisation came through at last in March, 1947. But Elizabeth was not around to congratulate him in person. She was away with her parents and sister on a royal tour of South Africa. Philip's photograph travelled with her on the dressing table in her cabin aboard the battleship *Vanguard*, and they wrote to each other frequently during the long weeks of separation. The King felt that separation would give his elder

June 2, 1953: Elizabeth II is attended by her Maids as she arrives at Westminster Abbey for her coronation.

Buckingham Palace, the royal residence of over 600 rooms, is a self-contained community of its own.

The Queen's drawing room aboard the royal yacht, *Britannia*.

Surrounded by 80,000 acres stands Balmoral Castle, the royal family's holiday home in Scotland.

H. R. H. Prince Philip, Duke of Edinburgh.

The Queen Mother leaves Edinburgh's St. Giles Cathedral after attending the Thistle Service.

Elizabeth and Philip attend the annual Trooping the Colour Ceremony at the
Mall in London.

Prince Philip discusses rescue operations with a miner in South Wales.

A polo pony gets the royal treatment after a match at Smith's Lawn.

Princess Anne has inherited her father's forthrightness and his ready wit.

How to keep cool—the Duke's prescription.

The Queen's special love of horses is shared by her children.

Elizabeth,
with Prince Edward,
her youngest.

Prince Andrew prepares for a smashing score as cousin Linley (second from left) and classmates look on.

Princess Anne on board *Bloodhound*.

The Badminton Horse Trials are a regular favorite with the royal family.

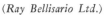

In the pony-jumping competitions, Princess Anne puts her mount over the jumps with the same dash and daring that her father displays.

Prince Charles discusses the Commonwealth Games with admiring competitors

... during a well-played match   ... accepting a royal reward.

Meditating.

Princess Margaret and Lord Snowden.

Lord Snowden and son Linley: water skiing.

On holiday in the Bahamas.

The royal procession moves slowly through London's cheering crowds.

daughter an opportunity to see things in their true perspective and establish in her own mind the fact that she was really in love with Philip. But shrewd and sensible though he was in this, the King, during those weeks in Africa, failed to notice another, less happy, romance beginning to bud almost under his very nose. For it was during the South African tour that the King's younger daughter, not yet seventeen, first formed an attachment for the royal equerry so often given the task of looking after her—Peter Townsend.

It was a pale Elizabeth who returned to England in May and danced a delighted jig on the deck of the *Vanguard* as it steamed into harbour. For her, the long years of waiting were almost over. It was now only a matter of weeks before her father's formal consent to her marriage was finally made public. Philip's father had died in 1944, but now, shortly after her return from South Africa, Elizabeth had her first opportunity of meeting his mother, who was staying at that time at Kensington Palace with her mother, the Dowager Marchioness of Milford Haven.

Philip was now at Buckingham Palace more often and more openly, driving his M.G. in through the wrought-iron gates and parking it in the inner quadrangle before slipping through a side door and taking the long flights of red-carpeted stairs two and three at a time. Then, as now, he scorned to use an elevator. He would make straight for the sitting room Elizabeth shared with Margaret and, once inside, would remove his jacket and make himself at home in his shirt sleeves.

On July 8, it was obvious to everyone who saw Princess Elizabeth that something very big was in the wind. Neither before nor since have I ever seen her quite so excited. For once, not even the long years of training could enable her to conceal her emotions entirely. Philip came to the palace again that evening —this time to stay overnight. He was given the Buhl Suite at the front of the palace on the second floor, a set of two rooms—bed-sitting room and bathroom—furnished with heavy, dark mahogany furniture.

I was given the job of looking after him, and unpacked his

valise for him, not an especially onerous duty. As at Balmoral, his wardrobe was the scanty one of the average young naval officer. Apart from the uniform in which he arrived at the palace, he had brought with him only a check suit, a tuxedo, two spare shirts, spare socks and shaving tackle. Still no pyjamas, bathrobe or slippers.

Philip was not around when I unpacked his things that evening, and my first real encounter with him came the following morning when I took him a small pot of tea at eight o'clock. He was still sound asleep when I entered the room and put the tea-tray on the small round-topped cabinet beside the bed. I moved to the windows and drew back the heavy brocade curtains as noisily as possible, hoping the combination of noise and daylight would serve to waken him. Still he slept soundly. I went through to the adjoining bathroom, leaving the door open behind me, and ran his bath for him—again making as much noise as possible. When I returned to the bedroom, Philip was blinking into wakefulness. Satisfied, I made my exit.

So far not a word had passed between us, but that evening I was again running his bath, having cleaned his shoes and pressed his tuxedo, when he breezed into the bedroom and came through to the bathroom. His movements were casual and relaxed, and he looked like a man on top of the world.

"I think we'd better keep the window curtains drawn," he said. I looked round at him, querying. "Otherwise people can look right in and see me," he explained. I glanced at the window and realised how right he was. A photographer with a telephoto lens perched on the Victoria Memorial would have got some excellent candid-camera shots.

"Very good, Sir," I said—he was no longer Prince Philip of Greece and not yet the Duke of Edinburgh—and went over to draw the curtains across the windows.

As I went out, Philip was starting to change for the private dinner party the King was giving to celebrate his daughter's engagement. At dinner Elizabeth wore her engagement ring for the first time. A large square-cut diamond surrounded by

[122]

smaller diamonds, it was a ring Philip's father had given to his bride-to-be years before, and which she, in turn, had now given to her son for his future wife. Philip had had the ring re-set, but had got the size a bit wrong. It was fractionally too large and even today, though it has been altered since, it is still loose-fitting, judging by the ease with which the Queen spins it round and round on her finger in moments of tension or impatience.

Next day came the formal announcement:

"It is with the greatest pleasure that the King and Queen announce the betrothal of their dearly beloved daughter The Princess Elizabeth to Lieutenant Philip Mountbatten, R.N., son of the late Prince Andrew of Greece and Princess Andrew (Princess Alice of Battenberg), to which union the King has gladly given his consent."

The following day Philip underwent his baptism of fire as a future member of the royal family. He looked much less relaxed than the previous evening as he squired his bride-to-be among crowds of excited guests at a palace garden party. You could follow Philip's progress about the gardens with ease that afternoon. Wherever he was, there the crowd was thickest. Everyone was eager to get a close look at this young man who had won the heart and hand of a future Queen.

Later, as the royal party sipped their tea from gold-rimmed cups in the red-and-white-striped marquee which did duty as a royal pavilion, someone remarked to the King, as dozens had done during the course of the afternoon, that the two young people made a handsome couple and that Philip was a very fortunate young man.

Replied the King, knowingly, "I only hope he realises what he's taking on. Being a Consort is much more difficult than being a Sovereign. It's perhaps the most difficult job in the world."

IV

November 20, 1947. I stood in the Grand Hall of Buckingham Palace, along with other footmen and pages, housemaids and cleaners, to watch the royal bride descend the marble steps on the arm of her father. It is the Royal Family's custom to invite the staff to gather in the Grand Hall for a privileged close-up on such occasions. The bride, slightly pale but composed, wore the pearl- and crystal-encrusted wedding gown which Norman Hartnell had designed for her with all the top-secrecy safeguards of a James Bond operation. And with good reason. While the dress was being made, bribes running to $1000 and higher were offered to members of Hartnell's staff for advance details of the design. To prevent any prying telephoto lens from peering over his shoulder, Hartnell whitewashed his workroom windows and screened them with folds of thick muslin. At night the design was carefully locked in the safe and the workroom manager maintained a watching brief on a camp-bed in the same room.

Fashion spies are continually probing for secrets which would enable mass-production manufacturers to turn out cut-price copies of royal fashions, and Elizabeth had no desire to be married in a gown of which secondary imitations were on sale in some chain store. More than once astute manufacturers have reaped a quick fortune from copying royal fashions. Copies of a silk coat the Queen wore for one visit to Paris were on sale in London the following day. Copies of a satin "magpie" dress, black at the back, white at the front, which she wore on another occasion, were on their way to the London stores within six hours. Copies of a tulip-shaped hat once worn by Princess Margaret sold in their thousands, from Toronto to Durban, from Pimlico to Melbourne. But pirating of royal fashions sometimes has wider beneficial results. Queen Mary's lace dresses were copied and sold to a degree which put the Nottingham lace trade back on its feet after years of recession.

Hartnell sent three of his assistants along to Buckingham Palace to help the bride into her wedding dress, but it was Bobo MacDonald, with characteristic calmness, who largely unravelled the well-nigh chaotic confusion of the wedding morning.

About everything went wrong that could conceivably go

wrong. The princess wanted to wear the pearls which her parents had given her as a wedding gift, but they were on display with the rest of the gifts at St. James's Palace. Sent to fetch them, Elizabeth's Private Secretary, John Colville, had considerable difficulty persuading those responsible for safeguarding the gifts of his identity and integrity. He was finally allowed to take the pearls only after agreeing to accept a three-man police escort to ensure that he really did take them to Buckingham Palace. The bride's tiara, the same one her mother had worn when she was married twenty-five years before, broke just as it was being fixed into position on her head. After hasty telephone calls it was rushed by car to a jeweler for emergency repairs. To top everything, with the bride on the point of departure, her bouquet of white orchids could not be found. It had been delivered to the palace earlier that morning, but from that point it seemed to have vanished. It was finally discovered in a refrigerator, where it had been popped to keep it cool and fresh.

There was rather less confusion in the bridegroom's quarters at Kensington Palace. Philip, dressed in the uniform of a naval lieutenant and wearing the sword which had once belonged to his grandfather, Prince Louis of Battenberg, was ready with time to spare. He walked out to the waiting car, only to have the time-keeping police officer on duty outside look at his watch and give a quick shake of his head. Philip went back inside again.

Despite his naval uniform, Philip, that wedding morning, was no longer plain Lieutenant Philip Mountbatten. Anxious that his daughter should not marry a royal nobody, Elizabeth's father had elevated Philip the previous day to the style of Royal Highness, granting him the titles of Baron Greenwich, Earl of Merioneth and Duke of Edinburgh. "It is," the King observed, "a great deal to give a man all at once, but I know Philip understands his new responsibilities on his marriage to Lilibet." He did not, however, give Philip the formal title of Prince. Despite this, Philip was popularly known as "Prince Philip" from then on, a title which Elizabeth herself was to regularise after she became Queen.

If Philip was tempted to kill those last few minutes of waiting with a quick cigarette, he resisted manfully. Previously a light smoker of cigarettes and, occasionally, a pipe, he had promised his bride-to-be that he would give up smoking. He smoked his last cigarette at the traditional stag party held in a private room at the Dorchester Hotel the previous evening to mark the end of his bachelor days. It was, by all accounts, a hilarious occasion of ribald jokes and robust horseplay, details of which, published subsequently in a magazine, were to bring about a rift between Philip and his cousin, David Milford Haven, who was also his best man at the wedding.

While Philip's mother was a guest at the wedding, his three surviving sisters, all married to German princes, were not invited. With World War II still fresh in public memory, the powers-that-be considered it inadvisable for Philip to parade his German connections at so early a date. But four days after the wedding, his cousin, Princess Marina, flew out to Germany with a firsthand account and a big batch of photographs for his sisters.

It was characteristic of Elizabeth, for all that she was Britain's future queen, that she should take the marriage vow in full, promising to love, honour and *obey*. The wedding provided London with its first real slice of colour and pageantry since pre-war days. The royal gold was brought out of storage to be reflected in the mirrored walls of the State Supper Room where the wedding "breakfast" was served. A few cynics queried whether such a festive display was appropriate to those immediate postwar days, but most of the public welcomed the occasion as a pleasing break with austerity. In any event, the wedding breakfast was neither extravagant nor ostentatious. The five kings, five queens, four princes and three princesses who were among the wedding guests feasted on nothing more sumptuous than filet of sole and casseroled partridge followed by ice cream, and the entire meal was over in twenty minutes.

I rode on the back of the open landau which conveyed the bride and bridegroom through the crowd-packed streets to Waterloo Station, where their honeymoon train was waiting. The bride travelled with her favourite corgi, Susan, snugly curled up on the floor at her feet. The route to Waterloo Station took us along Whitehall and past the Cenotaph, Britain's memorial to the dead of two world wars. A grinning Philip was so engrossed in acknowledging the cheers of the crowd that he failed to notice our approach to the Cenotaph. But Elizabeth, true to her long years of training, never misses a trick and, as she turned her head towards the Cenotaph and bowed slightly, I saw her give her newly acquired husband a quick nudge. Warned in the nick of time, Philip turned and hurriedly brought his right hand up in the naval salute.

V

Their honeymoon over, the newlyweds returned to London to await the renovation of their new quarters at Clarence House. This former home of the Duke of Connaught had not been lived in for thirty years, though the Red Cross had used part of it for wartime offices. It had no bathrooms, no electric light apart from a few makeshift wartime fittings, and even the old-fashioned gas lighting no longer worked. Bomb damage had done nothing to help, and when Elizabeth and Philip first inspected the place they had to pick their way over piles of rubble and debris through rooms with shattered windows. Renovation cost £55,000 and took more than a year to complete; meantime, the newlyweds lived in a third-floor apartment at Buckingham Palace. Sometimes they dined with the King and Queen, but more often, seeking the privacy all newlyweds desire, they ate alone in their own apartment.

During these early months of marriage, Elizabeth revealed a surprisingly new and curiously kittenish side to her nature. Until now, she had always been extremely serious and even rather prim. Brought up in the rarefied atmosphere of royalty, conscious of the high destiny which awaited her, and accustomed mainly to the company of people very much older than herself, she never knew the sort of freedom ordinary girls take for granted. She had been constantly surrounded by people who were excessively respectful to her, and in contact with a small number—her grandmother, her aunt, and her own parents—to whom she was respectful in turn.

Now, for the first time, she was constantly with someone she could treat on her own level, as he could her. Marriage opened a door into another world for her . . . a fresh, young, romantic, carefree world . . . and she responded in a fresh, young, romantic, carefree fashion.

I was setting the table in their apartment for breakfast one morning when the door into the bedroom suddenly flew open. Elizabeth raced out, flush-faced in nightdress and negligee, laughing as she ran. Philip bounded, whooping, in pursuit, a lean, athletic figure in a white bathrobe.

I continued laying the table as they dodged round it, this way and that. Then, spotting the open door into the corridor, Elizabeth raced through it. Philip charged after her, and the pair of them rushed away along the corridor. They did not come back. There was another entrance to their bedroom farther along the corridor, and presumably the chase continued through that.

With Clarence House still not ready for occupation, the first of their children, Prince Charles, was born at Buckingham Palace, appropriately perhaps in the selfsame Buhl Suite which Philip had occupied the night he came to the palace for their betrothal. Philip, casually shirt-sleeved after an energetic game of squash and a cooling-off swim in the palace pool, waited with his royal in-laws in their sitting room for the news of the baby's birth. Told he had a son, he was as excited as I have ever seen him, before or since. He dashed along to the delivery room to see mother and child, subsequently producing a big bouquet of roses, carnations, camellias and lilies-of-the-valley as a congratulatory gift for his wife.

I was passing the door of the Centre Room, which gives access to Buckingham Palace's famous balcony, when Philip's treasurer, "Boy" Browning, intercepted me. "Come on in," he said. "The Duke wants you to wet the baby's head." I went in. There was already a considerable crowd in the room, including Michael Parker, Philip's longtime friend and at that time his Private Secretary. Philip, still shirt-sleeved, was busy pouring champagne for everyone.

It was July of the following year before Elizabeth and Philip, with their baby son, could at last move into their new home at Clarence House. Soon after, Philip, resuming his Navy career at his own request, was sent out to the Mediterranean as first lieutenant aboard the destroyer *Chequers*. The sea runs in Philip's blood, as befits a grandson of the German prince who became Britain's First Sea Lord, and perhaps the biggest sacrifice he ever made for his wife was when he finally quit Navy life to undertake the infinitely more monotonous round of royal chores. On his wife's side, that first separation came as a considerable wrench. She was torn between a desire to be with her husband and the necessity for remaining behind with her baby son. She resolved the problem by commuting between London and Malta with almost the same casualness with which others commute between their city offices and suburban homes.

Those spells in Malta represent some of the happiest and most carefree days of her life. Philip, as a naval lieutenant, was an infinitely more content and more fulfilled human being than His Royal Highness the Duke of Edinburgh. In Malta, with protocol at a minimum, they enjoyed themselves as perhaps never before or since. Certainly Elizabeth had never known such a degree of personal freedom. She had her own car and drove all over the island as she never has in Britain. She watched Philip playing his first inexpert games of polo, her face draining of colour if ever he took risks or was thrown by his pony. They picnicked in rocky coves, sunned themselves in secluded bays, swam in the clear, warm water. Of an evening, they dined by candlelight without need of either a lady-in-waiting or a bulky royal body-guard.

It was in Malta that Elizabeth became pregnant again. She returned to Clarence House for the birth of Princess Anne, and Philip took advantage of some overdue leave to be with her. When he went back to the Mediterranean it was as lieutenant commander of his own ship, the *Magpie*, which he was to make pride of the flotilla by winning six of the ten races in a fleet regatta. Again, Elizabeth commuted between London and Malta to divide herself between Philip and the children.

But for both of them—for Elizabeth's new-found freedom and Philip's naval career—time was fast running out. The King's health was deteriorating, and Elizabeth found herself with many more duties as his daughter and heir. Philip was torn between naval career and royal life, but there really was no choice. Bidding farewell to the crew of *Magpie* on July 16, 1951, he said, "The past eleven months have been the happiest of my sailor life." They were also, as perhaps he guessed, the last eleven months of his sailor life. Any small, lingering hope that he might yet be able to resume his seagoing life at a later date was to go unfulfilled.

VI

With the death of her father and her own accession to the Throne, Elizabeth's relationship with Philip underwent a considerable change. Suddenly, literally overnight, at the still youthful age of twenty-five and after little more than four years of marriage, she became Queen Elizabeth II, the high office towards which she had been trained since childhood. Now, all at once, monarchy demanded the bulk of her time and energies. Dutifully and conscientiously, she responded.

She had promised on her wedding day to love, honour and obey her husband, and all this, in their personal life, she still did. But in public he had now to honour and obey her as his Sovereign. It was a complex and difficult situation demanding large sacrifices from both of them. With the Queen's decision to revert to her family name of Windsor, Philip found himself compelled to stand by and witness the bringing up of his children in another name. The Queen, for her part, had always said that she wanted more children. Now, for a time at least, she could not have them.

For her, those early years of monarchy, with so much to do, so much to learn, were the busiest she had ever known. For Philip, on the other hand, time hung heavily. He had given up his naval career to help his wife with the royal round and now found himself with very few royal duties. When the two of them moved back into Buckingham Palace, the Queen gave her husband the King's old study, contenting herself with what had formerly been her mother's sitting room. But she clung to her father's old desk . . . and to the work of monarchy which went with it. She had neither the power nor perhaps the inclination to delegate work to Philip.

There were, as Philip soon found out, no duties defined in the British constitution for the Queen's husband. He was a man without a meaning, a prince without power. He was not permitted to see the contents of the "Boxes" which reached his wife in endless succession. He was not allowed to be present when she talked with the prime minister on Tuesday evenings in the Wedgwood-blue-and-white Audience Room. In public, he must be careful never to usurp her royal prerogative by as much as a single inch. There was little for him to do . . . and perhaps nothing at all which, as an ex-naval officer, he could consider meaningful and worthwhile. From barking out orders on the bridge of a destroyer, he was reduced, quite suddenly, to merely giving orders to footmen and pages, valets and chauffeurs.

Fortunately, his sense of humour did not entirely desert him, even if perhaps it acquired a slightly more cynical flavour. At a university function in Australia during the world tour which followed the coronation, one couple were presented to Philip and the Queen as "Dr. and Mr. Robinson."

Philip raised a quizzical eyebrow. Mr. Robinson explained

hurriedly that his wife was a Doctor of Philosophy and therefore "the more important person."

"Ah, yes," sniffed Philip. "We have that sort of problem in our family, too."

Lacking a proper royal job of work, he set about devising ways and means of filling his time. He sent for books dealing with his predecessor in the tricky role of royal consort—Victoria's husband, Prince Albert—and read them assiduously. He toured the palace from top to bottom, inspecting everything from the fuel stores in the basement to the servants' bathrooms on the topmost floor. He came up with an idea for equipping the palace with its own laundry, but it never got off the ground. He worked out a plan for a new royal kitchen—smaller, more modern and much nearer the royal dining room. This time, his scheme was approved and the kitchen came into being. But royal chefs used it only briefly before going back to the old kitchen—a vast barn of a place which dates from Queen Victoria's day. Thereafter the expensive new sinks and cookers, refrigerators and vegetable racks in Philip's new kitchen went unused, and doubtless still are.

Philip also fulfilled a long-cherished ambition by learning to fly. He faced initial opposition from those who feared that the time would come, as indeed it has, when he would want to pilot his wife, the Queen. I was with the royal party on a return flight from New York when Philip, shirt-sleeved and in the dark glasses he wears to correct a small flaw in his vision, walked through to the flight deck and took over the controls. Philip now habitually pilots at least part of each trip as an antidote to boredom, and he was in fact flying one of the two Whirlwind helicopters forming part of the Queen's Flight only a few days before its twin crashed in December, 1967, killing the pilot, navigator and flight engineer as well as the Captain of the Queen's Flight, Air Commodore John Blount.

Where travel is concerned, there has been a big change in royal outlook in recent times, and many of the old rules have been discarded. Earlier in her reign, the Queen would never fly in the same aircraft as her son, Prince Charles, just as, when she was younger, she was never allowed to travel in the same aircraft as her father. But recently there has been more than one occasion on which mother and son, the Queen and the heir to the Throne, have flown together.

Where Philip is concerned, flying is indispensable. Without it, he would be quite unable to cope with the vast amount of public work he has attracted to himself over the years. Today, an ever-increasing percentage of his public engagements are carried out by either airplane or helicopter, as often as not with Philip himself piloting the machine. The first time Philip took off in a helicopter from the close-cropped lawn at the rear of the palace, the mallard and other wild duck which nest in the reeds around the royal lakes scattered in panic, while the Queen watched from an upstairs window. Today, the ducks are well accustomed to the sight of Philip's helicopter tree-hopping its way in or out of the palace grounds and scarcely turn a feather. But, as a safety precaution, firemen and a physician are always standing by as they did on that first occasion.

Another idea of Philip's, in those early days of monarchy, was to modernise and streamline the lofty, old-fashioned study he had inherited. Those responsible for maintaining the fabric of the palace were horrified at the idea, and quickly made it plain that whatever else he did he must on no account interfere with the ornate, richly-moulded ceiling. Philip met this opposition with a touch of true naval ingenuity. He did not touch the old ceiling. It is still there—high up and out of sight. Below it is the artificial ceiling Philip had installed to give the study a more streamlined look in keeping with the modern gadgets with which he has equipped it.

With the Queen's accession to the Throne, the halcyon, care-free days of early marriage were gone, never to be recaptured. The comfortable companionship they were to find in later marriage was still in the future. With the Queen now deeply involved in the work of monarchy, with Philip not yet having found any meaningful duties to fill the gap created by his retirement from the Navy, these years of marriage were perhaps neither the easiest nor the happiest. The situation was not helped by leaving Clarence House, the home they had planned, renovated and furnished together, and taking up residence amidst the much more impersonal atmosphere of Buckingham Palace, nor by the fact that Elizabeth was no longer completely free to play the wife to Philip's husband. No longer could she drop things at a moment's notice to go out and watch Philip in action at polo, or plod dutifully behind him as he banged away at pheasants and grouse. Her "Boxes" and the other manifold duties of monarchy had first call upon her time.

In the ordinary relationship of a king and queen-consort, as with any ordinary husband and wife, it is the king who copes with the office work of monarchy while his wife supervises the housekeeping of their palace home. But with Elizabeth and Philip, it was Elizabeth who did the office work *and* the housekeeping. Philip was not permitted by law to do the one, and could hardly be expected to undertake the other.

He did at this time devote some of his energies to overhauling the economics of the royal estates, Sandringham in particular, where his fact-finding visits were so probing that estate workers came to label them "Philip's naval inspections." He did much to streamline Sandringham and prevent its being the drain on his wife's purse that it had been on her father's. He created a profitable piggery there (and another at Windsor), he replaced exotic flowers with less colourful but more commercial mushrooms, and he started a ten-year plan for planting fresh timber.

But none of this filled the void in his life left by the naval career he had so dutifully sacrificed. Slowly, bit by bit, he created for himself his own special circle of royal duties and interests, concentrating particularly on those fields in which the Queen, as a woman, could hardly be expected to have much interest—science, sport, industry. Youth and education, too, became part of his orbit.

When he received an invitation to open the 1956 Olympic Games in Australia, he conceived the idea of also visiting people and places the Queen could hardly hope to visit—the trans-Antarctic expedition, lonely survey teams in the Falkland Islands, isolated communities and outposts of Britain's dwindling empire. It was perhaps the most adventurous royal tour ever undertaken. It took Philip into the backwoods and deep into pack ice, through storm-tossed seas and onto the slippery deck of a whaler, into the uranium mines of Australia's Rum Jungle and high into the Snowy Mountains. He was gone from mid-October, 1956, until February, 1957, and his long absence caused newspapers around the world to headline rumours of a rift between royal husband and wife.

Like any other couple, the Queen and Prince Philip have had their occasional differences. There have been times when the Queen has been deeply involved in her work perhaps to the detriment of personal relationships. Equally, there have been times when Philip has been insufficiently forbearing. He can, in private as in public, be sometimes furious, sometimes sullen, if things are not to his liking. As in less regal homes, there have been rare occasions at Buckingham Palace when a door has slammed behind him or he has stalked out without saying good-bye. But never have these occasional differences mounted to the degree necessary to justify those "royal rift" headlines of 1957.

To anyone at Buckingham Palace, the newspaper headlines seemed unjustified to the verge of the ridiculous. Philip and the Queen had parted on the best of terms, and as his adventurous trip ran its course the Queen looked forward to his return with a degree of excitement that was almost girlish. Ahead of Christmas, she tape-recorded a private greeting to be flown out to him. It was marked "Not to be opened till Christmas Day." Charles and Anne joined her in making the recording and even the royal corgis, Sugar and Susan, were rounded up for their barking to be recorded to give Philip a sense of home. And after Christmas, as the Queen prepared for her state visit to Portugal and her reunion there with Philip, I have never seen her more buoyant. Unlike Philip, who is more sensitive about such things than he cares to admit, she can shrug off most of what she reads about herself in the newspapers. But the stories of a "royal rift" hit deep. "How can they say such terrible things about us?" she asked Bobo, somewhat bitterly, on one occasion. And it was perhaps partly to show what she thought of the gossip that she raised her husband to the "style and title of Prince" once the two of them were reunited again.

VII

In more recent years, Elizabeth, assured and experienced in her role of monarch, has been able to devote increasing time and attention to her other roles of wife and mother without ever relaxing her firm grip on the reins of monarchy.

The first sign of a change in the delicate balance between wife and monarch came early in 1960, with the birth of her third child, Prince Andrew. And with this, nearly twelve years after the birth of Prince Charles and ten years after that of Princess Anne, the royal marriage entered upon a further and more companionable stage. The Queen, while taking the duties of monarchy no less seriously and conscientiously, seemed at last to understand that marriage, too, has its priorities and that there are some concessions which even monarchy must make to marriage. "Now we must see about a little playmate for Andrew," she remarked one day soon after the birth of her third child. The remark was made seemingly in jest, but she was not entirely jesting, as the subsequent birth of Prince Edward was to prove.

Philip, for his part, seems finally to have understood something of that sense of almost divine appointment his wife feels in regard to the monarchy. To her, monarchy is like a torch which has been handed down to her by her father and which she holds in trust for her son.

This better understanding on both sides has done much to

cement the fabric of their marriage. If, like many another long-married couple, they no longer view each other through the rose-tinted spectacles of honeymoon days, equally they are no longer subject to the strains and stresses of those years when the Queen was a largely inexperienced young monarch and her husband a man who had sacrificed one career and not yet established another.

It is no secret that Philip is often away from home for days, sometimes a week or more, at a stretch. Yet these absences, occasioned by the busy round of royal duties he has created for himself, have helped rather than hindered their marital relationship. Without them, Philip would be very much less of a man than he is, as is his old headmaster, Dr. Kurt Hahn, foresaw when he wrote in Philip's final report that he would "need the exacting demands of a great service to do justice to himself. His best is outstanding; his second best is not good enough. Prince Philip will make his mark in any profession where he will have to prove himself by a full trial of strength." Hahn had Philip's naval career in mind. In fact, Philip's "great service" and "full trial of strength" have come in his role as the Queen's husband.

Even if Philip is at home, royal husband and wife see comparatively little of each other in the course of the working week. Both have their own jobs to take them along different paths, though with joint purpose. But at weekends and during the long summer vacation they spend the bulk of their time together. At Windsor, like any country farmer and his wife, they stroll over to the Home Farm, Philip in sports jacket and flannels, the Queen in tweed jacket and tartan skirt, to look at the pigs and cattle. At Balmoral, on occasion, they load kids and picnic gear into a jeep-like Land Rover and take off for some hideaway in the heathery hills where Philip and Charles share the task of barbecuing steaks while the Queen and Anne mix batter for pancakes. They ride together a lot. The Queen enjoys walking. Philip is less enthusiastic unless he has a gun in hand and a dog at heel, but goes along to keep her company. The Queen, for her part, cheerfully endures wind-squalls and rain-showers to watch her husband in action at polo and happily trudges along behind him as he shoots grouse or pheasant. She still turns pale if ever he takes a tumble at polo. Philip is still quick to worry if ever she is even slightly unwell—and even quicker to rage if he feels she is being imposed upon.

Legally, except that his title of "Prince" is now official, Philip is still no more than the Queen's husband, though certainly no less. Yet while the Queen may heed only her official advisers in matters of monarchy, it is to her husband that she turns for guidance and advice in matters of family—or even when the needs of family and monarchy overlap, as in the upbringing and education of the son destined to succeed her on the throne.

In the privacy of their own apartment, she treats Philip always as head of the family, as indeed she regards him. At public banquets the Queen must sit at the head of the table, but in private it is Philip who sits where her father once sat. "Ask Papa," she tells the children if they seek parental advice. "He knows best." Equally, if the children indulge in something more than ordinary high spirits, it is Philip who delivers the necessary reprimand or occasional spanking.

Where the children's upbringing is concerned, the Queen allows herself to be guided almost entirely by her husband, recognising that he is the one with experience of the real world outside Buckingham Palace. Without Philip, the Queen would probably never have sent Charles to school, for the simple reason that the idea would never have occurred to her. She never went to school herself and would never have thought in such terms. It was Philip who realised how his son's character was being shaped under the petticoat influence of royal nanny and governess, and who persuaded the Queen to embark upon the big royal experiment which sent Charles in turn to Cheam, Gordonstoun, Timbertop and Cambridge.

The Queen is no molly-coddle mother. She believes that plenty of fresh air and plenty of outdoor exercise—in bad weather as in good—are beneficial to growing youngsters. As children, Charles and Anne had to spend part of each day, wet or fine, outdoors in the open air. The same applies to Andrew and Edward. The Queen has had a climbing frame installed in the palace garden to toughen young limbs, with a knotted rope slung from the branch of a tree to provide a further outlet for youthful energy.

In many respects, Andrew and Edward are permitted more freedom than Charles and Anne had as children. At the beginning of her reign the Queen made it a rule that the children should not invade her sitting room during what she regarded as her "working hours." Today, more experienced in her role as monarch, she can afford to relax the rule, and has often been seen working at her desk while Andrew or Edward played quietly in the room. The bottom drawer of an antique chest which stands against one wall contains playthings to amuse the youngsters on such occasions, and the Queen herself will sometimes take a break from work to join the children in rolling a ball for the corgis to chase. It was after such a game that one of the royal pages, failing to notice a ball lying in the middle of the room, skidded on it and performed an involuntary pirouette which almost deposited him in the Queen's lap.

I imagine the Queen and Philip had a good laugh about the incident when they met up that evening. So often serious in public, the Queen in private has a considerable sense of humour. There was an occasion when I encountered her in a corridor late at night following a royal banquet. She was tired, but in high spirits, walking along in her stockinged feet, her shoes in one hand, her tiara in the other. Seeing me, she put one hand to her back, bent forward and feigned a hobble. "Oo-er, me poor back," she exclaimed, in cockney accents which would have done credit to Eliza Doolittle.

Philip has an ever more uproarious sense of humour, and at the end of the day there is many a laugh in the royal apartment. In more than twenty years of marriage—they celebrate their silver wedding anniversary in 1972—they have never reached the stage of not knowing what to talk about when they are alone together. In the privacy of their apartment they chatter almost non-stop, the Queen's rippling, still girlish laughter mingling with Philip's robust guffaws as they talk over the events of the day.

6. *THE QUEEN AND HER RELATIVES*

I

ACH morning, between scanning whatever personal letters the day's mail has brought her and ringing for her Private Secretary to start the official business of the day, the Queen settles herself at the big, flat-topped desk which was her father's before her, picks up one of the two ivory-coloured telephones by her left hand and asks the duty operator to put her through to Clarence House. A direct line links the palace to Clarence House, and within seconds the Queen is engaged in animated conversation with her mother, as she has done almost every morning since she married and left home.

For the next five or ten minutes the two of them chatter away in mother-to-daughter fashion. Over the course of a week these morning telephone conversations will encompass almost the whole range of family life—how the children are coming along, what Philip is doing, Margaret and Tony's latest holiday—as well as horse racing, a topic of which neither the Queen nor her mother ever tires. Both are passionately addicted to the sport, though their enthusiasm taken different forms. The Queen

Mother is devoted to steeplechasing, the Queen to flat racing which she regards as less hazardous and more predictable.

Nine mornings out of ten the Queen Mother will be still in bed when her daughter's call comes through to Clarence House. Whatever else the two of them may have in common, their attitude to time is not among them. The Queen, like her father, is the very essence of punctuality, though perhaps not quite the inveterate clock-watcher the King was. She will permit an official Audience, scheduled for ten minutes, to run on for fifteen if the particular person or the topic being talked about happens to interest her. Her father never would. But where public functions are concerned she is always scrupulously punctual. The same is true of her personal life to a degree verging on the monotonous. Meals at Buckingham Palace are served precisely at the same time every day without variation, with the Queen sitting down at table practically on the stroke of the clock.

The Queen Mother, by contrast, has absolutely no regard for time (a habit in which Princess Margaret takes after her). She thinks nothing of coming down to dinner anything up to forty-five minutes late. On Sunday mornings she will still be putting on her hat and pulling on her gloves at Royal Lodge, her week-end retreat, at the precise moment that morning service is due to start in the small stone-built church she attends nearby. The Queen Mother is so often late for meals that when she is staying with her daughter at Balmoral or Sandringham, the Queen falls back on a daughterly trick to ensure that her mother gets to the table on time. "Dinner is at half-past eight," she will tell her page, "but I want you to tell Queen Elizabeth's page [she always refers to her mother as 'Queen Elizabeth' when talking to servants] that it is at eight o'clock." In the same way, though the Queen is up promptly at eight each morning, weekdays and weekend alike, her mother, though called at fifteen minutes to eight on her own instructions, seldom emerges from her bedroom much before eleven, by which time she has had her morning pot of tea, her breakfast (usually fruit), talked with her two daughters on the telephone, been through her mail and scanned the newspapers.

The Queen Mother's complete disregard for time was the despair of her husband. Many a time, with the two of them already late for an official function, I saw the King pacing impatiently up and down the corridor, looking at his watch, twiddling his big signet ring and snapping at his equerries as he waited for his wife. But not once did he snap at her when she finally emerged from her room. The Queen Mother could always charm her sometimes irascible husband as easily as she charmed and still charms everyone else with whom she has ever come into contact.

Even her tough old father-in-law, King George V, was not proof against her charm. She and her husband were on their way to dine with him one evening when their car broke down. Always in awe of his father, the Duke of York suggested that perhaps it would be better if they did not go at all, rather than arrive late. But the Duchess would not have it. She insisted on continuing the journey to Buckingham Palace, marched boldly into the dining room, where dinner had already started, took her place beside the King, switched on her most radiant smile and said, "I'm sorry we're late, Papa." Anyone else would have received the full blast of the King's temper. But to everyone's surprise he merely replied, "You're not late, m'dear. I think we must have started early."

The Queen Mother's smile is her trademark. "It must be put on," the occasional cynic will sneer. "No one could possibly smile all the time as she does." The cynics are wrong. The Queen Mother does smile all the time ... or nearly all the time ... in private as in public. She is a naturally happy and contented person and her peace of mind is reflected in her abundant smile, and, for that matter, in her comfortably plumpish contours. Though given to plumpness, she does not diet. On the contrary, she has a considerable weakness for things like cream and butter, and is constantly dipping into the boxes of chocolates and candy she always has scattered around her.

Less preoccupied with matters of state than her daughter, she finds time to derive real pleasure from the smaller things of life, and particularly from human relationships. She never passes a servant in a corridor without a smile and a word of greeting. Often, though already late, she makes herself even later by pausing to inquire about their wellbeing and the health of their families. She may be seldom seen at Buckingham Palace these days, but she still remembers those who worked for her, however humble their capacity, when she was Queen. Each December she attends the annual servants' ball and the first thing she does is walk straight to the far end of the ballroom and fall into animated conversation with the elderly cleaning women she remembers from her days in the palace.

I remember her coming to the palace one morning shortly after the Queen and Prince Philip had returned from one of their overseas tours. I was expecting the warm smile she flashed at me as I opened the door of the elevator for her to cross the landing to the Queen's room. I was not expecting the words which followed. "Thank you so much for everything you did for the Queen while she was away." I was taken aback to realise that she even knew I had accompanied the Queen.

The Queen and her mother have always got along remarkably well. Today they are more like two sisters in their relationship with each other than mother and daughter. They derive real pleasure from each other's company. With the house full of guests, the Queen will frequently and readily leave them to their own devices while she slips away with her mother for a long, quiet walk across the moors at Balmoral or beside the Thames at Windsor.

Unlike her counterpart, Queen Frederika of Greece, the Queen Mother made no attempt to retain the reins of power after the death of her husband. She was perfectly content to hand over, lock, stock and barrel, to her elder daughter and her daughter's husband. Indeed, far from hanging on, there seemed a possibility at one time that grief would drive her into premature retirement and cloistered seclusion. But time proved a great healer and bit by bit she emerged from seclusion to play a full, if subsidiary, role in public life.

In a way, it would have been perfectly understandable had she attempted to cling to her old position. During the years of her husband's monarchy, she was, to a quite considerable extent, the power behind the throne. The King himself acknowledged the fact again and again, publicly as well as privately. "Your mother is more than merely clever," he said once to Elizabeth. "She is wise." And he paid public tribute to his wife with the words, "There have been times when my task would have been almost too heavy but for the strength and comfort I have always found in my home."

It was the Queen Mother who persuaded her despairing husband to try yet one more course of treatment for his long-time stammer. As a result, though the stammer was not completely cured, the King was able to control it except at moments of extreme tension. During his years of monarchy his stammer occasionally made itself audible in his public speeches and broadcasts. But within the privacy of the home where he found so much "strength and comfort" you would never have realised that he had a stammer at all. At family gatherings you could always hear his voice plainly above the general hum of conversation as he talked on his favourite topics—his wife, his daughters, shooting and farming—with no sign of his impediment other than a slight mispronunciation of his *r*'s which caused them to emerge as *w*'s.

At public functions, during his early days of monarchy, it was the Queen Mother who carefully steered her husband towards any small group of people who might otherwise have been overlooked, exactly as Philip was to do later with the Queen. Like Philip, too, she was quick to utter those all-important words which thawed the ice and made conversation possible between a nervous king and his tongue-tied subjects.

In a way, the Queen Mother and Prince Philip are two of a kind. Both are outsiders who married into the royal family and finally found themselves, however reluctantly, with leading

[145]

roles to play. Given any freedom of choice, the woman who is now the Queen Mother would never have elected to be Queen. Indeed, she twice rejected proposals of marriage from the man who eventually became her husband for fear of what would be involved if she married into the royal family . . . "Never again to be free to think or speak or act as I really feel I should think, speak and act." When monarchy finally forced itself upon her husband and herself, her acknowledgement of her new status was matter-of-fact in the extreme: "Well, we must take what is coming to us and make the best of it."

Similarly, Prince Philip, given any freedom of choice, would undoubtedly have preferred to remain at sea and pursue his naval career. There was perhaps an echo of the Queen Mother's attitude in the words he used as he packed his white tropical uniforms for the last time: "It looks as though it will be a long time before I want those again."

Their natures, like their circumstances, run curiously parallel. Having accepted their roles, both came to enjoy being at the centre of the royal stage. A Frenchman watching the Queen Mother lay a foundation stone, a trite enough task which she had performed a score of times before in public life, was moved to comment, "She makes it seem something fresh and exciting." Similarly, Philip manages to inject freshness and a sense of excitement into even so mundane a chore as opening an exhibition or touring a factory. With both, their emotions are close to the surface. The Queen Mother, moving through the blitzed, rubble-strewn streets of London's East End during the wartime blitz, had tears in her eyes. When Buckingham Palace was bombed, she was, in a curious way, almost glad. "Now I shall feel I can look the East End in the face," she said. Similarly, Prince Philip, visiting the Welsh mining village of Aberfan after the disaster which killed 144 people, 116 of them children, was ashen-faced and had to be restrained from jerking off his jacket and grabbing a spade to help with the rescue operations.

With so much in common, it is not surprising that mother-in-law and son-in-law get along well. Whenever they sit together

[146]

at mealtimes there is good-natured ribbing, and wherever the Royal Family gather the two of them inevitably get into a huddle, talking animatedly and laughing heartily.

The Queen Mother has proved herself as wise a mother-in-law as she was a wife. Just as she has never interfered in matters of monarchy since her daughter became Queen, so has she refrained from interfering in matters of family. I have heard it said that she did not approve of Philip's plan for sending the children to boarding school. If this is true, then she certainly kept her counsel largely to herself. On one occasion when she might easily have been tempted to interfere she carefully refrained from doing so. Prince Charles had not long since started at Gordonstoun. The Queen Mother, who was staying at Birkhall on the Balmoral estate, sent her car to fetch him one Sunday so that he could spend the day with her. When the time came for him to go back, he burst into tears. He was unhappy at Gordonstoun, he said, and begged her not to send him back.

"But you must go back," she told her 13-year-old grandson. In response to his tearful protests, she added, "Remember that we all have to do things we don't like in life." She settled him in the car and sent him off with a smile on her face, but it was perhaps one of the rare occasions when her smile was more than a bit forced.

While she may disregard clocks, the Queen Mother continues to live by the calendar. A week each winter and another in summer are always spent at Sandringham, as they have been for years. Each spring she goes to Scotland for a week's salmon fishing. The Queen Mother is as enthusiastic and expert at fishing as the Queen is at deer-stalking. The year of her sixty-fifth birthday was one of her best seasons ever, and she hauled a dozen salmon from the tumbling waters of the Dee in the course of her week's stay.

Neither mother nor daughter cares a hoot for fashion when in pursuit of their respective quarries. For deer-stalking, the Queen wears tweed knickerbockers, a matching tweed jacket, stout brogues on her feet and a head-scarf over her hair, binoculars and a hunting rifle slung about her, and sets off with a tall stalk-ing-stick—not unlike a shepherd's crook—to help her plod her way through bracken and heather, boulders and bog. For salmon-fishing, the Queen Mother is garbed equally suitably, if non-fashionably, in rubber waders which come up to her waist, a waterproof jacket, and a shapeless felt hat which she ties in place with a scarf fastened beneath the chin.

When she goes to the races, the Queen Mother allows for every possible variation of Britain's always uncertain climate. Into her car with her go warm, fleece-lined boots, two spare pairs of shoes, a pair of plastic overshoes, three or four head-scarves, a raincoat, a tweed coat, an umbrella, a fur rug, a foot muff and even a hot-water bottle.

The Queen Mother's personal involvement in the racing scene came somewhat late in life. She was only a year short of her fiftieth birthday when she acquired a half-share in her first horse, an Irish-bred steeplechaser named Monaveen. "The milk-cart horse" as he was known, having drawn a milk float at one stage of his varying career, won four races in his first season under royal ownership and topped it by running fifth in the Grand National, Britain's toughest steeplechase. The Queen Mother had found a fresh outlet for her always enthusiastic nature. Over the next 18 seasons to 1967 she owned over fifty steeplechasers at one time or another, notched up 160 winners and amassed a total of £75,000 in winnings.

At this writing she has still not achieved a victory in the Grand National, her greatest ambition, though it eluded her only by mischance in 1956. Her entry, Devon Loch, 100–7 second favourite, had cleared the last of the thirty jumps and was a full fifteen lengths ahead of its nearest challenger, with no more than fifty yards to go to the post. The crowd was yelling its head off in anticipation of a seemingly certain royal victory when it was as though Devon Loch suddenly tried to clear a fence which did not exist and came down spread-eagled with the jockey still in the saddle. By the time the Queen Mother's horse had struggled to its feet again it had been passed by every other rider still left in the race. A subsequent medical examination revealed no cause for this sudden strange behaviour, and what really happened remains a mystery to this day. My own theory is that Devon Loch was startled by the great roar which went up from the crowd as royal victory seemed in sight. The Queen Mother, of course, was extremely disappointed. But she took her disappointment in true sporting fashion. "Ah, well, that's racing, I suppose," she said.

Each summer the Queen Mother spends two weeks at the ancient Castle of Mey, in northern Scotland, which she bought and renovated as an antidote to widowhood. Then she motors south for a further six weeks at Birkhall while her daughter is at Balmoral. The remainder of her time, except for her official tours, is spent at Clarence House, a few yards from the palace. Weekends find her retreating to the cosy intimacy of Royal Lodge at Windsor, where her late husband's desk is still set out as it was in his lifetime with leather blotter, silver inkstand and travelling clock, photographs of Lilibet and Margaret as children, and a photograph of the Queen Mother in the flapper fashion of the 1920s when she was first courted by a king's son.

Even more than the Queen, she is a lover of fresh air and outdoor life. She enjoys walking, whatever the weather, adores the smell and crackle of a leaping log fire, likes eating out of doors when Britain's climate permits, and has a habit of tossing doors and windows open wide wherever she goes. At Sandringham, one biting cold winter's day, Elizabeth came through into the big family room known as the Saloon to find the main door open wide with a chill blast howling through. She told me to close it. "The place is like a refrigerator," she commented. The Queen Mother, the inevitable fur wrap about her shoulders, looked up from one of the interminable games of solitaire with which she fills in her time. "It's my fault, darling," she interposed. "I thought the room was a bit stuffy and was letting in some fresh air."

Since the death of her husband she has been to a large extent a woman alone . . . and perhaps sometimes lonely. Books, solitaire, and television have been the main companions of her leisure hours. Like the Queen, she is a woman with scores of acquaintances, but few really close friends. She has never thought of re-marrying and the only crack in her otherwise placid disposition came when an American newspaper published a rumour that she was contemplating marriage to her Treasurer, the late Sir Arthur Penn. With no nonsense about royal reticence, the Queen Mother promptly authorised a statement which castigated the story as "complete and absolute nonsense." They were said to be "Her Majesty's own words." In fact she used at least one rather stronger word.

She is a voracious reader with a liking for tough thrillers and historical novels, especially those with a Scottish background. She belongs to a subscription library, has books delivered in batches of half a dozen at a time and often gets through them at the rate of one a day. Unlike the Queen, she loves dressing up and is never happier than when decked out in elaborate confections of buttons and bows, furs and feathers, full-skirted crinolines and sparkling tiaras. She adorns herself with a mass of jewelled accessories, yet somehow contrives never to look over-dressed. Her flamboyant style of dressing has never surrendered to the dictates of current fashion and has about it always an essential air of timelessness. Though she has lived alone, except for servants, since Margaret's marriage, she still clings to the custom of "dressing" for dinner each evening. A few yards along the road at Buckingham Palace, the Queen has long since discarded the custom save when she is entertaining guests, and one can hear echoes of that girlish plea, "Don't be old-fashioned, Mummy."

The Queen Mother clings also to her tradition of sipping an aperitif before dinner. Her favourite is a champagne cocktail which she mixes herself by placing a single sugar lump in the glass, impregnating it with two or three drops of angostura bitters, then covering it with brandy, and finally filling the glass with champagne to which she adds a slice of orange. She is a hearty eater and her dinner, as often as not, will run to five courses. She will start with soup, proceeding by way of fish, then meat and vegetables, to a dessert—perhaps steamed pudding or strawberries and cream—before finishing up with biscuits and cheese. A hearty meal, but also a lonely one, with only the servants for company. No wonder that she eats with the television set switched on and with long pauses between mouthfuls as she soaks up the peak-hour programmes.

II

Warm and sunny though the Queen Mother's nature is to outward appearances, there is one small corner of her being which remains bleak and icy. This is the corner reserved for her brother-in-law, the Duke of Windsor. In the days when her husband was still Duke of York and his brother, David, was Prince of Wales, the brother-in-law and sister-in-law were also close friends. The Prince of Wales was a frequent visitor to the York home at 145 Piccadilly, where he found a measure of relaxation in the evening session of children's games with his two small nieces, Lilibet and Margaret Rose, and their parents. But with his own accession to the throne and subsequent abdication, the relationship underwent a change. Almost as though she had never quite forgiven him for stepping down from the Throne, the Queen Mother—the Queen, as she then was—was noticeably never at home at Buckingham Palace on the rare occasions when the Duke of Windsor called round to see the younger brother who was now King in his place. It cannot have been merely coincidence that on every occasion when the Duke visited the palace she found herself with some other engagement, sometimes slipping out of the palace by the garden entrance at almost the same time that her brother-in-law was coming in the King's Door and climbing the semicircular flight of steps known as the King's Stairs.

If the Queen Mother has permitted old sores to rankle over the years, at least she has not been alone in this. On a humbler level, they rankled too with Frederick Smith, who served the

Prince of Wales and became his personal page when he succeeded to the throne as Edward VIII. But loyalty to the Crown was stronger in Smith than loyalty to the man, and when King Edward abdicated and left the country, it was noticeable that Smith did not go with him. Instead, he stayed on at Buckingham Palace as page to the new King, George VI. It was rumoured among the other palace servants that Smith, when he learned of his master's intention to abdicate, had so far forgotten himself as to round on him with blunt and bitter words. Perhaps this was one of the things George VI had in mind when he jotted down in his diary, "One or two curious incidents happened later re. the servants." In the years which followed, Smith, like the Queen Mother, was always absent when the Duke called. As soon as he knew that his former master would be calling, Smith would ask the King if he could be relieved at his post outside the door of the King's study for the period of the visit. Permission was always given, and another page would take over until the Duke had been and gone again.

It is doubtful if there is a living soul who knows how the Queen Mother really felt about the abdication. Neither in public nor in private has she ever said a word about it, but her action of quitting the palace whenever her brother-in-law was expected has spoken louder than any words over the years.

Further evidence of the strength of her feelings may perhaps be seen in the fact that she played no part in the lowering of what the Duchess of Windsor has called "the family-designed asbestos curtain," which took place when the aged and ailing Duke entered the London Clinic for eye surgery in February, 1965. First of the Royal Family to visit the Duke in hospital was the Queen herself. There Elizabeth and the Duchess met, by the Duke's bedside, for the first time in nearly thirty years. The Queen's visit to the Clinic was not listed in the official Court Circular, the reason given being that it was "a personal and family matter." That it was also something more was shown by the fact that the Queen was accompanied by her Private Secretary. Some interpreted this as foreshadowing a welcome for the Duchess of Windsor at Buckingham Palace and the granting to her of the style of Royal Highness. But despite a second visit to the Clinic—this time accompanied by one of her Assistant Private Secretaries—the Queen has made no move in the years since to elevate her aunt-by-marriage to full royal status.

Others of the Royal Family also visited the Duke at the London Clinic and met and talked with his wife. For his sister, the Princess Royal, it was an opportune reunion with the brother she had seen so seldom over the years. She died unexpectedly only thirteen days later. Another visitor was the late Princess Marina, widow of the Duke of Kent. Had he lived, her husband might perhaps have effected a family reconciliation. Of the four royal sons of George V—David (Duke of Windsor), Albert (the Queen's father, the late King George VI), Harry (Duke of Gloucester), and George (Duke of Kent)—David and George were always the closest. But Kent met an early and tragic death in a wartime air crash.

Yet though others of the Royal Family visited the Duke in the London Clinic, the Queen Mother did not. However, two years later she walked over to chat briefly, shaking hands with the Duchess and accepting a kiss on the cheek from the Duke, at the unveiling of a memorial to the Duke's mother, Queen Mary. The ceremony, at Marlborough Palace, was officially described as "private," though witnessed by a crowd of more than a thousand people. Perhaps it was the so-called "private" nature of the occasion which prompted the Windsors to accept the Queen's invitation, though, hurt and angered by continued refusal to grant the Duchess the style of "Royal Highness," they had previously declined invitations to Elizabeth's wedding, Margaret's wedding, and the wedding of the young Duke of Kent.

Be that as it may, it seems ironic that the occasion of partial reconciliation should have been a ceremony to the memory of Queen Mary, who was even more implacable than the Queen Mother in her attitude towards the Duchess of Windsor. In all the years between the abdication in 1936 and her own death in 1953, the Duke's regally imperious mother never once consented to meet the woman for whom he sacrificed the Throne. Her only concession in all that time was a letter, written years after the abdication, to which she added a brief footnote: "I send a kind message to your wife."

The Queen placed one of her cars at the Windsors' disposal for the ceremony and sent them back to France afterwards in an aircraft of the Queen's Flight. But she went no further... and in a television programme in which the Duke and Duchess took part before leaving London, the interviewer, while addressing the Duke as "Your Royal Highness," was careful to refer to the Duchess only as "Your Grace."

The decision not to grant the Duchess of Windsor the title of "Her Royal Highness" was taken by King George VI shortly after his brother's abdication. How far his wife, the Queen Mother, may have influenced him in this decision is something that only she knows. No mention of the King's reasons is given in his diaries... or, at least, in those extracts which have been published since his death. That Britain's then prime minister, Stanley Baldwin, and perhaps other government ministers of the time, had some say in the King's final decision is implicit in the method by which it was made public. The royal declaration was given effect by "Letters Patent under the Great Seal of the Realm," which means that it was a decision taken and a declaration made on the advice of the King's ministers. The *London Gazette* of the time recorded:

"The King has been pleased by Letters Patent under the Great Seal of the Realm bearing date the 27th day of May, 1937, to declare that the Duke of Windsor shall, notwithstanding his Instrument of Abdication executed on the 10th day of December, 1936, and His Majesty's Declaration of Abdication Act, 1936, whereby effect was given to the said Instrument, be entitled to hold and enjoy for himself only the title style or attribute of Royal Highness so however that his wife and descendants if any shall not hold the said title style and attribute."

The reasons which prompted the King to this decision were probably a complex mixture of the regal, the constitutional, the personal and the religious. His mother, Queen Mary, still at that time very much the fountainhead of the Royal Family, could not or would not bring herself to receive a divorcee. His wife, bitter about her brother-in-law's decision to abdicate and the regal burden it had placed upon the ill-equipped shoulders of her husband, was not prepared to accept her new sister-in-law as a member of the family. The King himself was doubtless mindful of the fact that he was not only monarch, but also, as Defender of the Faith, titular head of the Church of England.

Whatever the King's reasons, his decision, communicated to his brother in a personal letter which reached him in France just before his marriage, left the Duke of Windsor a disappointed and embittered man. Constitutionally, it meant that his wife was destined to occupy not only a lower position than he occupied himself, but also a lesser position than the wives of his brothers, the Duke of Gloucester and the late Duke of Kent. This was something he could barely tolerate, and in the years which followed he made more than one attempt to persuade his brother to change his mind. From Lisbon, in wartime, he sought the help of Winston Churchill. Churchill wanted the Duke and Duchess, who had fled to Lisbon when the Germans overran France, to return to England, and was prepared to send a flying-boat to enable them to make the journey. But the Duke dug his heels in. He felt, he informed Churchill, that his wife had been slighted and ignored when they were previously in Britain. Churchill advised him to return just the same and see how things worked out. The Duke declined. Instead, he went to the Bahamas as Governor and Commander-in-Chief, a post he held until the end of the war, when he and his wife could return to their sanctuary in France.

Hurt and angered by the continued refusal to elevate his wife to the style of Royal Highness, the Duke, however irregularly, has contrived to bestow the title himself. In private conversation he has frequently referred to the Duchess as "Her Royal Highness" and servants at their Paris home have been instructed to address her thus. On one occasion when the Duke chanced to overhear a servant addressing the Duchess as "Your Grace" (her correct title), he snapped angrily: "You're not in England now, man."

Even at this late date it is unlikely that there will be any change in the Duchess' official status. The Queen, like her father before her, is head of the Church of England, and the Church of England is still opposed to divorce. So constitutionally the Queen's position, even if she desired to bring about a change, remains complicated and difficult. Moreover, she is not only her father's daughter, but very much a granddaughter of Queen Mary, with the same rigid, implacable outlook on the fitness of things.

This I saw very clearly when accompanying her on one visit to the United States. She was in New York for only one day, and the informally dubbed "royal suite" on the 28th floor of the Waldorf Towers had been placed at her disposal. Along with Bobo MacDonald, Ernest Bennett, her page, and James Mac-Donald, Philip's valet, I arrived at the hotel ahead of the Queen and was waiting at the entrance to the suite when she came out of the elevator. Her attention was attracted by a statuette of herself in her Coronation robes which stood on a side table, and she walked over for a closer look at it. As she turned away again her eyes lighted on the silver plaque which records the names of various notables who have occupied that selfsame suite on their visits to New York.

Until now she had been smiling, but suddenly her smile vanished and her eyes took on that look of icy regality they have if she is displeased for any reason. After she had gone through into the sitting-room of the suite, I inspected the plaque to see what about it had aroused her displeasure. Among those who had previously occupied the suite were the Windsors, listed on the commemorative plaque as "T.R.H. The Duke and Duchess of Windsor." "T.R.H.," of course, signifies Their—meaning two—Royal Highnesses, which, in fact and as far as the Queen is concerned, one of them is not.

III

Whether or not the rift between the Windsors and the rest of the Royal Family was due, in part at least, to the unforgiving attitude of the Queen Mother, there can be little doubt that the headline-making romance between her younger daughter and Group Captain Peter Townsend was partly her fault. Either she did not see what was happening, or she decided to turn a blind eye to it. Had her husband lived, the situation might not have developed to the extent it did. The late King George, much as he liked and admired Townsend, would soon have nipped the romance in the bud, as a passing incident, the year before the King's death, clearly showed.

The King and Queen were paying their regular, short, early-summer visit to Balmoral, the Queen to enjoy the salmon-fishing, the King to look over the estate and relax generally. Princess Margaret was with them, and they had also taken Townsend along in his dual role of Royal Equerry and Deputy Master of the Royal Household. It was a week of brilliant sunny weather, and one day the King and Queen decided to picnic on the heathery slopes overlooking Loch Muich. Two estate cars were brought round to the main door; two picnic baskets were made ready and stood waiting on the front steps. Princess Margaret and Townsend came out and stood waiting. As instructed, I placed one of the baskets in the King's car. I picked up the other and was on the point of placing it in the second car when the King and Queen came out.

"Why aren't both baskets going in my car?" the King wanted to know.

It was the Queen who answered him. "Margaret and Peter are going for a picnic of their own," she said.

"Oh, no, they're not," said the King loudly. "We're all going together."

With that he climbed into his own car and the Queen followed. I put the second basket in the King's car. Margaret and Townsend looked at each other, exchanged shrugs, and climbed into the second car. Then both vehicles drove off with the King leading the way.

At this time, Princess Margaret's growing attachment to Townsend was already a source of gossip among those who worked for the royal family. Whatever the King and Queen may or may not have known, few of their staff had failed to notice the developing relationship. At Balmoral and Sandringham, it was made plain by the way Margaret so often reserved the seat next to herself for Townsend at mealtimes. It was evident, too, in the frequent horse-rides and long walks they enjoyed together. At Buckingham Palace, where Townsend ate not with the family but in the Household Dining Room, things were perhaps a shade less obvious. But even there it was an open secret that Townsend was a frequent visitor to the princess' sitting-room.

Townsend, a hero of the Battle of Britain with eleven enemy aircraft to his credit, first came to the palace through the King's policy of appointing as temporary equerries young men who had distinguished themselves in war. Most of these war-hero equerries came and went within a comparatively short period, and Townsend was appointed originally for three months. But the King took an almost instant liking to the tall, slim airman with the thick black hair and brooding blue-grey eyes, and Townsend stayed at the palace, finally, for nine years. When Townsend first arrived, Princess Margaret was a leggy, slightly precocious chatterbox in her teens. When he finally went out of her life, she was a young woman in her mid-twenties. In between, she had undergone a deeply bitter-sweet experience which she was to take a long time to get over.

Townsend, at the outset, was a married man. He had married during the war after one of those brief, whirlwind courtships which were symptomatic of the time. The King gave him and his wife a grace-and-favour cottage to live in at Windsor, was soon calling him "Peter," and served as a godfather to his second son, Hugo. My first impression of Townsend was of a man who could virtually do without sleep. Many times he was on duty at the palace until half-past eleven or twelve o'clock at night, when the King retired, and it would be perhaps a further half-hour before Townsend could follow suit. Yet, snatching only a few hours' sleep, he would be up, shaved, dressed and out of the palace at five o'clock in the morning to catch the first train out to Windsor. After spending a brief half-hour with his wife and children, he would catch a train back to London in time to be on duty again, fresh and spruce, by nine o'clock. Similarly, though technically on duty, he would sometimes slip away at weekends to spend a few hours with his wife and family, and there was one Monday morning when he inadvertently greeted the King with the news, "Beautiful weather at Windsor over the weekend, Sir."

"How do you know?" asked the King gruffly. "You're not supposed to have been there."

For all his seeming gruffness, the King was an essentially human man, and he turned a blind eye to Townsend's unofficial absences. In a very short time, all the Royal Family were copying the King's example and calling Townsend by his first name. Between themselves, the King and Queen talked about him often in the most cordial and flattering terms. That they also talked of him to Queen Mary was revealed when the old Queen paid one of her rare visits to the palace.

She was met at the door by one of the King's equerries. In her forthright manner, she asked him his name.

"Peter Ashmore, Ma'am," he told her.

"Are you *the* Peter?" she wanted to know.

"I'm not sure, Ma'am," replied Ashmore, clearly confused by this turn in the conversation.

"If you are, you're made," said Queen Mary and off she stalked, the inevitable parasol clutched in her hand.

Townsend would indeed have been made had he not committed the mistake of falling in love with the King's daughter.

It was during the 1947 royal tour of South Africa that Townsend and the teenage princess were first thrown into each other's company. For all concerned, it was an extremely difficult and arduous tour. The King became so exhausted that he lost seventeen pounds in weight. The Queen had her work cut out in looking after her husband. Elizabeth was pining for Philip. Margaret, a rather precocious 16-year-old, was consequently left much to her own devices and tended to get bored. Townsend was assigned to keep an eye on her and keep her amused.

By the time the tour ended, Margaret and Townsend had become firm friends. That summer, at Balmoral, they started riding together. At Balmoral many of the hills are capped with stone cairns erected by Queen Victoria to commemorate royal marriages and similar family events. One day, as a joke, Margaret put down the first stone of a new cairn. After that it became a sort of game between them that whoever reached the hilltop first should add another stone. So friendship flourished and romance perhaps was born.

Whatever the other members of the Royal Family may have thought of Townsend, Philip, by now Elizabeth's husband, did not always view him in quite the same non-critical light. By some quirk of character, Townsend, who had shot down eleven German aircraft, disliked the organised shoots which were part of royal life at Balmoral and Sandringham. He might occasionally go off on his own in pursuit of a stag, but I never knew him to join in the shooting of grouse or partridges. Instead, he would walk with the womenfolk, indulging in polite conversation. This tended to irritate Philip, and on one occasion when his marksmanship was disturbed by frivolous chatter between Margaret and Townsend, he turned abruptly and snapped at them to be quiet.

August 21, 1951, was Margaret's twenty-first birthday. The family were again at Balmoral, and she spent part of the day riding with Townsend, using a sheepskin saddle he had given her. That evening, in a small private ceremony with romantic undertones, she handed Townsend a lighted torch which he bore aloft like an Olympic runner, scaling the slope in front of the castle and lighting the birthday bonfire which had been built at the top.

Margaret's growing attachment to Townsend was not known outside the palace. The newspapers published rumours of her coming betrothal to first one young man, and then another... the Marquess of Blandford, the Earl of Dalkeith, Billy Wallace (stepson of Herbert Agar, the American-born Pulitzer prize-winner), Lord Ogilvy. But never a mention of Townsend. At this time he was still married, though marriage was no longer the halcyon affair it had once been. He no longer rose at five o'clock in the morning to catch the first train to Windsor.

Any possibility that the King might have intervened diminished along with his health, and terminated finally with his death in February, 1952. The King's death, indeed, served to draw Townsend and Margaret closer together. With her mother absorbed in her own grief and her sister preoccupied with her new duties as monarch, Margaret turned for consolation to the only other person close to hand... Peter Townsend.

Ten months later he divorced his wife on the grounds of misconduct. By now he was living permanently at the palace in a cubby-hole bedroom only a few doors from the office where he worked as Deputy Master of the Queen's Household. At Easter, 1953, when the Queen Mother and Princess Margaret moved to Clarence House, Townsend went with them as Comptroller, living and working in a small house sandwiched between Clarence House and St. James's Palace.

By this time, astute newspapermen in Britain, the United States and elsewhere were beginning to put two and two together. Royalty does its best to ignore gossip and rumours, but those linking Margaret and Townsend could no longer be safely ignored. Something had to be done, and quickly. Arrangements had already been made for Townsend to accompany Margaret and the Queen Mother on their tour of Southern Rhodesia. Townsend, in fact, had been responsible for planning the tour with its visit to the Rhodes Centenary Exhibition in Bulawayo. Then, almost on the eve of departure, came the bombshell announcement that Townsend would no longer be going. Captain the Lord Plunket would go in his place, and Townsend would remain behind to accompany the Queen and Prince Philip on their subsequent visit to Northern Ireland. It was, as events quickly proved, the thin end of the wedge for Margaret and Townsend.

For Princess Margaret, that trip to Rhodesia was certainly not among her happier royal journeys. At one point she cancelled her official engagements and took to her room with what was given out as a "heavy cold," an indisposition coinciding with the news that Group Captain Peter Townsend was resuming duty with the Royal Air Force (from which he had been seconded all those years before to serve as Royal Equerry) and was being sent to Brussels as British air attaché.

By the time Princess Margaret and her mother returned to London he had already left Britain. In fact, he never returned to Buckingham Palace. He came back from Northern Ireland with the Queen and Prince Philip, stood chatting with them for a few minutes on the tarmac at London Airport, received a farewell handshake from Prince Philip and drove off into "exile."

It was over two years before he and Margaret met again. They wrote to each other during their months of separation, Margaret's letters reaching Brussels in the diplomatic bag. Occasional newspaper interviews with Townsend served to keep the love story alive in the public mind. "I came here because the position was impossible for us both," he was quoted as saying on one occasion. And on another, "I cannot answer questions because I am not the prime mover in the situation. My loyalty to Princess Margaret is unquestionable. I would undergo any difficulties because of that loyalty."

From Princess Margaret there were no such announcements. But the fact that she was still in love with Townsend and missing him showed in her changed personality. She was no longer the gay, happy, carefree princess who had sparkled like a well-cut diamond in the late-night round of parties, balls, theatres and nightclubs only a few years before. She continued to perform those public duties required of her, but the old sparkle and dash were missing. In private she was quiet and withdrawn.

August, 1955, brought her to her twenty-fifth birthday. Until then, under the cobwebby restrictions of the Royal Marriage Act of 1772, she could marry only with "the consent of the Sovereign in Council"—in other words, with the formal consent of her sister. But now, at the age of twenty-five, she was free, if she wished, to give twelve months' notice and marry whomever she pleased.

Seven weeks later Townsend returned to London, and it seemed that things were moving in the direction of marriage. Within hours he was closeted with Margaret in her pink-walled sitting room at Clarence House. They spent the weekend together at the country home of Margaret's cousin, Mrs. John Lycett Wills. They saw each other constantly over the next few days. Then they spent another weekend together, this time at the Uckfield home of Lord Rupert Nevill. But that was a fortnight later, and the atmosphere had changed considerably. Margaret's feelings may not have changed, but the weekend between—which she spent at Windsor with her sister and Philip —had brought her round, however reluctantly, to the idea that royal duty must come first.

In the family line-up for and against marriage to Townsend, Margaret may perhaps have hoped that Philip would be on her side. She saw him as the occasional rebel against convention that she is herself. But Philip puts duty first and expects others to do the same. When the three of them emerged from the dining room that evening, Margaret's face wore a look of obstinate defiance. The Queen was regal and unsmiling, and Philip had that look of chiselled sternness which Annigoni captured so successfully in his portrait. They went into the Queen's private sitting room and closed the door. When they came out again an hour later, Margaret had clearly been crying. Nevertheless, she turned and kissed both her sister and Philip on the cheek before going along to her bedroom.

Back in London, the Princess went to see the Archbishop of

Canterbury (to whom she is said to have delivered the now-famous line, "Archbishop, you may put away your books. I have made up my mind"). Five days later came her touching statement of renunciation: "... Mindful of the Church's teaching that Christian marriage is indissoluble, and conscious of my duty to the Commonwealth, I have resolved to put these considerations before others. ..."

IV

It was six months after her parting from Peter Townsend that Princess Margaret first encountered the man she was eventually to marry, though that first meeting made little impression upon her. The occasion was the marriage of two old friends, Colin Tennant, heir to Lord Glenconner, and Anne Coke, daughter of the Earl and Countess of Leicester, whose home on the Norfolk coast is close to the royal estate at Sandringham. Still looking pale and strained in the aftermath of the Townsend episode, Margaret flew to Norfolk with her mother to attend the wedding. Another member of the wedding party was a young photographer named Tony Armstrong-Jones, and Margaret first glimpsed him hunched over the camera with which he took the wedding pictures.

They next ran into each other, some considerable time later, at a society party in London, and this time the encounter was on slightly more level terms. Tony was there not in his professional capacity, but as one of the guests. In all that has been written about him, the fact is often overlooked that he was not simply some small, back-street photographer. While he was not yet in the photographic top rank, socially he was out of the top drawer. He was the grandson of a knight, the son of a countess (his mother married the Earl of Rosse after her divorce from his father) and the brother of a viscountess. He was educated at Eton and Cambridge, where he was cox of the crew which beat Oxford by 3½ lengths in the 1950 boat race. His photographic apprenticeship had been with Baron Nahum, a friend of Prince Philip.

The first public image which emerged when Tony's secret romance with Princess Margaret was finally revealed was of an offbeat young bohemian whose favourite garb consisted of jeans and a sweater. In fact, jeans and sweaters represented only one facet of a complex, many-sided, considerably talented young man with oodles of drive and energy. From his £5-a-week studio in unfashionable Pimlico Road, Tony wrote for permission to photograph the young Duke of Kent. He got it, and the Duke liked the photographs so well that he selected one as the official portrait to be issued for his coming-of-age. Tony took photographs of Lord Rupert Nevill's children. The Queen saw them and asked him to photograph Charles and Anne. This, in turn, led to the official photographs he took of the Queen and Prince Philip for their 1957 tour of Canada.

Margaret and Tony continued to run into one another at various social functions. Margaret, just emerging from the long period of nun-like seclusion which had followed her parting from Townsend, found the bright chatter of the young photographer from Pimlico Road a refreshing tonic. Perhaps, too, he reminded her of Townsend ... gentle and unobtrusive, attentive to women, with a happy knack of making any woman in his company feel wholly feminine. He invited her to see a revue called *Keep Your Hair On*, for which he had designed the sets. Margaret accepted, but the show flopped before she could get along. Instead, he took her to see the American musical, *West Side Story*.

This theatre date marked the beginning of a twelve-month courtship which was conducted with all the secrecy of a military operation. The Townsend episode had taught Margaret a lesson, and she was determined that no newspaper publicity should mar her new romance. When Tony was invited to Royal Lodge at weekends he arrived in a car filled with photographic equipment which he painstakingly unloaded and carted indoors. In fact, the equipment did not always go unused. He took a number of photographs of Margaret, and one of them was issued as the official portrait to mark her twenty-ninth birthday. Still in his guise of photographer, he spent several days at Balmoral that summer and at Sandringham in the week following Christmas. So carefully camouflaged were these visits that not even the most wide-awake servant suspected what was going on. To the royal staff Tony was simply "that photographer chap." At mealtimes Margaret was careful not to sit beside him as she had once sat beside Townsend. When the Royal Family and their guests went out shooting or picnicking, she and Tony never left together. They departed separately and linked up only when out of sight.

Apart from members of the Royal Family, few people were in on the secret of Margaret's new romance. One was her maid, Ruby Gordon, the married sister of the Queen's beloved Bobo. Ruby first went to work for the family soon after Margaret was born and, with the exception of an interval during the war years, continued to look after her, first as nursemaid and later as personal maid, until some years after her marriage to Tony. Ruby's own marriage to Norman Gordon was one of those romances which blossom among the royal staff from time to time. Norman, when they met and married, was one of the royal footmen, though he subsequently resigned his post.

Ruby and Margaret became giggling conspirators in preserving the secrecy of the new romance. More than once Ruby booked theatre seats in her own name so that Tony and Margaret could see a show incognito. They timed things carefully to arrive at the theatre after the curtain had risen and in the interval Margaret kept her face buried in the programme. She was never recognized. A head-scarf and dark glasses proved an effective disguise when she met Tony for a quiet meal at some country inn, or wandered round with him inspecting the contents of junk yards and antique shops.

There was one occasion, as a return gesture, when Margaret used her royal influence to obtain seats for a fully-booked show for Ruby and her husband. Hearing that the two of them very much wanted to see the show but had been unable to get seats, she told an equerry to telephone the theatre in her name. Seats were immediately forthcoming, of course, and there was a slightly unexpected sequel. Ruby and her husband were late arriving at the theatre and the manager, under the impression that he was expecting Princess Margaret, held the curtain for them.

Under the influence of Tony and the artistic world in which he moved and worked, a new, more "with-it" Margaret emerged from the royal chrysalis. She had her hair styled in a new, short fashion quite unlike the normal regal hair-do. She changed her mode of make-up to give her face a fresh, more piquant look.

Outside the family, only Ruby Gordon and one or two well-trusted friends had the slightest inkling of what was afoot until the formal announcement burst like a bombshell in February, 1960: "It is with the greatest pleasure that Queen Elizabeth the Queen Mother announces the betrothal of her beloved daughter the Princess Margaret to Mr. Antony Charles Robert Armstrong-Jones, son of Mr. R. O. L. Armstrong-Jones, Q.C., and the Countess of Rosse, to which the Queen has gladly given her consent."

Since her marriage, Margaret has successfully bridged the gap between two very different and sometimes conflicting worlds ... the intensely formal, perhaps old-fashioned world of royal pomp and circumstance, and the less formal, more restless, very up-to-the-minute world of photo sessions and movie studios, theatre rehearsals and bright, brittle chatter, which is her husband's background. Yet she remains today what she has always been—very much an enigma, an unpredictable personality who can be gay one moment and moody the next, switching with equal facility from comparative informality to regal rigidity. She wears the most professional make-up of any of the royal ladies, changes her hair-style almost as often as she changes her mind (helped these days by a collection of eleven topknots and hairpieces), is equally at home at a jazz concert or the ballet, is rather given to witty asides which are sometimes tinged with a touch of acid, and sings in her bath in a loud and melodious voice which would certainly have assured her of musical comedy stardom had she been anyone other than who she is.

I remember my first encounter with Princess Margaret. Three separate times at five-minute intervals I was sent to her room to tell her that dinner was ready. The others finally sat down without her, and twenty minutes later she decided to join them. She was singing at the top of her voice as she walked into the dining room and took her seat for dinner.

She is also an accomplished pianist and, in private, a considerable comedienne with a talent for mimicry. At Balmoral once, a new young footman—an Irishman—was given the task of taking Margaret's breakfast tray up to her. In error, instead of depositing it on the table in her sitting room, he marched straight into her bedroom with it. The princess was still in bed. The poor footman blushed scarlet and stammered his apologies in a rich Irish brogue which Margaret imitated to perfection for the benefit of friends and relatives over dinner that evening.

These days, Margaret cleverly dovetails the public duties of a professional princess with a private life which is considerably offbeat by royal standards. Yet even in her most informal moments she never forgets that she is a member of the Royal Family, nor does she allow anyone else to forget it. She is "Your Royal Highness" to servants at her Kensington Palace home, and "Ma'am" to her friends. She can be quickly offended if anyone trespasses upon her regal dignity, and has been known to leave a cocktail party where she felt there was a tendency to treat her too informally.

She is, in many ways, as different from her sister, the Queen, as chalk is from cheese. The Queen is punctual, reserved, serious, undemonstrative, even-tempered and always the same. Margaret is seldom punctual, often flippant, quick to anger and as quickly affectionate, seldom the same from one hour to the next. The Queen likes to be up and about of a morning, even on vacation. Margaret prefers breakfast in bed. At night, if she has no public engagement, the Queen is usually in bed at half-past ten or a little after. Margaret will happily stay up chattering until midnight or past. The Queen prefers to "dress down" in tweeds and similar simple outfits. Margaret loves dressing up. Margaret loves the social round of theatres and restaurants, nightclubs and cocktail parties. The Queen prefers the countryside, the company of dogs or horses. Charity shows apart, she seldom goes to the theatre. It is years since she touched the record-player in her sitting room, and about the only time she plays the piano these days is to join Margaret in a sisterly duet at Christmas.

Yet the virtues are not all on the side of the older sister. Unlike childhood days, when Elizabeth was always the neat, methodical one, Margaret is the tidier of the two today. Her desk is neatly businesslike, compared to the seeming clutter with which the Queen surrounds herself. Her recording discs are carefully stored and catalogued while the Queen's home movies are stuffed haphazardly into drawers and cupboards. And Margaret takes after her mother in thoughtful consideration. The Queen, perhaps because she has so much else to do, would need a reminder to buy a gift for one of her staff who was perhaps getting married. Margaret would buy one of her own accord.

Strikingly different though the sisters are in personality and temperament, they have things in common . . . the same springy, upright walk, the same regal wave, the same rather limp handshake. Their voices too are almost identical. If you cannot see them, it is virtually impossible to tell which of the two is speaking. I once answered a shouted summons from the Queen's sitting room with a brisk, "Yes, Your Majesty." But it was Margaret I saw when I walked in. "It's not the Queen," she said with an impish grin. "It's me."

Poles apart though they are in so many ways, the royal sisters are deeply devoted to each other. Throughout childhood and into their teens they were almost inseparable. "We're telepathic," Margaret would say jokingly. Whatever Elizabeth did, Margaret wanted to do, too. "I want a train as long as Lilibet's," she wailed at her father's coronation. "I was born too late," she lamented when she was forced to sit at lessons while her elder sister drove off in her own car. Over the years she developed a complete and absolute trust in everything Elizabeth did and said. Elizabeth reciprocated with the fussy protectiveness of an older sister. It is interesting to note that the headline-hitting spate Margaret went through during her late teens and early twenties coincided with Elizabeth's courtship, marriage and general entry into public life. Margaret was deprived of the companionship and guidance upon which she had relied for so many years. For the first time in her life she had to act upon her own initiative. Perhaps, too, she felt all at once a sense of sisterly rivalry. Either way, the results verged on the disastrous.

Her marriage, by contrast, has been wholly successful. Over the years since 1960 she and Tony have proved that they can jog along very well in double harness. While their backgrounds may differ, their natures are complementary. Margaret has always been a bit of a rebel against convention, and marriage to Tony has given her the opportunity of rebelling in the nicest possible way, one of the royal set in public and one of the jet set in private.

She and the Queen remain close. While they see somewhat less of each other these days, they still talk frequently on the telephone. They meet sometimes at Windsor at weekends and at Balmoral on holiday. Occasionally, but not often, they and their husbands go out in a foursome. The two men, on balance, get along well enough together. While their temperaments may be opposite—Philip's basically athletic and Tony's largely artistic—they have common interests. Tony has published a book of photographs, and so has Philip. Tony has built himself a desk from a massive slab of teak; Philip has constructed an intricate scale-model of Balmoral Castle. Tony has designed a new aviary for the London Zoo. Philip was equally responsible for designing the new fountain which stands in the gardens at Windsor.

In recent times, notably since her husband went back to working as a professional photographer, Margaret has again undertaken a dutiful share of royal chores. A run-down of her public engagements over a recent two-year period reveals a total of more than fifty functions, not counting a three-week tour of the

United States, a flight to Hong Kong to promote the sale of British goods, and a visit to Brussels for the same purpose. While many of these functions were the sort of thing Margaret thoroughly enjoys—charity balls, movie premieres and the Cannes Film Festival, for example—many were equally of a routine royal nature. As president, she attended the annual meeting of the Girl Guides. As commandant-in-chief, she paid a visit to the St. John's ambulance cadets. She opened a new hospital, a new art school, and a new police headquarters, visited a flying training school, a nursery training college, and several hospitals, and accompanied her sister for the launching of Britain's newest transatlantic liner, *Queen Elizabeth II.*

Inevitably there have been critical rumblings from time to time. There were criticisms that she was doing insufficient work to justify the increased (from £6000 to £15,000 a year) official allowance she received on marriage. There was criticism, too, because Tony didn't work . . . and still more criticism when he did work, accepting a post with Lord Thomson's *Sunday Times.* There was sniping and sneering when £65,000 of public money went towards renovating and modernising the Snowdons' 21-room apartment in Kensington Palace. In the best royal tradition, the Snowdons weathered each storm in turn—as they will weather others in the future—by laying low and saying nothing.

7. THE QUEEN'S WORK

I

PROMPTLY at ten o'clock each morning, except when she is away from Buckingham Palace, the Queen goes along to the second-floor sitting room which doubles as her study, settles herself at the flat-topped desk in the bay window recess from where she can look out on the palace gardens, and prepares to tackle the business of monarchy.

This was her mother's sitting room when her father was King. But the Queen, though she gave her husband the room which had been her father's study, retained his antique, flat-topped desk for herself as a symbol of the continuity of monarchy. The chair on which the Queen sits is embroidered in petit-point needlework which was worked by her grandmother, the late Queen Mary. The desk is so cluttered as to be almost invisible. A leather-bound blotting pad is flanked by a scribbling pad and a tray of pencils. A silver inkstand is dominated by a leather-bound paper rack holding her scarlet-crested notepaper. There is a tray for documents and correspondence, a loose-leaf engagement book, a brass carriage clock to keep her to time, a gilt-framed list of the day's appointments, a rotary calendar, a paste-pot, another tray containing pins, clips and rubber bands, a small glass bowl holding a moist sponge for sticking envelopes, and wax, candle and matches for affixing her seal to official letters and state documents.

There are, in addition, two telephones to hand, an adjustable desk lamp, and up to a dozen family photographs, including several of Philip, several of herself and Philip taken on their honeymoon, one of her mother, another of her grandmother, the late Queen Mary, and one of Charles as a baby. More photographs—these of her father—stand on a nearby side table.

To one side of the desk, within easy reach, a pedestal cabinet holds her collection of books on horse racing and the breeding of thoroughbreds. On the other side, within equally easy reach, is a table on which are piled the dispatch boxes, leather-bound in red, green, and black, which reach her in never-ending succession from the government offices in Whitehall and the prime minister's sanctum at 10 Downing Street. These are the famous "Boxes" which have plagued Britain's monarchs for generations and which pursue the Queen day in, day out, workdays and weekends alike, at home or on holiday. In them are government papers and Foreign Office telegrams to keep her up-to-date on national and international affairs, and state documents requiring her signature to make them effective. The reading the Queen must do each day covers not only the whole panorama of political life in Britain, but also communications from the Commonwealth countries, for she is Queen of Canada, Australia and New Zealand no less than of the United Kingdom of Great Britain and Northern Ireland.

The first Box of the day, the words "The Queen" lettered in gold on the lid, has already arrived and awaits her attention. But first she deals with whatever personal mail her page has left for her on her desk. She opens each letter in turn with a plastic paper knife (though there is a Fabergé paper knife with a jewelled handle also on the desk), scans it quickly and, like as not, stuffs it away in a drawer with the intention of answering it later. Time, however, is always against her, and the pile of unanswered personal mail mounts steadily. From time to time the Queen will set about reducing the pile with a lightning blitz, penning letter after letter so hurriedly that her handwriting in places tends to become an almost illegible scrawl.

Her personal mail scanned, if not answered, the Queen unlocks the leather-bound dispatch box, sifts its contents and rings for her Private Secretary, Sir Michael Adeane. He arrives carrying a flat wicker tray containing more official documents and correspondence requiring her attention. The next half-hour, with Sir Michael's help, the Queen deals with the more important of her official correspondence, sometimes waiting for his advice, sometimes indicating forthwith the sort of reply she feels meets the case. With the passage of the years, as her own experience of monarchy has grown, the Queen has become more assured in her own decisions. There may be a state document requiring her formal assent, which she signifies with a flourishing *Elizabeth R* quite unlike the scrawling signature she appends to her personal letters. There may be the draft of a speech for her to read and approve (she seldom disapproves), plans for a future royal tour to be discussed, and nearly always there is the necessity for her to be briefed concerning one or more of those she will be receiving in Audience later that morning.

Some point may arise which requires the advice or assent of Prince Philip. A flick of a switch on the mahogany-faced control panel at the Queen's left elbow puts her in instant contact with Philip in his streamlined, gadget-filled study just along the corridor. Installed on Philip's suggestion, this internal communications system enables the Queen to contact all parts of her 600-room palace without troubling either a page or a telephone operator. A flick of a switch can put her straight through to any of her three secretaries, her Lady-in-Waiting, the children's nanny, even her chef.

Sir Michael is followed by one of the Queen's two Assistant Private Secretaries—Sir Martin Charteris or Mr. Philip Moore—with more documents and engagement lists to be perused and approved, more correspondence to be noted and answered. Except for items of very minor routine, every letter reaching Buckingham Palace is seen by the Queen at one time or another, and most are answered either by her or in her name. The only letters that go ignored and unanswered are those from obvious cranks like the mysterious "Elizabeth" who wrote week after week for several years claiming to be the rightful Queen of England. People with more legitimate grievances often write to the Queen in their attempts to gain satisfaction. She seldom intervenes directly, but she nearly always passes the letter on to the appropriate official or department with a request that the complaint be fully investigated. A request from the Queen is still a royal command, and over the years not a few small wrongs have been righted in this fashion.

Her Private Secretary and Assistant Secretaries dealt with, the Queen plugs away steadily at the contents of her Box—and any others which have arrived since she originally seated herself at her desk—in an unremitting race against time. It is a race without end which she can never hope to win, a life governed by the clock and the calendar and her engagement pad. She finishes the contents of a Box, locks it, rings for it to be collected. A glance at the diminutive platinum wristwatch on her left wrist informs her that it is time now to move on. But first she reaches for her black leather handbag, brings out her lipstick and mirror, and freshens her make-up. Then she walks back through the dining room to the Wedgwood-blue-and-white Audience Room at the far end of the royal apartment.

Because this is where she receives her official callers, including the prime minister on Tuesday evenings for a 90-minute session which keeps the Queen informed of the "state of the nation," it is often pictured and described as the Queen's study, though in fact it is not. The major part of her working life is spent in the less formal, more feminine, atmosphere of her sitting room. But only a very few privileged visitors ever succeed in penetrating that royal sanctum. The majority get no farther than the Audience Room, where the Queen stands to greet each visitor in turn

[175]

before motioning him to a seat in one of the two beige-pink armchairs. She sits herself on a matching chesterfield.

Between half-past eleven and one o'clock each day, the Queen will receive perhaps eight or nine visitors, allocating to each of them an average of ten minutes. Foreign ambassadors newly arrived in London enter in full diplomatic uniform to present their credentials to her. Britain's own ambassadors report to her—as well as more fully to the Foreign Secretary. She receives new judges and retiring judges, bishops and archbishops, governors and governors-general, admirals, field marshals and air marshals, the top brass of Britain's civil service, the heads of charitable organisations, and so on and so forth. With each, thanks to Adeane's concise, informative briefing, she is able to talk knowledgeably in the slightly higher pitch her voice tends to adopt on public and official occasions. Occasionally it happens that the visitor shares her own enthusiasm for horses and horse racing. If so, the Queen needs no briefing in order to talk expertly and at length. The tone of her voice drops and time flies by unheeded, with the result that subsequent visitors find themselves shunted in and out of the Audience Room at top speed as the Queen tries to catch up with lost time.

From time to time, the end of the morning is taken up with a meeting of the Privy Council, the present-day version of that witan of wise men called together by Alfred the Great. There are about twenty Privy Council meetings in the course of an average year. Usually they are held at noon in the 1844 Room at Buckingham Palace, though they have also been held at Windsor, Balmoral, and Sandringham, aboard the royal yacht *Britannia*, and even at Goodwood on one occasion when the Queen was staying there for the races. The latest list of Privy Counsellors available at this writing totals 321 names, including Cabinet ministers, archbishops, senior members of the Queen's Household, and distinguished members of the Commonwealth. Canada has the distinction of having its own Privy Council as well as being represented, nominally at least, on that of the United Kingdom. Prince Philip is a Privy Counsellor, as is his uncle, Earl

[176]

Mountbatten of Burma. So is the Queen's uncle, the Duke of Gloucester. But only those required for the business in hand, usually four or five (a quorum is three), are summoned to a particular meeting. By long tradition, the business of the Privy Council is always transacted standing. Members are sworn to secrecy, though much of what is transacted in this day and age simply involves the royal endorsement of what is required by Cabinet or Parliament.

II

Sometimes the last visitor of the morning will have been invited to stay on for lunch, and the Queen is doubly delighted if the visitor happens also to be a personal friend. Former President Eisenhower comes into this category and has several times lunched with the Queen. But more frequently the Queen lunches alone. Philip, dashing busily around to fulfill the hectic spate of public engagements he has built up for himself over the years, is seldom home for lunch.

Philip has undergone a very considerable transformation since his wife first succeeded to the throne, and so has the position of Prince Consort which he occupies in fact, if not in title. That he has not yet been raised to the formal style of Prince Consort is perhaps because he has no wish to be too closely linked in the public mind with his predecessor. Victoria's husband, Prince Albert, never commanded the public popularity Philip rates today. His character, in so many ways, was too much against him. He was an intellectual, a stiff, unbending man with reserved, pedantic traits. Unlike Philip, he cared nothing for sport, a shortcoming which caused him to be tagged as "un-English." So great was the prejudice against him that during the Crimean War (which he tried hard to avert) it was even rumoured that he was selling state secrets to Russia. This is not at all the sort of image with which Philip wants to be linked, and the reading up he did on Albert when his wife first came to the throne was perhaps as much to guard against possible pitfalls as anything else. Yet there was perhaps an echo of Albert's lament, "I am only the husband and not the master in the house," in Philip's early grumbling complaint that he felt "like a lodger" at Buckingham Palace.

Philip has Albert's energy without his stiffness, the same desire for social improvement without Albert's air of do-good priggishness. Albert wrote, "Means must be found not for diminishing riches, but to make facilities for the poor." Philip has declared, somewhat similarly, "I see no advantage in a prosperous and powerful state if it is to be achieved at the expense of human freedom and happiness." Albert considered that Britain's main evil was "the unequal division of property and the dangers of poverty and envy arising therefrom." A century later, Philip insists that "all people are primarily citizens and not just workers with a bit of private life."

Yet it is impossible to imagine Britain's present-day Foreign Secretary writing to Philip, as Lord John Russell did to Albert, seeking guidance on his future dealings with Germany. Philip is careful to steer clear of any overt connection with politics or international affairs, as indeed he should. Albert saw himself as "permanent private secretary to the Queen and her permanent minister." These words come very close to pinpointing Philip's present-day role, though he is far too shrewd and diplomatic to make a similar claim. Philip's role in royal life is a difficult and contradictory one. Like Albert, he has the masculine attributes as head of the family, but must always remain constitutionally subordinate to his wife. He must be popular, but never more popular than the Queen. He has to be, at one and the same time, a royal prince and a man of the people. These conflicting roles he fills remarkably well.

Where public life is concerned, Prince Philip these days is often busier than the Queen. Over the years he has built up for himself a staggering list of posts, presidencies and patronages. Yet he accepts office only where he feels he can play a real and worthwhile part, and consistently turns down approaches from those he feels are looking only for a royal figurehead. Even so, his list of official positions at this writing occupies 81 closely printed lines in *Debrett*, running like a thread of royal purple through the whole warp and weft of British life. Equally, the list reflects the man and his interests . . . Grand Master of the Guild of Air Pilots and Navigators, Commander in Chief of the Air Training Corps, Commodore of the Royal Yacht Squadron and admiral of seven yacht clubs, Trustee of the National Maritime Museum, Chairman of the Awards for Industry Committee, Chancellor of the Universities of Wales and Edinburgh, Vice President of the British Horse Society, and President of, among others, the National Playing Fields Association, the English Speaking Union of the Commonwealth, the Royal Society for the Prevention of Accidents, the Central Council for Physical Recreation, the Royal Society of Arts, the British Amateur Athletic Board, the International Lawn Tennis Club, the Royal Areo Club, the National Federation of Young Farmers' Clubs, and the World Wildlife Fund (which some people feel accords ill with his own reputation as a marksman and hunter).

Even when he is at home at Buckingham Palace and not zipping about the world in helicopters and jet planes, Philip is seldom still and never idle. He even walks as though always on the verge of breaking into a canter, and about the only time his pace of life moderates is when he has to match his wife's measured tread on occasions of national ceremony.

Even at weekends and during vacations his pace never slackens. No man to lie abed late, he is up sharp at eight o'clock even on holiday—still earlier if he plans to go duck-shooting—for another non-stop round of sports and games which have ranged, over the years, from polo to oil painting, from shooting pheasants, partridges and wild pig, to modelling Balmoral Castle on a detailed scale which included diminutive handles to the two-inch doors. He regards a change as being every bit as good as a rest; as he phrases it himself, "The essence of the exercise is to vary it if you can."

His working day starts around ten o'clock in the morning, as does his wife's, but it invariably outdistances hers in both time and variety. She is through, most days, in time for afternoon tea at five o'clock, and has had a brief break for lunch. Philip is seldom in for lunch, never bothers with afternoon tea (which he regards as a waste of time), and sometimes is not in for dinner. It is often after eleven o'clock at night when he finally arrives home.

I was in the Queen's private dining room on one occasion when Prince Charles, home from school, asked his mother if "Papa" (accent on the first syllable) would be in for lunch.

"In for lunch?" sighed the Queen. "If he takes on much more, he won't even be in for breakfast."

A typical Friday not long ago began with Prince Philip standing alongside the Queen in the Grand Hall of Buckingham Palace to bid a royal farewell to a Middle East monarch paying a state visit to London. Hardly had the visitor's cavalcade of horse-drawn carriages, with its accompanying escort of plumed and plated cavalry, trotted out through the palace gates than Philip was on his way by Rolls-Royce to the Design Centre in London's Haymarket, where he ran his eye over the prize-winning designs, before going on to Millbank to present the Council of Industrial Design Awards and sit down to a working lunch with the chairman of Vickers, one of Britain's major aircraft and engineering concerns. Nearby a royal helicopter stood waiting. Lunch over, Philip piloted himself to the old Battle of Britain airfield at Biggin Hill, 18 miles south of London, where he fired a Very pistol to open the International Air Fair before hedge-hopping another ten miles to the neighbouring Redhill airfield for a chat with members of the Tiger Club. A quick flip back to Buckingham Palace, with his helicopter scattering the ducks on the royal lake as it skimmed down to land on the palace lawn, enabled him to change into a tuxedo in time for a publishing dinner at Claridge's Hotel, which he was forced to leave immediately after the speech-making in order to join his wife aboard the royal train for an overnight trip to the adjoining counties of Rutland and Warwickshire. The train journey enabled them to get a night's sleep while travelling and to appear fresh and unjaded throughout a packed Saturday involving visits to four towns where they inspected schools, factories and youth organisations, as well as the ceremonial opening of a commemorative gateway celebrating the 400th anniversary of the school where rugby football was born. Eager to obtain some relaxation during what was left of the weekend, they discarded train travel in favour of flying the eighty miles back to London Airport, a shirt-sleeved Philip at the controls, and drove straight on to their hideaway home in the Queen's Tower at Windsor Castle.

Hectic though they sound, those two days are by no means atypical of Philip's frenetic workaday life. He is not a man who likes to delegate things. If he flies, he prefers to be at the controls himself. If he makes a speech, he must write it himself . . . which accounts for the point and pithiness of much of what he says, including such down-to-earth vulgarisms as his enjoinder to British exporters to "get their fingers out." By contrast, his wife's infinitely more formal speeches, carefully designed to say little and to avoid even a hint of controversy, are written for her by others, mainly by her Private Secretary, Sir Michael Adeane.

Philip's views are usually his own, and when working on what he considers an important speech he likes to get into the mood of the occasion. He switches on his tape-recorder, mounts the lectern in his gadget-filled study and delivers his speech to an invisible audience. Subsequent playbacks of the tape enable him to dot the i's and cross the t's of what he wants to say.

Through his speeches, his public engagements, and the many organisations with which he is so actively connected, Philip has become perhaps the most important dimension of identification between monarchy and people. His position remains nebulous and largely unofficial, but it becomes increasingly hard to imagine British public life without him.

With his ruggedly masculine outlook, firm opinions, forthright speeches, and down-to-earth wit, he stands—and has the freedom to stand—between the Queen and the outside world, both linking them and serving as a necessary buffer. He was asked once if he did not resent the constitutional limits of his position. He replied, "The fact that I do not have to toe the party-line all the time is the reverse of restriction." And this, up to a point, is true. He can say things the Queen may not say. He can go places where she cannot go. Over the years, Philip, in effect, has become the front-man for the monarchy, its mouthpiece, its supreme, ever-extended public relations officer. He has broadened the impact of the monarchy on national life and enhanced its image . . . though not always without difficulty, having occasionally laid himself open to the charge that he has lowered the dignity of the Crown. In a "swinging" Britain where mini-skirted models and long-haired pop singers are the new nobility, the monarchy still contrives to retain a safe, almost static, essentially old-fashioned outlook, and this Philip, despite his own contemporary, forward-looking attitude, is quick to defend. "I entirely agree that we are old-fashioned," he has said. "After all, it [the monarchy] is an old-fashioned institution."

III

To those outside the framework of British life, it is difficult—if not impossible—to convey adequately the Queen's role. To a foreigner, at first glance, it might seem perhaps that she does nothing beyond approving and underscoring what others have already done, serving purely as a rubber-stamp, without which the whole machinery of government and national life could go on just as well.

Up to a point, of course, this is true. Government and national life would hardly cease if the monarchy ended tomorrow. But it would operate differently and perhaps less smoothly. It has been said many times that the Queen serves as a symbol of unity and continuity. Yet she is more than merely a symbol. Her years of monarchy, which are also years of knowledge accumulated from the endless succession of leather-covered dispatch boxes, have rendered her more knowledgeable in matters of state than many of her ministers. And behind her, when she talks with the prime minister, is a wealth of knowledge and wisdom gathered from all the prime ministers who have gone before. She serves as a link between one government and the next, one Commonwealth country and another.

True, she has no direct power, and in constitutional matters she can act only on the advice of her ministers. Her only rights are "to be consulted, to encourage, to warn," and even those rights are more limited than they were in the days of her great-great-grandmother. Queen Victoria, on Albert's advice, may have toned down a Foreign Office dispatch to the United States and perhaps, in consequence, have averted conflict between Britain and America. It is doubtful if the Queen could interfere to the same extent today. Yet it is curious that the more power has been transferred from monarch to Parliament, the busier successive monarchs have become. Overwork contributed in no small degree to the tragic and early death of the Queen's father, and today his daughter is kept busier than any civil servant with an endless spate of paperwork and an endless round of public engagements.

But if the Queen's present-day powers exist largely on paper, one vital task remains within her royal prerogative which has been handed down to her from the days when monarchs actually ruled and did not merely reign. It is still the Sovereign who appoints each new prime minister, and the Queen, by constitutional tradition, can do this entirely on her own authority if she wishes. Usually, of course, the choice is abundantly clear-cut. It would be pointless to appoint anyone other than the leader of the party which commands a majority in the House of Commons. But the resignation of a sick Anthony Eden following Suez found the Conservative party, which had a majority in the Commons, with no obvious successor to take over as prime minister. There were several possible contenders for the post, notably the intellectual R. A. Butler and the Edwardian-looking Harold Macmillan. Of the two, Butler was the more widely fancied among those claiming political know-how, but it was left to the Queen to make the final decision. Before doing so, she sought advice from the elder statesmen of the Conservative party—Churchill, whom she had long regarded as the backbone of England, and the Marquess of Salisbury, one of whose ancestors had been the righthand man of her ancestor, the first Elizabeth. In the end she appointed Macmillan rather than the more widely fancied Butler, though how far the choice was really her own and how far she may have felt obligated to follow any advice given to her by Churchill and Salisbury is a matter for conjecture.

To a degree which seems remarkable to foreign eyes—but which Britons take completely for granted—the Queen is Britain, the supreme head of the British constitution, the apex of the nation's formal and official life. It is the Queen who summons Parliament, and dissolves it again when it has run its course. Every Act of Parliament is enacted in her name, and none of them is law until she has given her regal consent. Yet by one of those curious contradictions with which British heritage bristles, she cannot refuse assent to anything which Parliament has determined. As the historian Walter Bagehot pointed out, a British monarch must even sign his or her own death warrant if it is first approved by both Houses of Parliament.

The Queen heads every major department of British life. The government is "Her Majesty's Government," not "the British Government." British passports are issued "in the Name of Her Majesty." Cabinet ministers are her ministers, state departments are her agents, civil servants are her servants. Overseas envoys present their letters of credence to her at Buckingham Palace. She is the fountainhead of justice, and her royal arms appear behind the head of every judge and magistrate in Britain's courts. The armed forces and the police alike serve her and not the state. War is declared and peace concluded in her name. Even the mails are carried under her insignia.

She is in everything and of everything. She is head of the Established Church of England, with prayers said for her every Sunday in churches and cathedrals throughout the land. She appoints bishops and archbishops (though on the prime minister's recommendation). Her health is toasted at every formal banquet and dinner, and it is considered a flagrant breach of good taste to light a cigar or cigarette before glasses have been charged and raised to "The Queen." She is the fountainhead of honour and even the Beatles are proud to be numbered among the recipients of the orders, medals and decorations she awards in her twice-yearly Honours List. She lends her name and patronage to all manner of national institutions and charities. Through her travels up and down Britain, with their accompanying ceremonies of tree-planting and ship-launching, hospital openings and factory inspections, she continues to bring a much-needed touch of glamour to the humdrum monotony of national life. Through her wider travels she seeks to preserve Commonwealth unity and to win friends and influence people on behalf of Britain.

No one can say how much the Queen may have achieved over the years in smoothing out differences and cementing good relations, perhaps in the course of her worldwide travels, perhaps in the privacy of her Wedgwood-blue-and-white Audience Room at Buckingham Palace. Even future history will reveal only fragmentary glimpses of what she may have accomplished. Yet the sum total of her achievements is perhaps far greater than anyone realises.

To the British, she has to be all things to all people. The task is difficult, almost impossible. She must remain always regal without seeming too imperious or offhand. She must be reserved without being shy, religious without being priggish, glamorous without being sexy, modest without being prudish, dutiful without being dull. If she errs, it is on the side of modesty and dullness. Yet this is surely to err on the right side of the ledger. As she has said of herself many times, "I am not a film star."

Perhaps the British expect too much of their Queen. The older generation of Britons still regards her with a degree of veneration which almost reaches deification. To them, she is inviolate and sacrosanct, above criticism. Writers and public speakers, though they may occasionally attack royal officials and even snipe at Prince Philip, continue to fight shy of criticising the Queen herself. One writer who did so was subsequently spat at in the street. Another had his face slapped in public. Such is the depth of Britain's feelings where the Queen is concerned.

Sometimes this veneration of the Queen verges upon the ridiculous. A jockey who objected to the way a royal horse was ridden in a race at Longchamp, Paris—an objection upheld by the French stewards, who disqualified the royal horse—was treated by some fellow-Britons as though he had been guilty of high treason. But the Queen, when she heard of what had happened, subsequently sent her racing manager to Newmarket to see the jockey concerned and inform him that she, for her part, bore no hard feelings.

The Queen herself is eminently sensible and level-headed where her royal prerogative is concerned. Unfortunately, some of those around her sometimes suffer a rush of blood to the head on her account, and bring the monarchy into ridicule and disrepute. Local dignitaries, in particular, are not infrequently guilty in this respect. On one occasion when the Queen and Philip were involved in a ten-minute tree-planting ceremony, the officials concerned, far outdoing Sir Walter Raleigh, had a quarter-mile strip of fresh turf specially laid—and torn up again afterwards—so that the royal couple should not soil their shoes. Elsewhere, equally fussy officials demolished a street refuge so that Philip should have a clear drive through the main street of their town. At a railroad station where the Queen was expected, workmen were sent round to cover the signs labelled "Gentlemen" with tactful pieces of blue cloth so that they should not offend royal eyes.

A statistical summary of the Queen's engagements over a recent 12-month period gives some indication of what her "work" involves, though it excludes the part that is carried out unseen and unsung within the confines of her private sitting room at the palace. In the course of that more or less average year she gave 287 audiences (26 of them to the prime minister), and held four banquets, four garden parties, 15 luncheon parties, and seven receptions. She gave 11 sittings to artists and photographers. She left Britain on two overseas tours, one of which involved a total of 57 full-scale public engagements. She went to a further 41 functions in various parts of London, 20 more in other parts of Britain, and attended nine formal lunch and dinner parties and some half-dozen charity entertainments.

The Queen's luncheon parties are an innovation—there was nothing like them in her father's time—and bear the imprint of Philip's forward-looking, experimental personality. The object is to let the Queen talk on a relatively informal basis with a wide cross-section of people . . . politicians and trade unionists, businessmen, scientists and educationalists, painters, writers and actors, even pop singers and sporting celebrities. A typical luncheon party would perhaps find the Queen and Prince Philip sitting down to eat and talk with an eminent surgeon, an actress, a fire chief, an author, a lawyer, the headmistress of a girls' school, a television announcer and perhaps a hospital matron. Heavyweight boxer Henry Cooper, racing driver Graham Hill, film stars Julie Christie and Tommy Steele, actress Dora Bryan (who played the title role in the London production of *Hello Dolly*) and Russian cosmonaut Yuri Gagarin have been among the Queen's luncheon guests at varying times.

By royal standards, these parties are relatively informal. The guests, seldom more than a dozen, assemble amidst the Corinthian columns of the Bow Room, where the young Victoria announced her intention of marrying Prince Albert. Sherry and martinis are handed round and a Royal Equerry introduces the guests to each other. No pomp or ceremony attends the Queen's arrival. She merely strolls into the room with her husband, her corgis scampering ahead of her. Philip usually joins the guests in a martini while the Queen chats over a glass of sherry or possibly orange squash. After about half an hour of preliminary chatter, the Royal Steward announces, "Luncheon is served, Your Majesty," and the Queen, still chatting with one or other of her guests, leads the way into the adjoining 1844 Room.

The Queen is sufficiently superstitious not to want thirteen people sitting down at table together, and the number of luncheon guests is calculated accordingly. If the number should ever resolve itself to thirteen, perhaps through last-minute illness, the Queen overcomes the difficulty by asking the Queen Mother or Prince Charles to join the party or, failing that, asking her equerry to drop out. At Balmoral or Sandringham, where one solution is impracticable and the other impolite, she resolves the problem by having a second, smaller table set alongside the main table. It is placed so closely that the two tables appear to be one and the same, but the seating of two or three guests at the smaller table overcomes superstition.

The luncheon table is oval-shaped. The Queen sits not at the end, but midway along with Philip facing her so that, between them, they can more easily keep the conversation going. Her corgis follow her in and curl up under the table at her feet. A typical menu would consist of melon or prawn cocktail followed by roast lamb or veal, a sweet such as water ice or apple meringue, and cheese and crackers. Then comes fresh fruit. (Actress Dora Bryan, when she lunched at Buckingham Palace, helped herself to some grapes and then found herself in the embarrassing position of not knowing what to do with the pips. As elegantly as possible she removed them from her mouth and heaped them at the side of her plate. She need not have worried. The Queen, when she eats grapes, does exactly the same.) The meal concludes with coffee and a choice of brandy or liqueurs. Cigars and cigarettes are handed round, though neither the Queen nor Philip smokes.

Conversation continues throughout the meal, ranging over a wide variety of topics according to the occupations and interests of the guests. Subtly the Queen and Prince Philip divide their attention, talking mainly to guests on their right during the early part of the meal and switching to those on their left when the sweet is served. The meal over, the whole party returns to the Bow Room until the Queen shakes hands with each guest in turn and finally withdraws as a sign that it is time for everyone to leave.

A state banquet, staged in honour of some visiting president or monarch, is vastly more formal and elaborate. The setting is the palace ballroom, a vast, glittering arena some 123 feet long, 65 feet wide and 45 feet high, its walls hung with Gobelin tapestries depicting Jason's quest for the Golden Fleece, illuminated by six magnificent chandeliers and dominated at one end by the gold and crimson canopy which overhangs the throne.

For weeks ahead of a state banquet, Walter Fry, the Yeoman of the Gold, and his two assistants are kept busy readying the fabulous royal collection of gold plate. Clad in aprons of green baize, they work away behind the thick, safe-like doors of the gold pantry, burnishing knives and forks, plates and cups, trays and salvers with chamois leathers, a special powder, and a selection of soft brushes. The extent of the job can be judged from the fact that the total collection weighs around five tons, and some of the table centres are so massive that it takes four men to lift them into place without damaging the table.

As the day of the state banquet approaches, twenty housemaids are set to work to dust and polish the vast ballroom. Damask tablecloths more than a century old are brought out of storage in the basement linen room, lifted onto wheeled trolleys and taken upstairs to the ballroom, where they are carefully unrolled to cover the state dining table and its nineteen extensions. On the day itself, Buckingham Palace is choked with servants, over 150 extra footmen, pages, chefs and porters having been hired through an employment agency to supplement the resident staff. Footmen and pages don the state liveries which are stored in mothproof steel boxes in the palace basement. The pages dress in black and gold tunics with black knee-breeches, white stockings and black pumps. The footmen are in scarlet knee-breeches with tunics of scarlet and gold. But no longer do they "powder" their hair with a messy mixture of soap and water, flour and starch, as they did once. Prince Philip put a stop to that practice, considering it old-fashioned and unmanly.

Flowers and plants are imported and banked thickly in the corners of the ballroom, roses, lilies and orchids intertwined with purple grapes providing a mass of colour which rises to a height of some eight feet. More flowers fill the gold vases dotted about the tables. But not in front of the Queen. The flowers in front of her float in a shallow gold bowl so that her face is visible to all.

At six o'clock on the evening of the banquet the Queen personally checks the ballroom, pausing here and there to thank those responsible. Her formal entrance to the banquet, some three hours later, is vastly different from the casual way she walks into the Bow Room for a luncheon party. Dressed in a state gown with its accompanying jewelled finery, a tiara glittering on her head, she makes a stately and dignified entrance to the strains of the National Anthem. Members of her court precede her in tailcoats and knee-breeches, walking backwards in front of her with lowered gaze. Guests around the dining tables stand to attention, facing in her direction.

It is the Queen's boast that a Buckingham Palace banquet runs like clockwork. That it does so is a tremendous feat of organisation, with a whole regiment of helpers to hump the food from kitchens to ballroom—a quarter-mile steeplechase with two flights of stairs as the principal obstacles. Much of the credit is due to Robert Smith, the Palace Steward. Standing immediately behind the Queen as she eats, the dignified Smith is well placed to observe when she is ready for each course and when she has finished. A press-button concealed in his hand enables him to ensure that each course is served throughout the ballroom at the same time that it is placed before the Queen and her main guests. The press-button is linked to miniature traffic lights hidden among the banked flowers on either side of the throne. Amber lights are the signal for servants to move into place with the next course. When amber turns green, they start serving. It is as simple—and as streamlined—as that, a system ensuring that there is no question of the Queen racing ahead to the dessert course while guests at the far end of the vast ballroom are still waiting for the soup.

To prevent it from being scratched, the royal gold is carried to and from the ballroom in large leather buckets. Ten men tackle the washing-up—a task which continues long after the last guest has departed. As each item is washed and dried, Walter Fry methodically checks it off in his record books. It is seldom that anything goes astray, though I recall an occasion when a gold fork was missing. It was found only after a long and worrying search. It had been inadvertently dropped into one of the waste bins along with the food scraps.

IV

London offers the tourist more free shows than any other city in the world, and in most of them the Queen has the leading part. Each separate occasion of pomp and ceremony reveals a different facet of her many-sided role as monarch. There is the charitable Queen who distributes the traditional Maundy Money at Easter. There is the fountain of honour who leads her Knights of the Garter to their annual service of dedication in St. George's Chapel, Windsor. There is the head of state who opens Parliament each November. There is the commander-in-chief who reviews her troops each summer in celebration of her official birthday. There is the elegantly dressed society Queen who drives the length of the racecourse in her open carriage on each day of Royal Ascot. And there is, in striking contrast, the humble woman with downcast eyes who represents the conscience of a nation as she stands silently before the Cenotaph in Whitehall on Armistice Day.

The annual ceremony of the Royal Maundy is amongst the oldest of royal traditions, its origins lost in the mists of time. It was certainly being observed by Edward I as far back as the thirteenth century, and possibly for half a century or more before that. In earlier times, the custom was for the monarch to emulate Christ by washing the feet of the poor as a sign of humility and compassion (though the present Queen's namesake, Elizabeth I, took good care that her courtiers washed the feet first before it was her turn). That custom was abandoned in the reign of George II, but resurrected by the Queen's grandfather,

George V, though in rather different form. At today's ceremony, on Maundy Thursday (the day preceding Good Friday), usually at Westminster Abbey, though the venue is sometimes varied, the Queen distributes alms to as many old men and old women as the years of her age. These alms include the traditional Maundy Money, silver coins to the value of one, two, three and four sterlings, the Norman coin from which the present pound sterling and sterling silver are alike descended. While the coins of the Royal Maundy are specially minted for the Queen, they are still legal tender in Britain, though it is highly unlikely that any ever find their way over shop counters in the ordinary course of business. They are far too highly prized by those who qualify for them. Should poverty force anyone to part with the coins, he can be assured of receiving far more than their face value from collectors and dealers eager to acquire them. One man who received Maundy Money from the Queen in the first year of her reign has had frequent offers of $300 and more for his set of four small silver coins in their velvet-lined case.

The Most Noble Order of the Garter is the highest of Britain's nine orders of chivalry and one of only three (the others are the Most Ancient and Most Noble Order of the Thistle and the Royal Victorian Order) which the Queen bestows personally. Its origins, like those of the Royal Maundy, are lost in antiquity. It is known that the Order was founded by Edward III in 1348 with a blue garter as its symbol. But why a garter? Legend has it that one of Edward's favourites, the Countess of Salisbury (though another version replaces the Countess with Edward's wife, Queen Phillipa), dropped her garter while treading a stately measure during the course of a royal ball. Observing the tittering smiles of his nobles, the King picked up the fallen garter and fastened it round his own leg with the rebuking remark, *"Honi soit qui mal y pense"* ("Dishonour on him who evil thinks"). Today the number of Knight Companions in the Order is still limited to twenty-four, the figure originally set by Edward III when he conceived the idea of resurrecting the Round Table of King Arthur. A small number of royal princes (Prince Philip, the Duke of Gloucester and the Duke of Windsor) and foreign monarchs are included additionally as Royal Knights and Extra Knights.

The ceremony of investiture takes place in the Throne Room at Windsor Castle, the Queen wearing her Sovereign's mantle of blue velvet lined with white satin as she buckles the blue and gold embroidered garter on the left leg of the new knight. For a Lady of the Garter the traditional symbol is fastened on the left arm. The Queen herself, as a princess, was first made a Lady of the Garter by her father a short time before her marriage in 1947. Her husband-to-be, Prince Philip, was similarly invested as a Knight of the Garter eight days later. In 1968–21 years later–it was the Queen's turn to invest her eldest son, Prince Charles.

Following the ceremony of investiture, the Queen leads her knights in procession from the castle to the ornate Chapel of St. George, where they sit beneath their colourful banners for the solemn service of dedication in accordance with the ancient maxim of the Order: "Be bold not only strongly to fight but also to offer yourself to shed your blood for Christ's faith, the liberties of the Church and the just and necessary defence of them that be oppressed and needy."

The state opening of Parliament is one of Britain's oldest ceremonies, dating back in one form or another nearly 1000 years, to the days when William the Conqueror and successive Norman kings, in their attempts to win over a Britain they had already conquered, summoned the great men of the land to attend them in council. These councils–at Gloucester on Christmas Day, at Winchester at Easter, and at Westminster (where Parliament now sits) at Pentecost–were the beginnings of British parliamentary government. In those days, of course, it was the king who had the main say; today the situation is very different. The Speech from the Throne which the Queen delivers each time she opens Parliament afresh may be drafted in personal terms, but it is in fact written for her by the prime minister and she must by law read it word for word as written.

The crown she wears to open Parliament is not the weighty St. Edward's Crown which she wore for her coronation, but the lighter, somewhat less historic, Imperial State Crown. Even so, it is a spectacular object. Set into the framework are four rubies, eleven emeralds, sixteen sapphires, 273 pearls—and a staggering total of 2,783 diamonds, including the Second Star of Africa, a magnificent stone of 309 carats. Legend insists that one of the sapphires was once worn on the finger of Edward the Confessor, and one of the rubies glinted in Henry V's helmet at the Battle of Agincourt.

The crown is heavy enough for the Queen to need practice if she is to wear it with ease and dignity. To enable her to do this, she usually has it brought over to the palace from the Tower of London, where it is normally displayed along with the rest of the Crown Jewels, a few days ahead of the actual ceremony. During those few days she wears it in her workaday role about the palace to accustom herself afresh to its weight and balance. Looking every inch a queen from some children's storybook, she will sit at her desk, tackling her correspondence, the crown winking and glinting with every turn of her head.

Even the Queen's youngest child, Prince Edward, is now accustomed to the sight of "Mummy" wearing this splendid headgear as she sips her afternoon tea, and Philip no longer even grins, as he did once, if she should sit with it on her head of an evening as she relaxes over a crossword puzzle. The trickiest bit of practice comes when she feeds her dogs, but a sort of bob-and-curtsey motion contrives to keep the crown neatly balanced on her head as she places the feeding bowls where the dogs can get at them.

For her state drive from Buckingham Palace to Parliament, she travels in the Irish State Coach, a relic of Victoria's day, drawn by the famous Windsor Greys and accompanied by a mounted escort of Household Cavalry resplendent in plumed helmets and glinting breastplates. In place of her crown, the Queen wears a diadem of diamonds and pearls, designed in the form of Maltese crosses interspersed with roses, thistles and shamrocks, which has been worn in turn by every Queen and Queen Consort since the days of Victoria. While the Queen is on her way from Buckingham Palace, another, smaller procession is also moving towards Parliament from the Tower of London. A single carriage conveying the Imperial State Crown is escorted, as the Queen herself is, by a mounted detachment of Household Cavalry. Troops lining the route present arms, just as they do to the Queen, as this symbol of monarchy passes by on its velvet cushion.

Many points of British history converge on this day. Before the ceremony, the Parliament buildings are carefully searched by Yeomen of the Guard equipped with pikes and lanterns, just as they have been ever since Guy Fawkes and his fellow conspirators tried to blast Parliament into the Thames with twenty kegs of gunpowder back in 1605. In keeping with yet another tradition, the Queen, once robed and crowned, takes her seat in the House of Lords—never in the House of Commons. Constitutionally she is not permitted to enter the Commons, though her father was granted the unique privilege of doing so when he expressed a wish to see how the building had been rebuilt after its wartime gutting by German bombers. He was the first monarch to be allowed inside the Commons since Charles I swooped down on Parliament some three hundred years before and arrested five of its members. Today, even the Queen's messenger, a dignitary with the faintly horrific title of Gentleman Usher of the Black Rod, has the door of the Commons ceremonially slammed in his face when he goes to summon its members to attend upon their Queen in the neighbouring House of Lords. To gain admission and deliver his message he must first knock three times with his staff upon the oaken door.

The origins of the annual ceremony of Trooping the Colour are obscured in history, as with so much else that surrounds the monarchy, but today it takes the form of a military review in honour of the Queen's official "birthday." The date fluctuates,

[195]

falling usually on the second Saturday in June—Saturday so that London's traffic is disrupted as little as possible, June so that there is a reasonable chance of Britain's always uncertain weather remaining fine for a few hours. Because of this, the ceremony in fact usually takes place nearer Philip's birthday—June 10— than the Queen's real birthday, which is April 21.

Just as she finds it necessary to practise wearing the crown ahead of each fresh opening of Parliament, so the Queen must re-accustom herself to riding side-saddle for the ceremony of Trooping the Colour. Expert horsewoman though she is, she normally rides astride, a masculine fashion considered too un-regal and inelegant for so important a ceremony. So each year, ahead of the parade, she goes along to the indoor riding school in the royal mews at the back of the palace to practice the more difficult side-saddle method of sitting a horse. For the actual parade she wears a long riding habit of dark blue—carefully de-signed to conceal the black riding breeches she wears beneath— calf-length black boots fitted with spurs, a black tricorne hat decked with the plume of whichever Guards regiment is being specifically honoured that year, and a scarlet tunic of the same regiment.

As for the opening of Parliament, the Queen is escorted by a plumed and breastplated detachment of the Household Cavalry as she rides her horse from Buckingham Palace to Horse Guards' Parade. There the five foot regiments of the Brigade of Guards —the Grenadiers, the Coldstreams, the Scots, the Irish and the Welsh Guards—are drawn up in motionless, arrow-straight lines in readiness for her inspection.

Because of the difficulty of timing exactly the pace of the ceremonial ride from palace to parade ground, this is one of the few functions for which the Queen is sometimes late. Un-officially, of course. Officially she is *never* late, and the clock in the turret, having been held back for her arrival, always strikes the hour of eleven at the exact moment that she wheels her horse onto the parade ground. It is surreptitiously advanced again afterwards to make up for lost time.

The Queen inspects her troops and then positions her mount at the saluting base while the regimental colour being honoured that particular year is "trooped"—borne high—through the ranks of assembled guardsmen. This is followed by an intricate series of drill movements in which both guardsmen and cavalry participate, after which the Queen stations herself at the head of the whole colourful array and leads them back along the Mall to Buckingham Palace. There she centres herself between the stone pillars of the main gates to take the final salute.

But not even in June is there any hard-and-fast guarantee that Britain's weather will cooperate. I remember one year when the day appointed for the ceremony dawned in a downpour of rain. The Queen had not been in the best of health for some time past—indeed, an operation to relieve a long-standing sinus condition was to become necessary soon after—and Prince Philip suggested, not unreasonably, that she should postpone the ceremony against better weather. Together, the two of them walked along a corridor to where they could look out one of the front windows of the palace at the pelting rain. Along the Mall the crowds were already massing six and eight deep beneath a forest of umbrellas.

The Queen looked out, then turned back to her husband. True to the "show-must-go-on" spirit of Britain's monarchy, she said, "We must go. I can't possibly disappoint them."

8. THE QUEEN'S YEAR

I

PARTLY by custom, partly by circumstance, and partly by her own inclination, the Queen's life, like that of her father and grandfather before her, is governed by the clock, the calendar, and royal tradition. Her father bred racing pigeons, so she must, too (though she seldom actually sees the birds bred and raced in her name). Her father and grandfather collected stamps, so she does the same. Her father, grandfather, and great-grandfather all journeyed at set times to Balmoral and Sandringham. She continues the pattern.

Her sister may have broken away from traditional royal timekeeping with occasional holiday jaunts to Sardinia and the Caribbean, but the Queen has not...nor perhaps has she any wish to do so. In her private life as in her public life, with rare exceptions, she continues to do the same thing at the same time on the same day at the same season of the year. The pattern starts with the publication of her New Year's Honours List on the first day of January, and continues without variation until her annual telecast the following Christmas. In between come ship launchings and tree plantings, hospital openings and charity matinees, banquets and luncheons, smiles and handshakes, six weeks at Windsor in the spring, trips to Sandringham, the long summer respite at Balmoral. Most people would find such a fixed way of life boring and monotonous in the extreme; the Queen does not.

Almost invariably her year begins with a visit to Sandringham, the remote, rambling, bleak-looking country mansion which her great-grandfather, Edward VII, built for himself in the flat, windswept Norfolk countryside, 105 miles northeast of London. Sandringham is an unwieldy place and requires a regiment of servants when the Queen is in residence. It is draughty, too. The gales which howl in from the North Sea penetrate every nook and cranny. Yet it is a place for which the Royal Family have long had a deep affection. George V always called it his "home"—Buckingham Palace, by contrast, was simply his "house in London." George VI once said that at Sandringham "I can forget for a little while that I am King." Given their choice, both would infinitely have preferred to live as country gentlemen at Sandringham rather than reign as monarchs.

For both of them, the wide, flat expanse of Sandringham—extra land purchased by the Queen's father brought the estate to its present total of around 17,000 acres—represented a world of their own. For George V it was a world where even time was different. While the rest of Britain worked to Greenwich Time, George V, once he had escaped from London to Sandringham, lived by "Sandringham Time," with the clocks set half an hour ahead of the rest of the country. By doing so, he reasoned, he gained an extra half-hour of daylight for the pheasant and partridge shooting which was his favourite pastime. This harmless eccentricity irritated his eldest son so much that the Duke of Windsor's first act, when his father died at Sandringham and he became King in his stead, was to stalk downstairs and order the clocks to be set to the correct time.

Sandringham today, though renovated and modernised by the installation of such things as central heating and an electric elevator, still remains much as it was in the days of the Queen's great-grandfather, a hotch-potch of long corridors, unexpected stairways and high-ceilinged rooms, some of which are stuffed like museums with the accumulated knickknacks of successive royal reigns, among them Queen Mary's almost priceless collection of exquisite trinkets by Fabergé, the renowned goldsmith of Tsarist Russia.

The Queen, though she has not quite the same links of birth and childhood to tie her to Sandringham as her father and grandfather had, has inherited their feeling of affection for the draughty rooms and wide, windswept acres. She loves to roam the woods and fields with her dogs, a raincoated, head-scarfed figure who might easily pass, at first glance, for any ordinary farmer's wife. She likes nothing so much as to drive the three miles to Wolferton with a bunch of freshly scrubbed carrots for her favourite stallion, Aureole, pausing to chat expertly with the stud groom.

The Queen is proud of the fact that in Aureole she has a stud to more than rival her great-grandfather's famed Persimmon, the celebrated stallion whose larger-than-lifesize statue still dominates the old royal stud farm at Sandringham. But the Queen is not so ostentatious as was her great-grandfather. No outsize statue of Aureole commemorates the small fortune in prize money and stud fees he has earned over the years. Instead, the Queen has settled for a small gold statuette which occupies pride of place in the new, modern drawing room she has created for herself in what is now the Queen's Tower—it was formerly known as the Victoria Tower—at Windsor.

Unlike Sandringham and Balmoral, which are the Queen's private property, Windsor Castle, like Buckingham Palace, belongs to the state. For more than eight centuries it has been the main stronghold of Britain's monarchs. The keep (or Round Tower), from which the royal standard flies whenever the Queen is in residence, is the oldest part of the castle, dating back to Henry II. But the mound on which it stands, a carpet of yellow daffodils when the Queen moves to Windsor with her court for a six-week period over Easter, was moated and fortified even before that.

Over the centuries the castle has been extended, altered, and renovated by successive monarchs. It was Edward III who first began turning it from a castle into a palace. Edward IV built the graceful St. George's Chapel where the Knights of the Garter have their annual dedication service. Charles II started the magnificent range of state apartments. George IV added a host of further towers and battlements—though by his time they had become far more ornament than defensive necessity. The Queen, since her accession to the Throne, has remodelled several of the rooms in the Queen's Tower. Philip has re-designed the garden and converted the old Orangery, where exotic plants once flourished, into an indoor swimming pool.

In striving to achieve greater comfort for herself in what is still in essence a mediaeval fortress the Queen has been somewhat handicapped by the work of her ancestors. It is, after all, difficult to do much in the way of remodelling rooms whose walls are more than six feet thick. Her father experienced the same difficulty before her, overcoming it in one instance by the removal of several tons of masonry for a new bathroom to be constructed within one of the walls. The Queen has been similarly ingenious in reconstructing the old Victoria Tower so that it now includes a modern kitchen, a nursery, a large and essentially feminine bedroom, and a light, airy study.

But her greatest achievement has been the conversion of the gloomy old Oak Dining Room into a modern drawing room. The ancient walls of time-blackened oak are now hidden by a décor of white and gold, with the elaborate plasterwork of the ceiling similarly highlighted in gold. Gold drapes hang at the windows and the floor is close-carpeted in a cheerful cherry-red. She has furnished the room with comfortable sofas and armchairs and some antiques which are not quite what they seem. One of a pair of matching antique Chinese cabinets conceals a cocktail cabinet; the other hides a record-player. It is in this room, lit at night by a huge chandelier of glittering crystal, that she keeps the gold statuette of Aureole, her favourite and most successful racehorse.

II

Racing is without doubt the Queen's favourite pastime. Apart from Royal Ascot in June, she is seen on Britain's racetracks much less frequently these days than was once the case, but her interest in horse racing and, more particularly, the breeding of thoroughbreds is as strong as ever. She reads *The Sporting Life* daily, receives race results on the ticker-tape her father had installed in Buckingham Palace, subscribes to a weekly guide to current racing form, and spends hours painstakingly updating her own racing and breeding records.

Prince Philip does not share her interest in the sport. Royal Ascot apart, he has hardly ever been seen at the races. Even at Ascot he spends most of his time watching cricket on television before slipping away for a quick game of polo.

To see the Queen at the races is to catch a fleeting glimpse of a very different person from the serious-faced monarch of other public occasions. The racetrack is perhaps the one place where the iron mask of royalty slips a little to reveal the woman behind the queen. As she stands in the royal box watching the races, or strolls across to the paddock for a close-up glimpse of the runners, the Queen, for once, is completely oblivious of the staring crowd around her. She has eyes only for her race-card and the runners, and her face is alight and alive as at no other time. As she studies the horses, talking animatedly—and expertly—with those around her, she even forgets to acknowledge the bows and curtsies accorded to her.

The start of a race finds her eyes glued to her binoculars, her excitement showing in the way she hops from one foot to another and in the shouts of encouragement or dismay which escape her lips. Her movie camera is always close to hand, but in the excitement of the moment she not infrequently forgets to use it. So it was that she omitted to film the finish of the

King George VI and Queen Elizabeth Stakes, Britain's most valuable race, the year she won it with Aureole.

Within the confines of her private apartment, watching the races on television, she is completely uninhibited, and her cries of exhortation and admonition—ranging from "Ride him!" to "You're too soon, you fool!"—can be heard clearly through the closed door of her sitting room. If a public engagement prevents her from even watching television when she has a horse running, she will detail one of her staff to look in for her. The task fell on me one weekend at Windsor when the Queen had a horse named High Veldt racing at Hurst Park. She told me to use the television set in her private room. "I don't think he'll win," she said, "but I want to know how he's run when I get back." (Sadly, her forecast proved only too accurate.)

The Queen's love for racing comes more from her mother than from her father. Though the late King had fourteen horses in training at the time of his death, his interest in racing was never more than lukewarm. His wife, on the other hand, though she owned only one horse at that time, a steeplechaser named Monaveen, was so keen that she would shelter under the trees on a day of torrential rain when hardly anyone else was at the track in order to see the animal race. Her enthusiasm has grown with the years . . . and so has her string of steeplechasers, with a total of 22 either racing or being readied for future race commitments at this writing.

The Queen has no interest in steeplechasers, for the simple reason that she cannot breed from them when their racing days are over. And, to her, the breeding of thoroughbreds is every bit as enthralling as the actual racing. The success attending her efforts in this direction was clearly seen during the 1967 flat-racing season, when horses sired by Aureole won a total of more than £30,000, while others sired by St. Paddy, one of Aureole's earlier offspring, notched up a further £38,000. As an owner the Queen was somewhat less successful, winning 14 races and a total of £13,522 in prize money.

For the annual June festivity of horse racing and high fashion known as "Royal Ascot," the Queen fills Windsor Castle with her race-going cronies, among them usually the Duke and Duchess of Beaufort, trainer Jeremy Tree, and Lord Porchester and his American-born wife, Jean. The house party may also include Lord Rupert Nevill and his wife, Anne, who is an American on her mother's side, Lady Zia and Sir Harold Wernher, and perhaps the Wernhers' daughter, Myra, and her husband, Major David Butter. The Queen Mother will move over from Royal Lodge to Windsor Castle, along with Margaret and Tony. The young Duke and Duchess of Kent swell the house party, as do Princess Alexandra and her husband, Angus Ogilvy, a man of many directorships who has not permitted marriage into the royal family to disturb his business activities. Even at Royal Ascot he not infrequently slips away from the racing to attend his office in the City of London. For the benefit of the younger members of the Royal Family, the Queen also invites up to a dozen of the younger race-going set. Prince Philip is there too, of course, though Royal Ascot by no means has the same appeal for him as it does for the Queen and her friends.

With the exception of electricians, plumbers, and housemaids (the permanent staff at Windsor already includes these), most of the Buckingham Palace servants are switched over to help look after the Queen's guests. Reinforcing them are dozens of additional footmen, pages, under-butlers and chefs hired through the medium of an employment agency.

To be the Queen's guest at Windsor during Royal Ascot—or, indeed, to be invited to Sandringham or Balmoral Castle for the shooting at other times of the year—is to live, however briefly, in the grand manner of old-time royalty which has today almost vanished from the face of the earth. Apart from cleaning their own teeth, the Queen's houseguests are hardly required to do a thing for themselves from the moment they climb out of their cars in the quadrangle fronting the Tower Door until they climb into them again at the end of the week. Their cars are promptly whisked away to be cleaned and polished. Their luggage finds its way unseen to their allotted rooms, where their clothes are unpacked and meticulously pressed before being hung in wardrobes. Dinner each evening finds baths drawn in readiness and evening gowns and tuxedos laid out and waiting. No man need wrestle with his cufflinks. A valet does this for him. No lady need struggle with a reluctant zip-fastener. A lurking maid is instantly to hand at such moments. And no one need worry about discarding clothes. These can be—and are—simply dropped in a heap on the bedroom floor to vanish the moment their owner's back is turned. When next seen they are again spotless and immaculate—laundered, pressed, shoes polished—ready to be worn.

Dinner in the white-and-gilt State Dining Room is heralded by the aroma of smouldering lavender as a liveried page conveys the swinging burner through the long, wide corridors in accordance with age-old custom. Drinks in the adjoining Crimson Drawing Room, so named on account of its draperies and furnishings, precede dinner. In the dining room, where a portrait of Queen Victoria looks down in seeming disapproval from above the marble fireplace, the massive sideboards groan under the weight of ornamental gold plate and valuable antique china brought over from Buckingham Palace. From behind a gilt grille, crammed into a room so small it is disrespectfully known as the "Black Hole," a band from the Brigade of Guards dispenses background music ranging from the Beatles to the waltzes of Johann Strauss.

Including Royal Equerries and Ladies-in-Waiting, as many as forty people may sit down to dinner, ranged round the long, solid mahogany table. The Queen and her husband sit facing each other midway along. The meal runs to four courses followed by fresh fruit, and each course is accompanied by a choice of the appropriate wines. The food is served by pages and footmen resplendent in semi-state liveries of scarlet and gold. The plates are of gold, as are the cutlery, the condiment sets, the serving dishes, the coffee pots and the massive, gleaming trays on which everything is borne into the room. Except perhaps in the immediate vicinity of Prince Philip, conversation around the table as the meal runs its course tends to be concentrated on horses.

A page discreetly waylays new guests before dinner to inquire what time they require calling in the morning, whether they prefer tea or coffee on waking, and exactly how they like it. Those who have stayed at Windsor before receive no such inquiry. Charles Oulton, the Royal Steward, knows by heart the special preferences of everyone who has ever been the Queen's guest. Those who prefer their coffee black, their tea without sugar or with glucose instead of sugar, can be sure of getting it precisely that way. Those who prefer whisky to wine at dinner will get that, too, without asking. Those who prefer Turkish coffee after dinner will get that, equally automatically. Guests who stay at Buckingham Palace are assured of equally personal attention and Queen Frederika of Greece, the second time she was Queen Elizabeth's guest, was amazed to find herself automatically served with her favourite Greek breakfast.

At Windsor, even waking in the morning is a luxurious and pleasurable experience of muted sounds... the soft rattle of the tea-tray being set down on the bedside table, the quiet swish of curtains being drawn back from the tall windows, the gentle splash of water as the bath is filled in the adjoining bathroom. A complete range of the day's newspapers, from the lofty *Times* to the tabloid *Daily Mirror*—and not forgetting *The Sporting Life*—comes with the tea-tray. Evening clothes discarded the previous night are stealthily removed, their place taken by jodhpurs and hacking jackets for those who are going riding, tweeds for those who contemplate a leisurely stroll, sport shirts and flannels for those indulging in a round of golf on the nine-hole course. For the ladies, breakfast is served in bed. The men are expected to make their way to the dining room where gold dishes on electric hot-plates are filled with bacon, sausages, kidneys, mushrooms and eggs in almost every conceivable guise. For those who prefer something cold there is a choice of ham or tongue, sliced on the spot by an attendant page.

The Queen and Prince Philip breakfast alone in their private dining room. After breakfast, as always, the Queen deals with her mail and the contents of any "Box" which awaits her attention. Only when this is done does she join those of her guests whom she has invited to go riding with her that morning. This morning ride, which starts as a leisurely jogtrot across Windsor Great Park, invariably ends in a hectic five-furlong sprint round Ascot racecourse, a royal legacy handed down to the Queen from the distant days of Queen Anne, another monarch with a passion for horse racing. Wearied of the long trek from London to Newmarket, the corpulent Anne set up her own racetrack at the rear of her castle at Windsor. In consequence, her descendant, Queen Elizabeth II, is the only monarch to own her own racecourse, which she operates, however, on a strictly non-profitmaking basis. There was one year when the Queen nearly came to grief in this unofficial race which she and her house-guests refer to jokingly as "The Windsor Castle Stakes." She was in the lead, head down, galloping hard, when there was a warning yell of "Look out!" She glanced up to spot a broken wire trailing across the track and flattened herself along her horse's neck in the nick of time to avoid it.

Everyone, whether riding, walking or golfing, is back at Windsor Castle in time for a quick change and a quick lunch before joining the Queen, sharp at fifteen minutes past one, for the really serious part of the day's proceedings—the races and the traditional cavalcade which opens each day's racing. This is a dressy affair. The men array themselves in morning suits of striped trousers and tailed jackets with elegant toppers, their womenfolk in fashionable gowns and elaborate hats the cost of which is a strict secret between them and the country's leading fashion designers. A fleet of chauffeur-driven cars speeds the royal family and their guests to a spot known as Duke's Lane where a convoy of seven open carriages drawn by the famed Windsor Greys awaits their coming. The Queen and Prince Philip ride always in the first carriage along with the Duke of Beaufort who holds the traditional post of Master of the Queen's Horse. The Queen Mother rides in the second carriage, along with Princess Margaret and Lord Snowdon. Others of the royal family share the remaining carriages with the Queen's house-guests on a rota basis which ensures that each guest will take part in the opening cavalcade on at least one occasion. Complete with outriders, postillions and footmen, all clad in their scarlet and gold semi-state liveries, the procession presents a colourful spectacle as it proceeds at stately pace along a course lined with cheering race-goers to the royal box.

As an additional diversion for her guests, the Queen usually books a block of seats at the grandiloquently named Theatre Royal in Windsor for one evening of the week. On other evenings she stages impromptu movie shows in a room converted for the purpose by the installation of a full-size screen and dual sound projectors. Her guests sit in a miscellaneous collection of armchairs and garden chairs, with rugs available for those susceptible to draughts, to watch the pre-release screening of new films which the Queen hires from the major distributing companies. On yet another evening the valuable Persian carpets are rolled back in one of the three state drawing rooms and dancing takes place into the small hours, winding up with a bacon-and-egg breakfast. Sometimes, on these occasions, the dance turns into an informal royal ball with a hired orchestra to provide the music. Sometimes, even more informally, the Queen simply borrows some of Princess Margaret's huge collection of discs and dancing takes place to the music of a record-player.

III

By contrast with the elaborate dinner parties given at Windsor during Ascot week, the occasional private parties the Queen gives at Buckingham Palace—or during one of her ordinary weekends at Windsor—are relatively informal. However, there is no such thing as complete informality, in the normal sense of the phrase, in the small, tight royal circle. Not even the Queen's closest friends would dream of dropping in on her unexpectedly. They wait always to be invited. Such invitations are not necessarily in writing. They may be by word of mouth if the Queen chances to run into one of her friends at the racetrack, for instance, in which case they are always confirmed later by a telephone call from a Royal Equerry. Even a private dinner party at the palace is very much an evening-dress affair. Punctuality is of the essence. To ensure that they are not too early—and certainly not late—the Queen's friends usually contrive things so that they arrive in the vicinity of the palace some minutes ahead of time, either parking their cars briefly under the trees along the Mall or circling the palace block so that they drive in through the gates exactly to the minute.

The Queen greets her guests with a handshake (for the men) and a brush of cheeks (for their wives). She addresses them by their first names and sometimes, with very close friends, even by nickname. Lord Rupert Nevill's wife, Anne, for instance, is "Mickey" to the Queen. But her friends know better than to adopt reciprocal informality. Even relatives such as the former Pamela Mountbatten and her husband, designer David Hicks, bow or curtsey to the Queen when she greets them. Equally, with the exception of a privileged few relatives who address her as "Lilibet," her childhood nickname, they carefully refer to the Queen as "Ma'am" throughout the ensuing evening and to Philip as "Sir."

Philip himself pours the drinks. The available selection usually includes a very cold, very dry martini he has mixed to his own formula in a silver cocktail shaker. Philip himself may have one of his own martinis or alternatively a gin and tonic, for which he acquired a taste during his Navy days. The Queen usually has a very dry sherry before dinner, though she seldom takes more than one or two small sips.

The programme for the evening seldom varies more than fractionally. If the Queen and her friends are going on to the theatre and there is insufficient time for a sit-down meal, she lays on a snack of smoked salmon, cold ham, scrambled eggs and toast with champagne to drink. The food is set out on a cloth-covered card table with an electric hot-plate to keep the eggs warm. Guests serve themselves and sit round on the available chairs and sofas nursing their plates on their knees.

Sometimes the Queen will go to the house of one of her friends for dinner after the theatre. But she prefers not to do so. She does not like eating late. If she cannot sit down to dinner at her usual time of eight or half-past, she prefers to have nothing more substantial than a glass of orange juice before retiring. In this, she is very different from her mother and sister, both of whom will happily tuck into a full four-course meal after an evening at the theatre.

Even the most informal of the Queen's private dinner parties involves not less than a dozen servants. It requires three chefs to cook the meal, two kitchen porters to clean up after them, and two maids to prepare the toast and coffee. A footman conveys the food from the kitchen to the dining room, where he hands over to an under-butler who sets it out on the sideboards. It is served by the palace steward and two pages. Wines are dispensed by a wine butler helped by an assistant who conveys the bottles from the cellar to the dining room.

For those who dine with the Queen there is no difficulty over what cutlery to use for a particular course or which glass to drink from. The Queen dislikes an overcrowded table. In consequence, the Georgian-design silver cutlery embossed with the royal crest and the long-stemmed, tulip-shaped glasses engraved with her EIIR cypher are changed for each course.

There is, incidentally, no truth in the story that forks are always placed upside down on the royal table to avoid any repetition of the incident when an overwrought monarch hammered on the table to emphasise a point and impaled his hand on a fork. The forks at Buckingham Palace are placed the same way up as elsewhere.

No cloth covers the top of the oval-shaped, highly polished mahogany table which can be extended to accommodate a dozen or more guests. Instead, each guest has a personal place-mat which may be from one of several sets, the designs ranging from hunting scenes to views of London. The Queen and Prince

Philip sit facing each other across the oval width of the table, with the royal corgis curled up at the Queen's feet in patient anticipation of the cashews or hazelnuts she usually slips them later. In the centre of the table is a silver statuette of the Queen on horseback in the feminine-style Guards uniform she wears for the annual ceremony of Trooping the Colour. Flanking it are four silver figures of Guards officers, their swords raised in salute. On either side are candelabra of heavy antique silver, in each of which three candles burn steadily throughout the meal. The small personal condiment set in front of each guest is equally of antique silver. The dinner plates are of white china, gold-rimmed and bearing the royal cypher.

The meal is usually a simple one, starting with either clear soup or fish, the soup accompanied by sherry, the fish by some suitable white wine. The main course is dictated by what has gone before. Soup is usually followed by roast chicken, fish by filet of steak, saddle of lamb, or lamb cutlets. The main course usually carries a choice of white or red wine. The Queen always picks the white, though she has very little even of that, usually switching to either water or orange squash. The main course is also accompanied by a salad of lettuce, chicory and tomatoes served on kidney-shaped glass plates. Philip is not normally a gourmet. But he is fussy about salad dressing and at one time even went to the extent of having the necessary ingredients sent up from the kitchen so that he could mix his own dressing. A sweet follows the main course. Fresh fruit salad is one of the Queen's favourites. Another of her favourite sweets is made by scooping out the flesh of an orange or pineapple, mixing it with water-ice of the same flavour and restoring it to its original case for serving. She avoids fattening sweets such as pies and puddings.

Among their personal friends, most of whom they have known for many years, there is little need for either Philip or the Queen to lead the conversation over dinner. They allow it to take its natural course, flea-hopping from subject to subject though, usually, horses tend to predominate. No topic is officially taboo, though certain subjects are avoided out of deference to the Queen's position. She would, for instance, never dream of discussing either politics or religion, and the modern trend for talking sex at the dinner table has not yet penetrated the royal dining room, nor is it likely to do so. Horses, dogs, children, farming, shooting, polo, fashion, films and theatre remain as relatively safe topics for conversation which seldom sparkles, as it does at one of Princess Margaret's dinner parties, and is hardly ever controversial.

The sweet course is followed by a savoury, perhaps cheese souffle or Scotch woodcock or devils on horseback. Cheese is never served at dinner, though there is an ample cheeseboard for luncheon parties.

The savoury eaten, the table is completely cleared except for the candelabra and statuettes in readiness for the ritual ceremony of fruit and port. A hand-painted plate of delicate china is set before each guest along with a silver knife, fork and spoon and a crystal fingerbowl reclining on a small lace mat. Hand-painted dishes matching the plates are borne round from guest to guest for them to make their choice of peaches and oranges, apples and bananas, black and white grapes. Strawberries and cherries are also in evidence at the right season. At the same time the wine butler circulates the table in a clockwise direction with a cut-glass decanter of vintage port, starting with the Queen (though she has never been known to take port) and ending with the guest sitting on her immediate right. The circuit completed, the decanter is left on the table in front of Philip so that those guests who wish to do so can replenish their glasses. In accordance with tradition, the decanter can circulate only in a clockwise direction. Thus, if a guest on Philip's right requires the port he or she gets it only after the decanter has made full circuit of the table. Coffee and brandy follow with a wide choice of liqueurs for those who prefer them. Cigars and two types of cigarette, Virginian and Turkish, are handed round, though neither the Queen nor Philip smokes. For her small private dinner parties the Queen has discarded the old tradition by which the ladies leave the room while the men tuck into more port, though it is still carried on at her house parties at Windsor, Sandringham and Balmoral. On these occasions it is not unknown for Philip to become so engrossed in the ensuing all-male conversation that his wife has to send her page along to remind him of the necessity for rejoining the ladies.

As an after-dinner diversion for her friends the Queen usually arranges a film show in the private movie theatre at the rear of the palace. She and her guests sit in comfortable armchairs on a raised platform at the back. Members of her staff are invited along to fill the rest of the seats. It is very much a personal affair. A telephone on the table beside her enables the Queen to contact the projectionist when she is ready for the show to start or to tell him if she wants the sound or vision adjusted as the programme proceeds. There is usually a cartoon or short comedy followed by a newsreel and a main feature film, which may be a British comedy or thriller or an American musical or western.

Neither the Queen nor Philip has any liking for slow-moving emotional or psychological dramas, infinitely preferring a film with plenty of plot and action. If things are slow on the screen, they are not above adding their own interjections, though perhaps not to quite the extent that the Queen's father did when he was alive. "For heaven's sake, get on with it, man!" the King would shout if the hero was perhaps too slow and dreamy in his lovemaking. Philip's occasional wisecracks are couched in lower terms audible only to those nearest to him, while the Queen has a habit of forecasting aloud what she thinks is going to happen next. In the semi-darkness of her private movie theatre she gives full play to those inner feelings she is so good at concealing in public. A comedy sequence will invariably reduce her to peals of hearty laughter, while a moment of screen suspense has even been known to wrench a throaty scream from her.

IV

Late summer, when the London "season" of palace garden parties and diplomatic receptions has run its course, marks the traditional shift from Buckingham Palace to Balmoral, the Royal Family's mock castle in the Scottish Highlands. Windsor is a real castle, steeped in history and tradition. Balmoral, on the other hand, is the Victorian concept of a castle, owing much of its design to the ideas of Prince Albert. The result is a cross between a German *schloss* and the Highland stronghold of a clan chief, a curious creation of towers, turrets and imitation battlements, bowmen's slits and winding defensive stairways, which might have come from the Disney film version of some mid-European fairy tale, the more so on a sunny day when the granite stonework sparkles as though coated with sugar frosting. A marble statue of Prince Albert in Highland dress dominates the main hall, a temptation which successive generations of royal children—indeed, even royal grown-ups in their moments of frivolity—have found themselves quite unable to resist. Hardly a visit passes without some occasion on which the statue is adorned with muffler and cap, and I recall one occasion, in the course of celebrating a royal birthday, when lipstick and rouge were also used to enhance poor Albert's appearance.

The imprint of Queen Victoria and her beloved Prince Consort is still strong at Balmoral. Successive royal owners have done little to change the original décor of tartan carpets, tartan window drapes and pelmets, tartan-covered furnishings, mounted stags' heads, and embossed wallpaper which still bears Victoria's VRI cypher. Indeed, the stags' heads continue to increase in number, some of the more recent additions bearing the inscription "Shot by the Queen" or "Shot by the Duke of Edinburgh." The carpet and curtains in the spacious drawing room are patterned in the grey-and-red Balmoral tartan which was designed by Prince Albert and which the royal family since have continued to regard as their personal tartan. The castle is filled with heavy,

[214]

solid, old-fashioned Victorian furniture. The tattered standards of Scottish regiments hang in the marble-floored entrance hall. Prints and paintings by Landseer, Queen Victoria's favourite artist, still hang one above the other in pairs in the Victorian fashion. The walls of the dining room are almost hidden behind portraits of Victoria and Albert and their numerous offspring. Mounted rams' heads, which once served as mobile snuff-boxes for Victorian dinner parties, still adorn the sideboards in the main hall. Highland shepherds carved in marble serve as lamp-holders in the drawing room, though the candles of Queen Victoria's day have given way to candle-shaped electric lamps.

Though less publicised than her addiction to horse racing, deer-stalking is one of the Queen's favourite pursuits. She shot her first stag on the heather-clad hills of Balmoral when she was still a girl in her teens. There has scarcely been a royal holiday at Balmoral during which she has not engaged in at least one stalking expedition and, indeed, she was even out stalking deer when she was three months pregnant with Prince Andrew.

The Queen's stalking expeditions are quite unlike the highly organised grouse shoots, with their dozens of loaders and beaters, which Prince Philip leads across the moors at Balmoral. For deer-stalking the Queen sets off with only two gillies (Scottish gamekeepers) for company. One carries her hunting rifle, the other a packed lunch of ham sandwiches, crackers and cream cheese, and some apples. There is also a warming flask of Scotch whisky in the lunch pack, though the Queen seldom if ever resorts to it. She is equipped with a stout stalking stick to help her traverse the rougher terrain, and is warmly clad in masculine-looking knickerbockers, a woollen sweater and tweed jacket, woollen stockings and stoutly spiked shoes. A silk scarf keeps her hair in place and long-range binoculars are slung round her neck. Either she or one of the gillies also carries an extending telescope.

A jeep-like Land Rover conveys the party to the nearest accessible spot to the stag earmarked for stalking. Usually it is a beast with a "bad" head—small or malformed antlers—and unsuitable for breeding. Seldom does the Queen stalk a stag with a fine head, and then only if it is too old to breed. She was on her way back from one stalking expedition when one of her gillies spotted a fine old stag which had become separated from the main herd. Excitedly he pointed it out to the Queen as a suitable target.

"Oh, but that's old Charlie," protested the Queen. "I can't possibly shoot him. He's been around here for years."

Pursuit may continue for six or seven hours as the Queen works her way within rifle range and down-wind of the stag she is stalking, scrambling up rocky slopes, wading through mountain streams, crawling Indian-fashion through soggy bog or prickly gorse, perhaps ploughing through deep snow in the upper reaches. Once in position she invariably kills with a single shot. She is a crack shot with a rifle and from time to time practises on a leaden target shaped like a full-grown stag which stands in the castle grounds. Only once, to my knowledge, has she returned after merely wounding a stag. She was very young at the time, and her father, when he learned what had happened, promptly ordered her to go out and finish the beast off. "You must never leave a wounded animal," he told her. However, it was late and dark by then, and an obliging gillie undertook the mission for her.

The 80,000 heathery acres of Balmoral offer the Queen and her family a combination of privacy and personal freedom they can find nowhere else. The tall pines, the crystal-clear salmon-filled waters of the River Dee, and a range of rugged mountains dominated by the perpetually snow-clad peak of Lochnagar join forces to keep them safe from rubbernecking sightseers. Camouflage netting is skilfully employed as an additional defence at one spot where the road from Braemar to Ballater passes within binocular range of the dining room windows. Not even this combination of natural and man-made defences has been completely proof against the prying telephoto lenses of enterprising photographers, but it is seldom penetrated, and then only briefly.

The Queen and her family usually head for Balmoral in early

August, travelling from London on an overnight train which the Queen pays for out of her own purse, even down to purchasing travel tickets for the royal corgis. Nearly half the staff of a Buckingham Palace go with her to reinforce the small skeleton crew which keeps Balmoral Castle aired and dusted throughout the remainder of the year. Until the local station was closed under Britain's national scheme to render its railroads less uneconomic, she alighted from the train at the small Scottish township of Ballater, where a convoy of cars waited to whisk her the remaining eight miles to Balmoral. Nowadays the train can take her only to Aberdeen, some 42 miles farther off.

Once at Balmoral, safe from the public gaze, the Royal Family can happily slip into the favourite, time-tested clothes they keep there from holiday to holiday. The Queen usually wears a tartan kilt with a tweed jacket, switching the kilt as the mood takes her. Sometimes she wears the grey-and-red Balmoral tartan which her great-great-grandfather designed, sometimes the Royal Stewart dress tartan, and sometimes the hunting Stewart. Philip, too, wears a kilt at Balmoral. The youngsters alternate between kilts and jeans. Prince Charles must have been about eight or nine when the wearing of a kilt—or, rather, what went under it—became the subject of a wordy battle between him and his nanny. His nanny insisted that he should wear a pair of tartan shorts beneath the kilt as he always had done. Charles had other ideas. "I'm not wearing those," he protested stoutly. "Papa doesn't." Whatever Prince Philip may or may not wear under his kilt, Charles, on that occasion, finally had to do as his nanny wanted.

At Balmoral the royal children are permitted to run wild to a degree not possible elsewhere, a fact of which Anne and Andrew, the more extroverted of the Queen's four children, take full advantage . . . not always without incident. Anne was once galloping her pony through a copse at the rear of the castle when she ran smack into an improvised line one of the servants had rigged up to air linen in the Scottish tradition. She was plucked bodily from the saddle and dashed to the ground, fortunately without serious injury.

Royal life at Balmoral is still lived in the old tradition of the Scottish lairds. Every morning, as the clock in the castle tower strikes the hour of nine, the Queen's piper paces up and down the granite chippings at the front of the castle, skirling the wild, sweet strains of Scotland's traditional airs. Each evening, after dinner, a team of four pipers, eagle feathers protruding jauntily from their tam-o'-shanter headgear, stalk into the dining room and parade round the table, pipes going full blast. A visit to the Highland Games at nearby Braemar to watch husky Scots perform such feats as throwing the hammer (a 16-pound metal ball on a steel-wire handle) and tossing the caber (the 20-foot trunk of a larch tree) is a traditional feature of the royal stay.

Another is the Gillies' Ball held in the castle ballroom, for which the royal family deck themselves out in full Highland dress. It is a gay occasion which both the Queen and Prince Philip thoroughly enjoy. Indeed, it is one of the very rare occasions on which the Queen seems less inhibited than her husband. She declines to wear a tiara in case it impedes her dancing and is not above giving tongue to the gleeful yells which considerably enliven some of the more exuberant Scottish dances. She and Philip always head the opening grand march and then separate, as do others of the Royal Family, to join sets made up of gillies and their wives, royal servants, and soldiers from the guard-of-honour, for a lively Eightsome Reel and the succeeding dances. This mixing of royalty and commoners sometimes produces curious reactions. A battle-hardened sergeant of the Black Watch who found himself dancing with the Queen Mother on one occasion was subsequently discovered in the castle yard with tears of emotional excitement streaming down his leathery, weather-beaten cheeks.

While the Queen's two-month stay at Balmoral is perhaps the most relaxed period in the royal year, the discipline of the clock still exerts itself. The Queen and Philip are still called at eight o'clock each morning, as they are at Buckingham Palace. Breakfast is still served at nine o'clock. Except at weekends or in stormy weather, Philip leaves the castle for the grouse moors promptly at half-past nine each morning. For the Queen, there is still work to be done. Future overseas tours involve reading up on the places and people she will be visiting. Her Boxes and correspondence pursue her as always. She works after breakfast at a desk by the window, dressed in the riding clothes she will require at eleven o'clock when she goes to the stables to join Anne for an hour's canter by the side of the silvery Dee. Returning to the castle, she closets herself with her Private Secretary, who travels to Scotland with her, living in a grace-and-favour house a few miles away, and gets through further work.

Then she changes from her riding rig into a tweed jacket and tartan kilt, adds a raincoat as protection against the inevitable Scots mist, and is off to join Philip and the others of the shooting party for a barbecue lunch, cooked on the portable outfit Philip bought for himself during a royal tour of Canada. After lunch the Queen follows the guns until shooting ends for the day at four o'clock. She returns to the castle, feeds her dogs and, as though she has not walked enough, goes out with them for a further brisk trek. Another change—this time into a silk or woollen dress—finds her ready for afternoon tea, after which she has a further session with her Boxes and her Private Secretary before joining the rest of the family and such guests as she has staying with her in the drawing room. This is a time of day normally devoted to the younger children, and it is not at all unusual for the Queen to remove her shoes, persuading others to do the same, to play tag with the children in the main hall or join them in a game of hide-and-seek in corridors and cupboards. A bath and a change into evening dress and she is ready for dinner, a long, leisurely meal which may last until ten o'clock or even half-past, its menu varied by the inclusion of such Scottish delicacies as grouse and venison, salmon and trout.

The Queen Mother frequently drives over from her house at nearby Birkhall to join her daughter and son-in-law for dinner. Margaret and Tony may come with her, or they and their two children may already be staying with the Queen at Balmoral. In any event, the castle is usually crammed with guests . . . relatives such as the Duke and Duchess of Gloucester, the young Duke and Duchess of Kent, Princess Alexandra and her husband, friends such as the Porchesters and the Nevills, the Brabournes and the Ogilvys. The prime minister may be invited for a weekend. The minister preaching in the little stone church at Crathie, which the Queen attends every Sunday, is always invited to stay at Balmoral as the Queen's guest.

Saturdays and Sundays provide a variation in routine. Grouse shooting is forgotten and the Queen and Philip devote themselves to the children, sometimes taking them over to Loch Muich for a fishing expedition, sometimes going for a picnic in the hills where the Queen and Anne mix batter for pancakes while Philip and Charles do the cooking on the portable barbecue. Such trips are usually made by Land Rover, but once when Anne was rather younger she preferred to go along on her bicycle. However, when the time came to return home, she was too tired to pedal back. Her father hoisted her into the Land Rover, telling the Queen to drive back while he followed on the bicycle. Unfortunately, his weight proved too much for Anne's pint-sized bicycle, and it collapsed under him, the front wheel buckling to such an extent that he could not even push it. With the rest of the party now out of sight, there was nothing for it but to hoist the machine on his shoulders and trudge a weary two miles back to the castle.

V

Either just before or immediately after her stay at Balmoral, the Queen spends a few days at the Palace of Holyroodhouse in Edinburgh, where her programme is a telescoped version of what she does in London—a garden party, perhaps an investiture, perhaps a banquet for Scottish dignitaries. The Scots are always sensitive about their links with England and its royal family— there are even objections to the Queen styling herself Elizabeth

II on the grounds that the earlier Elizabeth was never Queen of Scotland—and from time to time they rumble that she uses Holyroodhouse too little.

If so, she can hardly be blamed. This collection of gaunt and gloomy rooms, where Mary Queen of Scots once lived and where her Italian favourite, Rizzio, was murdered, is more like a museum of Scottish history than a contemporary royal residence. There are rooms in which it would be no surprise to see Rizzio's ghost suddenly materialise. In particular, to walk through the long picture gallery, where Bonnie Prince Charlie once danced the night away, can be quite awe-inspiring. Unlike the Queen's own well-lighted gallery at Buckingham Palace, the one at Holyroodhouse is a high, echoing chamber of age-blackened timbers, hung with sombre, time-darkened portraits in which only the eyes seem to be alive, staring and following your progress as you walk through.

The Queen returns to London from Scotland in good time for the state opening of Parliament and the Remembrance Day service at the Cenotaph in Whitehall where she stands in silence for two minutes before laying a wreath of blood-red poppies to the memory of those who died in two world wars. The pattern of her paperwork continues and the programme of public engagements in and around London is resumed, broken by an occasional trip to Sandringham, where the pheasants and partridges are now ready to be added to the stocks of grouse stored in the royal deep-freeze against future banquet commitments.

The approach of Christmas is the only time of the year when the Queen goes out shopping. Normally, the bulk of her shopping is done for her by her staff. Where more personal items are concerned, stores are only too willing to send a selection to Buckingham Palace for the Queen to make a choice. But her Christmas shopping she likes to do on the spot. She goes to Fortnum and Mason, the Piccadilly store where elegant young men in black jackets and striped trousers dispense jars of caviar and pots of preserved ginger with the air of collectors handling precious objets d'art, and to Harrods, the equally luxurious emporium in Knightsbridge.

The Queen is the twelfth British monarch to shop at Fortnum and Mason, which is perhaps only as it should be, since the firm was originally founded by one of Queen Anne's footmen with money obtained by the simple expedient of selling royal candle-ends. As the hundreds of candles in the royal chandeliers were replaced daily, whether used or not, he and succeeding footmen amassed small fortunes until Victoria's husband, the economically minded Albert, realised what was going on and put a stop to the practice. It was Albert, too, who ended the custom of placing a fresh bottle of whisky beside the Queen's bed each night and whisking it away the following morning, invariably unopened. Yet in some respects this idea of footmen's "perks" still continues at Buckingham Palace. During my time there, any fruit left over on the breakfast trays (though not on the dinner table) was always considered the legitimate "perk" of the footman concerned.

The Queen, when she goes Christmas shopping, is greeted ceremoniously by the store manager and escorted by him from department to department. Her purchases, which she restricts to gifts for family and friends, leaving her housekeeper to buy the gifts she gives her staff, include furniture and china, toys and books, food delicacies, scarves, handbags and gloves. Mechanical toys have a particular fascination for her, and one year she surprised those who were with her by insisting upon trying out a toy space-gun which discharged a shower of coloured sparks. Another year she called me into her sitting room to watch while she put a clockwork monkey, bought for one of the children, through its paces, much to the consternation of her pet corgis.

With the exception of very close relatives, she does not buy specific gifts for specific people. Instead, she buys whatever takes her fancy—sometimes two or three of the same thing—and decides later who shall receive what. Once selected, each gift is accompanied by a small card of good wishes which she writes out by hand. Similarly, she insists upon signing all her Christmas cards personally, despite the fact that they run into several hundreds. She would not dream of sending a card, as many people do these days, on which her name was merely printed. The Christmas cards she signs and sends out each year go to relatives, friends, members of her personal staff, government ministers and ambassadors, and those overseas monarchs and presidents with whom she is on friendly personal terms.

Each year she receives far more cards than she sends out. She likes to look through them all, even those from people she has never heard of, and any with horses on them stand a good chance of ending up on the royal mantlepiece.

Those of her staff who are not spending Christmas with her at Sandringham or Windsor, as the case may be, receive their gifts from her before she leaves London. The rest get theirs at a small ceremony on Christmas Eve. Gifts for the staff range from perhaps half a dozen pairs of stockings for a junior maid to complete dinner services and cutlery sets for those who have been with her for many years. Philip helps out with this annual ceremony, enlivening the affair in his usual spontaneous fashion. "Only just in time," he quipped—a reference to my receding hairline—as he handed me a pair of hairbrushes one Christmas. Always curious about how things work, he once dismantled a new-style coffee percolator intended for one of the staff and then found that he could not fit it together again. Unperturbed, he handed over the collection of bits and pieces. "If you can't put it together again, get another and charge it to me," he said.

To leave themselves free for church on Christmas morning, the Royal Family also exchange their own gifts on Christmas Eve, standing around a tall Christmas tree gay with coloured lights. But for the younger children there is also a bulging stocking at the foot of the bed when they wake on Christmas morning. Here again the Queen prefers the personal touch and refuses to buy ready-made Christmas stockings. Instead, she uses discarded nylons, filling them with things she has bought herself. She also makes up a Christmas stocking for each of the royal corgis. For

[223]

each corgi there is a packet of dog biscuits, a tin of chocolate drops, a new rubber bone and a rubber ball.

The Queen is called extra early on Christmas morning. In company with Prince Philip and others of the family she goes to church for early communion and again for morning service. After that, she is free for the day . . . though this was not always the case. Until a few years ago, she had to hurry through lunch in order to prepare for her Christmas Day telecast. Nerves taut at the prospect of what is always for her a considerable ordeal, she did little more than peck at her turkey and Christmas pudding before dashing off to submit herself to the attentions of the make-up man and undergo a quick last-minute rehearsal. But these days, with her telecast pre-taped weeks ahead, she is free to enjoy her lunch in the same leisurely fashion as everyone else . . . and watch herself on television afterwards if she wishes to do so. The change also has the advantage that copies of the film can be flown out in advance to Commonwealth countries for screening at the most convenient time locally.

At Christmas, the Queen, like her father and grandfather before her, likes nothing so much as to surround herself with relatives. It is perhaps the one time of the year when the whole of the Royal Family (with two notable exceptions) are all together in one place at one time . . . the Queen, Philip, their children, the Queen Mother, Margaret and Tony and their youngsters, the Duke and Duchess of Gloucester and their grown-up sons, the Duke and Duchess of Kent and their children, Princess Alexandra and her husband and children. The notable exceptions are the Duke and Duchess of Windsor.

Except for the younger children, who have their meals in the nursery, they all sit down together to a festive board groaning with nuts and candy, figs and dates, peaches, grapes and crystallised fruit. Gaily-coloured bonbons and cottonwool snowmen filled with toys, trinkets and paper hats add to the fun; holly, mistletoe and a leaping log fire augment the atmosphere of a truly Dickensian Christmas. Dinner in the evening has the additional touch of candlelight, and everyone is in evening dress, the menfolk in tuxedos and black bow ties and the ladies in long evening gowns offset by sparkling jewellery.

The Royal Steward carves the turkey with due ceremony. The Christmas pudding, a sprig of holly perched on top, brandy-blue flames dancing around it, is carried in by one of the royal pages. After dinner there are games, charades, often a treasure hunt, a family sing-song round the grand piano. Everyone does his or her piece, with Princess Margaret usually the life and soul of the party. She and the Queen will frequently join forces in a rip-roaring duet... perhaps "The Rain in Spain" from *My Fair Lady* or "You're Just in Love," the contrapuntal duet from *Call Me Madam.*

Equally festive and high-spirited is the family party on New Year's Eve. True to the Scottish ancestry on her mother's side of the family, the Queen still observes the ancient Scots custom of "first footing" at New Year. She waits just inside the front door, her family and relatives around her, as the clock strikes midnight. As the chimes die away, the door opens and in walks the traditional "dark man" (usually one of the royal footmen) bearing a lump of coal which the Queen accepts as the symbol of continued good health and good fortune during the next twelve months.

9. *TRAVELS WITH THE QUEEN*

I

I TAPPED on the door of the Queen's sitting room and walked in to collect the royal corgis for their customary afternoon run in the palace grounds. A huge map of Canada, some nine feet long by six feet wide, was spread out on the available floor space between the Queen's desk and the marble fireplace. The Queen was down on her hands and knees in front of the fire, studying the map. Beside her, also on their hands and knees, were Prince Philip and her Private Secretary, Sir Michael Adeane. Yet another royal tour had reached the planning stage.

The Queen is much the most travelled monarch in British history. Within a few months of her coronation, she was setting out on a royal tour which was to take her right round the world. In the first seven years of her reign she had already done more globe-trotting and undertaken more state visits than any monarch before her, and today the sum total of her travels stretches several times round the globe.

As Sovereign, she has opened Parliament in places as far apart as Canada and Australia, Malta, Ceylon and New Zealand. By doing so, she has made it abundantly clear that she is as much Queen of these countries as Queen of Great Britain. And her visit to the United States in 1957 was made as Queen of Canada. "When I go to the United States," she said in a Canadian broadcast just prior to the visit, "I shall be going as Head of the Canadian Nation to pay a state visit to the Head of our great neighbouring country."

She has paid similar state visits to most of the countries of Europe. In Africa she has been to Nigeria, Ghana, Liberia, Sierra Leone, Gambia, Ethiopia, Uganda, Libya and the Sudan. Farther east, she has been to Turkey, Iran, Nepal, India and Pakistan. To the west, she has visited Guyana (when it was British Guiana), Trinidad and Tobago, Grenada, St. Vincent, Barbados, St. Lucia, Dominica, Montserrat, Antigua, St. Kitts-Nevis-Anguilla, the British Virgin Islands, the Turks and Caicos Islands, the Bahamas and Jamaica. She has sampled hot dogs in Chicago, roast pig in Tonga (eating it with her fingers in accordance with local custom), and the soapy-tasting kava which is the national drink of Fiji. She has watched sheep-shearing in Australia, heard Maori war chants in New Zealand, and witnessed a Zulu war dance in Africa, the famous Calgary Stampede in Canada, and a game of American football in the United States. Last year she visited the countries of South America; next year she goes again to Australia.

Philip's travels over the years have been even more wide-ranging. In addition to all the places he has been with the Queen, he has travelled north to the Yukon and the Arctic Circle, south to the Falkland Islands, Deception Island, the South Shetland Islands and the Antarctic. He has been to lonely, isolated spots which the Queen, as a woman, could scarcely hope to see... the Seychelles, Papua, Tristan da Cunha. He has visited Malaya and Singapore, Sarawak, Brunei, Hong Kong and the Solomon Islands, the Galápagos Islands (subsequently appearing on television to introduce a film about their unique wild life), Mexico, Morocco and Zanzibar, Argentina, Brazil and eight other South American countries.

Royal travels fall into four main categories—state visits, royal tours, visits with a specific purpose (as when Philip went to Canada in 1967 to attend the conference of the Royal Agricultural Society of the Commonwealth) and private visits. A state visit is what the name implies, a courtesy call paid by one head of state to another, and the Queen, like any other head of state, pays only one such visit to any one country. She may of course visit the same country again subsequently, either officially or privately, but these would not be state visits.

Because its object is simply an exchange of courtesies between two heads of state, a state visit normally lasts no more than three days. If the Queen stays longer it is usually in a private capacity. The official programme includes a public welcome and a state drive through the capital, an exchange of gifts, a state banquet by the host country with a reciprocal function on the visiting side, usually a visit to the opera or ballet, and perhaps some sightseeing on an official and historic level.

A royal tour lasts longer—sometimes considerably longer—and has a rather different function. Normally restricted to the countries of the Commonwealth, its main object is to enable the Queen to see as much of the country, its people, and their way of life as can be reasonably telescoped into the available time. Also, of course, it enables her to be seen by the people she has come to see. Instead of staying almost exclusively in the capital, as she does on a state visit, she undertakes a whistle-stop tour from city to city, town to town, village to village, received at each stopping place by the local mayor and other civic dignitaries. She will accept a bouquet, make a brief speech, perhaps inspect a guard-of-honour or plant a tree commemorating her visit. She may visit a local hospital, factory, or suburb. The bigger centres of population will perhaps lay on an official luncheon or banquet, barbecue or ball in her honour. There is usually some sort of open-air gathering for the local schoolchildren, so that they can file away a memory of the Queen with which one day to regale their grandchildren.

Because she goes only where the government of the day feels

she should go, the Queen's travels give a pretty fair idea of the diplomatic climate as it affects Britain. Old enmities die hard, and it was not until thirteen years after ascending the throne that she could pay a state visit to Germany, though she had three sisters-in-law living there as well as dozens of distant blood relatives descended, like herself, from Queen Victoria. As yet she has not visited Soviet Russia or any other country beyond the Iron Curtain. The day she does will signify a distinct thaw in East-West relations. Spain has not yet been included in her visiting list. Nor has she been to South Africa since she became Queen, though she spent her twenty-first birthday there as a princess. On the other hand, she has been to the United States three times since ascending the Throne (and once before that as deputy for her sick father).

Even the shortest state visit involves not less than six months of planning and preparation. A tour of any magnitude, like the Queen's six-week visit to Canada and the United States in 1959, will be more than a year on the drawing-board. On that occasion, the final red-bound schedule for the tour ran to 344 closely printed pages. Arrangements included linking the royal yacht to the mainland telephone service whenever it was in harbour, ensuring that the Queen received official documents and correspondence as usual (though in diplomatic pouches instead of the traditional Boxes), and leap-frogging three special cars ahead of the royal party by air so that they were awaiting the Queen at each fresh stopping place.

The actual plans for a royal tour are drawn up by the host country. They are, of course, submitted to the Queen for her approval, and she sometimes comes up with an improving suggestion. Ahead of her visit to Washington, for instance, she noticed that the draft schedule had her aircraft touching down in the capital after dark. This, she felt, might well disappoint a lot of Americans hoping to see her, and she suggested that a daylight landing should be substituted.

While she may make occasional suggestions of this sort, the Queen seldom, if ever, turns down arrangements made on her behalf. The Canadian Government, perhaps unwisely, decided to include Quebec in the schedule for her Canadian centenary visit in 1964. Despite reported threats that her visit would see Quebec turned into "a second Dallas," she still went there, riding through the streets in a bullet-proof Cadillac while police sharpshooters kept watch from rooftops against the possibility of assassination, and riot police waded into jeering, booing French-Canadians with their truncheons. "Fancy having to put up with this sort of thing," sighed Bobo MacDonald, who, as always, was in the royal party. "Don't worry about me," the Queen replied. "Nobody's going to hurt me. I'm as safe as houses."

While the actual details of a royal tour are arranged by others, there is still a fair amount for the Queen herself to do. In particular, she has to familiarise herself with the places she will be visiting and the more important people she will be meeting in each stopping place. Most formidable task of all for a woman who is not really interested in clothes, she has to commission, approve, and try on a whole new wardrobe. For a tour of any considerable duration the Queen will need fifty or sixty new outfits if she is to have something suitable for each different type of public engagement and not wear the same outfit too many times. She will need coats, suits, day dresses, cocktail dresses and evening gowns. If the programme includes a state banquet, then she will also need a state gown. With its elaborate hand-worked design, usually embodying the national flower of the country she is visiting, a single state gown can involve months of work. Even the more ordinary clothes she will wear have to be suited not only to the country she is visiting, but also to the time of year when she will be there. Equally, they must be designed to ensure that she can climb in and out of cars with decorum, is clearly visible from a distance, and has considerable freedom of movement.

The two fashion designers who provide the bulk of her wardrobe—Norman Hartnell and Hardy Amies—first submit preliminary sketches for her approval. Each sketch is a miniature full-length portrait so that the Queen can see what she will look like in the finished outfit. A sample of the material to be used is attached. As work on the wardrobe progresses, fittings take up an increasing amount of the Queen's time. She will spend many afternoons in her dressing room with one or other of her designers and his several assistants crouching and bobbing around her.

There are, additionally, hats and shoes to be made and tried on. The Queen has a matching pair of shoes for each outfit, though in practice she often wears no more than half a dozen pairs in the course of a tour. With so much walking and standing involved, she tends to cling to those shoes she finds particularly comfortable. Sometimes, indeed, she will wear the same pair time after time, and this was so noticeable during a tour of Australia that a leading fashion writer was moved to pose the query: Has the Queen only one pair of shoes?

II

The Queen, when she undertakes a royal tour, travels with a staggering amount of luggage. Two truly queen-sized travelling wardrobes in blue leather, each six feet high and mounted on wheels to make for easier handling, hold her evening gowns. Also on wheels is a matching chest-of-drawers, in which gloves, stockings, handkerchiefs and lingerie are contained in neat layers, which she had specially made for her world travels. Hat-boxes and shoe-boxes in matching blue leather hold perhaps three dozen hats and twice that number of shoes. Half a dozen stout leather trunks hold coats and suits, dresses and furs. The state gown has a trunk to itself. A crocodile dressing case holds the 30-piece set of silver-gilt brushes and combs, hand mirrors and cosmetic containers which was one of her wedding gifts. A long, slender case of unique design, which she inherited from her grandmother, Queen Mary, contains umbrellas and parasols, each with a cover of fine chamois leather to protect the jewelled handle.

It is Bobo MacDonald's task to mastermind this mammoth wardrobe, ensuring that the right outfit and correct accessories, crisp and spotless, are in readiness in the right place at the right time. With the aid of an assistant dresser, sometimes two, and relying upon her excellent memory to recall which items are in which pieces of luggage, she hardly ever makes a mistake. In fact, I can recall only one occasion when she did. Even then, she had the correct outfit ready for the Queen to wear as the train neared the next stopping place. But for once she could not locate the right hat to go with it. She was furious . . . with herself and with everyone else in her immediate vicinity. The Queen, for her part, was quite unperturbed. "It doesn't matter," she assured the upset Bobo. "I'll wear what I have on."

Wherever she goes, the Queen always takes her cameras with her. She is an enthusiastic, spur-of-the-moment photographer, though her efforts cannot match the near-professionalism of her husband. Because she has travelled so widely and because she has so often been "where the action is," her private movies, amateurish though they are, are worth seeing. Over the years she has filmed Everest from the air, shark fishing in the Indian Ocean, water buck duelling to the death by a waterhole in Kenya, and a crocodile hunt in which Philip took part. She has filmed a tiger hunt in India, the ancient ceremony of Buddha's Tooth in Ceylon, the apes at Gibraltar, the spouting geysers at Rotorua in New Zealand, the armada of little boats which sailed out to greet her at Sydney, Australia, and the fire boats which welcomed her to Manhattan. There is one film which includes a quite hilarious sequence of Philip revelling in a messy crossing-the-line ceremony aboard ship on their way to Australia. Properly stored and catalogued, as Margaret does with her discs, the Queen's films would constitute a unique personal record of her world travels. But like so many other amateur movie-makers, the Queen tends to stuff them away in drawers and cupboards to gather dust, once she has shown them to her family and friends.

In addition to everything else she takes along, the Queen travels with her own hot-water bottle, her own feather-filled pillows, a cannister of her favourite China tea, her own toilet soap, supplies of barley sugar and her favourite chocolate-coated mints, even her own supply of bottled water. The bottled water is no mere royal whim, but a sensible precaution against possible constitutional upsets, which has proved surprisingly effective over the years.

In America, on one occasion, the Queen's cannister of China tea went temporarily astray. Faced with the prospect of making a pot of tea for her on arrival at the White House, I could locate only tea-bags in the presidential kitchen. I did what I could with them, but the resulting pot of tea was clearly far too weak and watery for the Queen's taste. Fortunately, the President's butler arrived at that moment to ask if there was anything we wanted.

"Yes," I said. "Tea—but in a packet, not tea-bags."

He nodded and went away, to return a few minutes later with a packet of tea, enabling me to brew a pot for the Queen in the English tradition.

Among the miscellaneous hand luggage containing cameras, soap, books, and crossword puzzles which travel with the Queen wherever she goes, is one with contents more valuable than the rest of the royal luggage lumped together. This is the case containing the Queen's jewels, a shimmering collection of tiaras, necklaces, brooches, bracelets and earrings, each piece in its own velvet-lined box. During my years as the Queen's footman, it was often my responsibility to convey this case and its almost priceless contents from place to place. It was not a responsibility which caused me any undue concern ... except on one never-to-be-forgotten occasion.

It was in New Zealand. The Queen had been staying overnight at a small hotel in New Plymouth. She and Philip had left that afternoon for Wellington. They had been gone only a few minutes when Bobo put her head over the bannisters and called down to me in the hotel lobby, "Have you seen the case?"

She could be referring to only one case.

"No," I called back.

[233]

"Well, it's gone," she said.

I took the stairs two at a time. Together, Bobo and I searched the Queen's bedroom. We looked in the cupboards, in the adjoining bathroom, even under the bed. There was no sign of the jewel case.

The manageress of the hotel came along. We described the case to her and asked if she had seen it.

She shook her head. Then she said, "What about the soldiers who collected the rest of the luggage? Did they take it, perhaps?"

A small detachment of New Zealand troops had been assigned to the royal party to manhandle the heavy luggage. I raced downstairs again, but the troops and their trucks had already gone ... and the luggage with them.

I got into a car with Bobo and Ernest Bennett, the Queen's page, and we set off in pursuit. But our car was delayed by the crowds who had turned out to see the Queen, and we finally reached the airport only to find that the rest of the luggage had been loaded into the baggage plane and was already airborne. There was only one thing to do and we did it: we boarded our own aircraft and continued the chase. It was late afternoon when we arrived at Government House in Wellington where the Queen was to stay for the following week. The royal luggage was being unloaded as we got there, and there was a miniature mountain of trunks and suitcases heaped on the front steps. Although there was nothing about it to distinguish the particular case which held the all-important jewels, I recognised it instantly. I heaved a big sigh of relief as I collected it and carried it inside and up to the Queen's bedroom.

"Thank heavens it's safe," said Bobo. "I never want to live through another day like this one."

Nor did I. A stiff drink seemed indicated, and I went off in search of one.

Voluminous though the Queen's own luggage is, it forms only part of the tons of trunks and cases involved in a royal tour. The Queen seldom travels abroad without an entourage of at least thirty people, each of whom has his or her own stack of luggage. Then there are all the miscellaneous items such as the souvenir gifts the Queen distributes as the tour progresses. Medals and orders, gold cufflinks and jewelled brooches, signed photographs and powder compacts embossed with the royal cypher—there is something for everyone, from governor-general down to maids, butlers, cooks and chauffeurs. For any head of state she is visiting there is a still more elaborate gift. On her 1957 visit to the United States, for instance, she took President Eisenhower a walnut table appropriately adorned with the battle plan for D-Day. In return, President Eisenhower gave her a portrait of Prince Charles he had painted himself.

Wherever the Queen goes, it seems that everyone wants to give her something. During that lightning visit to the United States she received, in addition to the portrait of Prince Charles, a gold-plated model of the Empire State Building, a pair of 18th-century spurs, a replica of George Washington's riding crop and a mink coat. In France she was given a Renault car, a Louis XV clock, the largest bottle of perfume in the world . . . and the smallest watch. From Nigeria she returned home with shawls and turbans, fans and furniture and a paperweight made from a tiger's paw. On her world tour she collected some four hundred gifts, from nylon nighties to a century-old tortoise egg. One tour of Canada resulted in 120 gifts, ranging from a gold-and-silver desk set to a pair of beaded gloves made by the Blackfoot Indians. Over the years she has amassed a considerable collection of brooches presented to her in the various countries she has visited. Philip has a similar collection of cufflinks.

The entourage which surrounds the Queen on her travels usually includes her Private Secretary, one of the Assistant Private Secretaries, the Press Secretary, an Equerry, a physician, her hairdresser, her personal detective (Chief Superintendent A. E. Perkins), the Sergeant-Footman (or his deputy), the Queen's personal page and personal footman, the indispensable Bobo and one or two assistant dressers, and a couple of Ladies-in-Waiting. Philip, if he is along, has with him his Private Secretary (Mr.

[235]

James Orr), an Equerry, his personal detective and one of his two valets. Completing the party are clerks, additional footmen and maids to look after the Ladies-in-Waiting.

The Queen, at this writing, has ten Ladies-in-Waiting. Senior of them is the Countess of Euston. As Mistress of the Robes it is her duty to attend the Queen on such ceremonial occasions as the state opening of Parliament. Next in line are the two Ladies of the Bedchamber, the tall, dignified Countess of Leicester and the Marchioness of Abergavenny. Like the Countess of Euston, both are long-time friends of the Queen. Then come the Women of the Bedchamber, four of them, Lady Margaret Hay, Lady Rose Baring, the Honourable Mary Morrison and Lady Susan Hussey. There are, additionally, three Extra Women of the Bedchamber. They can be called upon should illness upset the normal rota by which Women of the Bedchamber attend upon the Queen for periods of two weeks at a time, living with her at Buckingham Palace, theoretically on duty from the time the Queen gets up in the morning until she goes to bed at night.

In practice, the resident Lady-in-Waiting starts work around half-past nine when she receives a batch of the Queen's mail to peruse and answer. The letters she deals with fall midway between the top-level official correspondence, which is dealt with by the royal Private Secretaries, and strictly personal letters which the Queen prefers to answer herself. Into this middle stream, dealt with by the Lady-in-Waiting, come letters seeking charitable donations, requests for royal gifts to be auctioned for charity, letters concerning the royal children and letters from people (and there are scores of them in the course of a year) who merely want to wish the Queen well.

If the Queen has an official engagement outside the palace, then the Lady-in-Waiting goes with her, first checking with Bobo to ensure that whatever outfit she proposes to wear will not outshine or clash with that worn by the Queen. For state visits and royal tours, two Ladies-in-Waiting go along, a Lady of the Bedchamber to accompany the Queen to top-level functions and a Woman of the Bedchamber who goes along with her to less important engagements.

It is the Lady-in-Waiting's job to carry the Queen's umbrella, a light waterproof cape for her to slip over her coat if it should rain, and a brown leather grip containing all manner of things the Queen may need at short notice. Carefully packed and checked by the indispensable Bobo, the grip contains spare gloves for the Queen to put on when her own become soiled from too much handshaking, spare stockings in case she develops a run, spare shoes in case she wrings a heel, spare handkerchiefs, extra cosmetics, dark glasses for bright sunlight and a supply of barley sugar for her to suck while travelling.

Some of those in the royal entourage when the Queen sets out on her travels are covering the same ground for the second time. An advance party, usually including one of the Assistant Private Secretaries and the Queen's personal detective, along with the Master of the Household, invariably travels the planned route ahead of the Queen to check on arrangements. The Assistant Private Secretary times the proposed schedule at each stopping place, Chief Superintendent Perkins checks on the security arrangements, and the Master of the Household copes with the many questions posed by those who will be hosting the Queen. He tells them that the Queen prefers orange squash to orange juice, has little liking for exotic delicacies such as caviar and oysters, prefers her bed with its head against the wall, likes a full-length mirror in which she can inspect herself from head to toe before leaving for an official function, and requires a writing desk as part of her sitting room furniture wherever she stays, so that she can cope with official papers and correspondence between engagements. Prince Philip, they learn, likes a shower instead of a bath when he can get one, and prefers to stretch out at night in the longest bed available. When he stayed at the White House he was given the massive eight-footer which once belonged to President Lincoln, while the Queen slept in the 18th-century four poster in the Rose Room.

Despite such meticulous advance planning, small things inevitably go wrong in the course of a royal tour. The desk provided for the Queen is frequently inadequate for its purpose. Well-meaning hosts usually provide her with something small, elegant and antique, but quite incapable of accommodating the volumes of paper scattered around her as she works. Several times where this has happened I have had to forage around for a kitchen or dining-room table which offered a larger working surface. The provision of a full-length mirror is sometimes overlooked, and I remember one occasion at a hotel in New Zealand when we rectified the omission by taking down the long horizontal mirror in the ladies' powder room and installing it, end on, in the Queen's dressing room. To make the Queen comfortable in Nigeria a commercial refrigeration plant was installed in Government House to lower the temperature and humidity in the rooms she would be using. Fortunately, the wife of the Governor-General decided to sleep in the royal bedroom ahead of the Queen's arrival to try things out. She awoke in the night, teeth chattering, to find that the refrigeration plant had plunged the room almost to deep-freeze level.

Wherever the Queen goes, her personal staff gets there ahead of her, whisking through the rooms she will be occupying, altering them around to make them as much like her own apartment at Buckingham Palace as is humanly possible. There is a very practical reason for this. Only if everything is where the Queen normally expects it to be can she hope to adhere to her close-packed timetable.

So her dressing table is always set out with her hairbrushes to the right, clothes brushes to the left, her hand-mirror in the centre with her cosmetic containers in neat regimental rows behind it. Her desk or table top is similarly set out with the blotting pad immediately in front of her, her scarlet-crested notepaper in an upright rack behind, a tray of pencils to the right, a scribbling pad to the left. Her personal dispatch box, which goes with her everywhere, is placed on the far right-hand corner. The travelling chest-of-drawers is placed in her dressing room, with Bobo quickly tidying the drawers and ensuring that fresh handkerchiefs, stockings and similar items are all in their correct place. The clothes the Queen will be wearing for her next engagement are rapidly unpacked, pressed on the folding ironing board which Bobo always brings with her, and laid out in readiness.

The contents of the Queen's cosmetic containers vary according to the country she is visiting and the time of the year when she will be there. For the higher altitudes in India, for instance, she took along a moisturising foundation liquid. For more humid areas she uses a tinted lotion-powder which gives her face a matt appearance lasting for long spells without the need for retouching. In Australia, where she was exposed to blazing sunshine, she used a honey-gold face powder instead of the more customary pink tint.

The question of who does what in the course of a royal tour sometimes causes confusion. In one place where we stayed, apparently no one was instructed to make the Queen's bed. "But I thought the Queen was bringing her own maid," said the local housekeeper when she was asked about it. She looked pointedly at Bobo as she said it. "I am not a housemaid," retorted Bobo indignantly. "I am the Queen's Dresser."

Elsewhere, the Queen's page and I had to take over the task of serving the Queen and others at the top table for an official luncheon. The waitresses who should have done the serving were so overcome with nerves they were in no condition to serve anyone. There was yet another occasion when it would perhaps have been better if we had taken over, though in fact we did not. A wine waiter, too nervous to ask the Queen what she would like to drink, insisted upon thrusting a fresh glass of wine in front of her with each course. As a result, the Queen finished the meal with some six or seven glasses of wine, most of them untouched, jogging her elbow.

At the time of the royal visit to Perth, Australia, there was a poliomyelitis scare in the area, and strict precautions were enforced to ensure that the Queen's health was adequately safeguarded. Instead of staying for six days at Government House

[239]

in Perth, as had been planned, she used the liner *Gothic*, anchored twelve miles away in Fremantle harbour, as a floating headquarters. Whenever she went ashore, everything she might conceivably require—food, drink, table linen, cutlery—was loaded into a refrigerated truck and went along with her. We were serving the Queen a picnic luncheon during one of these shore trips when I was unable to find the cream cheese. The Queen often likes to finish a meal with cream cheese, and I had made sure that some went along with us for this purpose. But the compartment in which it had been stored was now empty. I looked in a number of other compartments without success, then asked the truck driver if he had seen it. He went red with embarrassment. "Seen it?" he said. "I've just eaten it, mate. I didn't know it was for the Queen."

III

Whatever the mode of transport—car or train, ship or plane—it goes almost without saying that the Queen travels in the grandest of grand manners. The Rolls-Royce cars she uses on her provincial tours of Britain must surely be numbered amongst the world's most luxurious vehicles. Their royal maroon coachwork is lovingly and laboriously created from no fewer than twenty coats of paint. They are cleaned and polished meticulously after every journey, however short, even if it is only from the royal mews to the front of the palace and back again. The pristine paintwork is inspected regularly for scratches which are almost unavoidable when the vehicle has to nose its way through tight-packed crowds. Indeed, the Rolls-Royce which Princess Margaret borrowed from her sister for her wedding-day trip from Buckingham Palace to where the royal yacht was moored in the Thames was so badly scarred by the buttons, brooches and handbags of the crowd that it had to be returned to the factory for complete renovation.

The Queen's cars are the only vehicles permitted to use Britain's roads without displaying a registration plate fore and aft. To further identify them they also have a winking blue light, similar to those used by police cars, mounted on the roof. Any car in which the Queen is actually riding also flies her royal standard and has her personal mascot—St. George and the Dragon wrought in silver—mounted on the radiator. In Australia so many royal standards became the property of souvenir-hunters that further supplies had to be flown out from Britain. But no souvenir-hunter is ever likely to acquire the St. George and Dragon mascot. Whenever he leaves the car, if only for a matter of seconds, the Queen's chauffeur, Harry Purvey, carefully unscrews it first and takes it with him.

In addition to a specially angled rear seat which makes the Queen distinctly visible to watching crowds, the Rolls-Royces are also fitted with detachable outer covers. Beneath them is a transparent inner lining which gives a clear view of the interior of the car from all angles. At night the interior is illuminated by fluorescent lighting which the Queen controls from a button beside her seat. Similar buttons give her fingertip control over the windows, the sliding roof, the glass division which separates her from the chauffeur, and an air-conditioning system which can circulate fresh, warm or refrigerated air. Each car is fitted with a push-button radio which she switches on sometimes to hear what the radio commentators are saying about her as she progresses through the crowds, and she was highly amused on one occasion to hear a commentator waxing eloquent over the green outfit she was supposedly wearing, when in fact she was dressed in red. As always, advance details of her outfit had been circulated to press and radio, but for once she had exercised the feminine prerogative of changing her mind at the last moment. The centre arm of the rear seat also conceals a small compartment in which she stores a reserve supply of barley sugar.

When she travels by train, the Queen has a coach to herself. The coach is divided into bedroom, sitting room and bathroom and also includes diminutive compartments for the Queen's Dresser and personal footman. Philip also has a coach of his own, similarly divided. The sitting room of the Queen's coach is comfortably furnished with two armchairs, two matching sofas, a desk at which she can work while travelling, and an occasional table on which there is always a vase of flowers, usually carnations, with a selection of newspapers and magazines, her crossword puzzles, chocolate-coated mints and barley sugar close to hand.

Airliners in which the Queen travels are usually specially adapted to provide her with a royal apartment in miniature. When she flew to New Delhi, for instance, her Comet airliner had its own tiny dining room to seat eight people, as well as a cosy sitting-room with the divans on either side of the sea-blue centre aisle converting into comfortable beds at night. Silver-grey drapes concealed two pint-sized dressing rooms, one for her and one for Philip, each with its own built-in wardrobe.

But of all the modes of transport at the Queen's command, easily the most luxurious is the royal yacht *Britannia* with its royal-blue hull, yellow funnel and a band of gleaming gold off-setting the snowy-white superstructure. Measuring 413 feet from stem to stern, with a mainmast so tall a hinge had to be inserted before it could pass under the bridges of the St. Lawrence Seaway, the royal yacht is nearly half the length of the liner *Queen Elizabeth*. Built at a cost of more than £2 million, it bears as little resemblance to an ordinary yacht as Buckingham Palace does to an ordinary house. It is, in effect, an air-conditioned floating palace, aboard which a wide, grey-carpeted, mahogany staircase leads down to a vast, luxurious drawing room of turquoise-coloured walls, hyacinth-blue carpet, gold drapes and chintz-covered armchairs. The only nautical notes which intrude are the painting of *Britannia*'s launching hanging above the marble fireplace, and a small round table mounted on gimbals to keep it constantly horizontal which came from the old royal yacht *Victoria and Albert*.

When the tall mahogany doors facing the fireplace are folded back, drawing room and anteroom combine into one vast water-borne reception hall in which as many as two hundred guests have been hosted at a time. The adjoining dining room with its ebony-edged dining table is similarly magnificent, with sliding panels which part to reveal a large-sized screen enabling the room to serve also as a private movie theatre. The mahogany sideboards which flank the walls, like the Hepplewhite chairs around the dining table, also came from the old *Victoria and Albert*. In contemporary contrast are the candelabra spaced at intervals along the table, which draw their source of illumination from the ingenious electrified runner on which they stand, an idea originating in the inventive brain of Philip's uncle, Earl Mountbatten of Burma. The table itself was originally designed to seat thirty-two people, but Philip, after taking a train-load of the palace staff to Portsmouth for a dummy run when the yacht was first fitted out, decided that this number was insufficient and had removable wings added to seat a further twenty-eight guests should occasion arise. Adjoining the dining room is the Royal Family's private kitchen, presided over when the yacht is at sea by Ronald Aubrey, the genial head chef from Buckingham Palace.

The Queen and Prince Philip each have a private sitting room leading off the anteroom. The Queen's room is essentially feminine, with white panelling, moss-green carpet, silk-shaded wall lamps and curtains of rosebud chintz. Philip's room, with teak-panelled walls, grey carpeting, functional lighting and a concealed cocktail cabinet, is contrastingly masculine. A model of the frigate *Magpie*, which he commanded during the closing stages of his naval career, stands in an illuminated case let into the panelling above the electric fire. Each sitting room is fitted with a built-in desk—the Queen's inlaid with green leather, Philip's with red—and telephones and an intercommunication system similar to that which serves Buckingham Palace. An electric elevator connects the sitting rooms with the royal bedrooms—they are too luxurious to be classed merely as cabins—on the deck above. Here too is a wardrobe room for the Queen's clothes, cabins for her dressers and Prince Philip's valet, and, looking out over the stern, a glass-enclosed sun lounge where the royal travellers breakfast beneath a large map on which the previous day's run is recorded.

The windows of the royal sleeping quarters are set at such a level that members of the crew, passing outside in the rubber-soled plimsolls they wear to reduce noise aboard ship, are unable to see in. The royal rooms are fitted with beds, not bunks, and, like the other rooms, are equipped with air conditioning. The Queen's room has a built-in wardrobe and is fitted with a long, low dressing table, rubber-topped to prevent brushes and combs slipping about unduly, which is fastened to the wall by large metal hooks at either end. When the Queen paid her state visit to Sweden, however, the North Sea was so rough and the yacht, not yet fitted with stabilisers, rolled so violently that the dressing table broke free from its moorings in the night, slid across the cabin and collided with the Queen's bed. Members of the crew were hurriedly summoned to re-fasten the dressing table to the wall while the Queen looked on in her dressing gown. "I thought we were under attack," she joked with Bobo. Even so, she fared rather better than her great-grandmother, Queen Alexandra, who was crossing the North Sea in the old *Victoria and Albert* when a sudden lurch sent her, her chair and her tea-things flying right across the dining saloon.

But however luxurious and comfortable the mode of travel, a royal tour or state visit is still a quite exhausting experience. To keep pace with her tightly packed schedule, the Queen will start at eight A.M. and still be on the go at one, two or even three o'clock the following morning. In between all the official engagements she still has to find time for her official papers and correspondence, as well as to change from one outfit to another in intervals which are sometimes far too short.

Open the official programme for any royal tour at almost any page and you would be surprised at the meticulousness of the arrangements and the intricacy of the timing. Let us look at the detail for just one day. It happens to be in Canada, but it could have been anywhere in the world.

10 A.M. Eastern Standard Time	Royal Party disembarks from the Royal Barge. The Mayors of Port Arthur and Fort William are presented.
10.05	The Queen and the Duke of Edinburgh enter an automobile and leave for a drive through Port Arthur.
10.08	Arrive St. Joseph's Hospital.
10.13	Leave St. Joseph's Hospital.
10.23	Arrive General Hospital.
10.28	Leave General Hospital. Drive past Dawson Court and the Ontario Hospital with brief stop to meet the Superintendent. Thence to Hillcrest Park. Brief stop.
11.00	Arrive at City Stadium. The Queen accepts a bouquet. The Mayor presents members of the City Council and their wives together with the Reeves of adjacent municipalities and their wives.
11.15	Re-enter automobile and leave for Fort William.
11.30	The Queen and the Duke of Edinburgh arrive at the boundary of Fort William and are received by the Mayor. Slow drive south on May Street to Victoria Avenue, west on Victoria Avenue to Brodie Street, east on Brodie Street to Donald Street, east on Donald Street to May Street, north on May Street to the Royal Edward Hotel.
11.45	Arrive at the Royal Edward Hotel. The President of the hotel conducts the Royal Party to their suite.
12.15 P.M.	The Mayors of Fort William and Port Arthur call for Her Majesty and His Royal Highness and conduct them to the Norman Room for a luncheon given by the cities of Fort William and Port Arthur. The Mayors each read an Address of Welcome and present it to Her Majesty.
1.40	The Queen and the Duke of Edinburgh leave for Chapple Recreation Centre. Slow drive north on May Street to Victoria Avenue, west on Victoria Avenue

to Syndicate Avenue, south on Syndicate Avenue to Ridgeway Street, west on Ridgeway to McKellar General Hospital. The Mayor presents the Administrator who presents the Matron and the President of the Medical Staff. The Queen and the Duke of Edinburgh re-enter their automobile. Slow drive west on Kingsway to Vickers, north on Vickers to Arthur Street, west on Arthur Street to Franklin Street, north on Franklin Street to Victoria Avenue, west on Victoria Avenue to Chapple Recreation Centre.

2.10   The Queen and the Duke of Edinburgh proceed to a special platform where they sign the City Guest Register. The Mayor presents officials and citizens of Fort William and their wives. Her Majesty accepts a bouquet.

2.15   The Queen and the Duke of Edinburgh see a Pony League baseball game and an exhibition of Canadian square dancing.

2.20   Her Majesty and His Royal Highness enter a jeep and are driven round the arena.

2.25   The Queen and the Duke of Edinburgh re-enter their automobile. Slow drive west on Victoria Avenue to Lillie Street, north on Lillie Street to Grandview Lodge Home for Aged, circle entrance and proceed north to turning basin at Fort William Sanatorium.

2.30   Leave for airport. Slow drive south on Lillie Street to Arthur Street, west on Arthur to Lakehead Airport.

2.45   Arrive airport. The Mayors of Fort William and Port Arthur say farewell.

2.50   The Queen and the Duke of Edinburgh emplane.

3.00   Royal plane leaves.

4.35 P.M. Mountain Standard Time   Royal plane arrives McCall Field, Calgary Municipal Airport. The Queen and the Duke of Edinburgh are received by the Minister of Agriculture who presents the Mayor of Calgary. The Queen and the Duke of Edinburgh sign the Distinguished Visitors' Book.

[246]

4.45	The Queen and the Duke of Edinburgh enter an automobile and drive to Southern Alberta Jubilee Auditorium. Fast drive to 32nd Avenue, slow thereafter.
5.20	Arrive Auditorium where a children's programme is in progress. The Queen accepts a bouquet.
5.40	The Queen and the Duke of Edinburgh leave for Fort Calgary House. Slow drive 10th Street N.W., 9th Street S.W., 8th Avenue and 2nd Street east.
6.05	Arrive Fort Calgary House at entrance to Exhibition and Stampede Grounds. The President of the Calgary Stampede is presented. Following presentations the Queen and the Duke of Edinburgh proceed to rooms reserved for their use for a brief rest and tea.
6.25	Leave Fort Calgary House for the Garden where the Mayor presents a number of citizens.
6.30	Walk from Fort Calgary House through an Indian village.
6.50	Leave for Grandstand.
6.55	Arrive at the Grandstand and watch chuck wagon races.
7.00	Her Majesty accepts an Address of Welcome from the citizens of Calgary.
7.30	The Queen and the Duke of Edinburgh re-enter their automobile and leave for the Barbecue.
——	Leave Barbecue for the Royal Train at Her Majesty's pleasure.

So there you are. One day of a royal tour ... except in the finer detail, exactly like the day before and the day to follow. Many people would find it monotonous and boring in the extreme. Strangely enough, the Queen does not. The pity of it is that she so seldom permits her inner enthusiasm to show in her face. It is often said that the Queen does not smile enough as she performs her royal duty, and this is true. Yet the truly surprising thing, to those who know what a royal tour is really like, is that she should contrive to remain so fresh and unjaded while submitting to so hectic and congested a schedule.

When I accompanied the Queen on the six-month round-the-world tour which followed her coronation, the pace was so terrific that I came back twenty pounds lighter than when I went. The Queen herself, though she does what she can to ease the strain, is noticeably trimmer in the figure and looks somewhat tired around the eyes at the end of a royal tour of any considerable duration.

Experience has taught her a number of tricks to help conserve her resources as a tour progresses. For her, one of the more considerable strains is the excessive amount of handshaking to which she must submit—literally thousands of handshakes in the course of a single day. The Queen eases the strain by always wearing gloves—otherwise her hands would be rubbed raw—and by proffering only the first three fingers of her hand in as relaxed a manner as possible. But even this cannot always guard against the nervous or excited attitude of those she is greeting, and there was an occasion in Australia when the Queen winced visibly as her small delicate hand was pulped in the vice-like grip of a professional sheep-shearer. Similarly, she makes use of an armrest whenever possible to ease the strain of the continuous royal wave.

Back aboard the royal train after a whistle stop, the first thing she does is to kick off her shoes and sit full-length on a settee to ease her aching leg muscles. A triple blast on the whistle, however, is the pre-arranged signal that there are people lining the track ahead. Without bothering to replace her shoes, she dashes in stockinged feet to the observation platform ready to return a greeting. And even when she has her feet up she is never completely idle. She will fill in time by pegging away at her correspondence or relax with a crossword puzzle. Philip, by contrast, prefers to stretch out full-length, with a cushion for a pillow, and cat-nap. He has a trick of waking to the minute without the necessity for setting an alarm or being called.

While she realises the necessity of it, the Queen herself, I think, is sometimes mildly amused by the meticulousness of the planning which goes on around her. During an official luncheon in Australia she happened to notice that her programme showed the meal as finishing at two o'clock but that she was not scheduled to leave until 2.17. For once the oddness of the timing piqued her curiosity, and she inquired about it. It was explained at some length that it would take her exactly seventeen minutes to leave the table, walk to the main door of the building, shaking hands as she went, and take her leave; it had all been paced out, rehearsed and timed in advance. The Queen could not resist one of her rare quips. "I hope I don't spill my coffee," she said. "It looks as though I won't have time for another cup."

But not even the most meticulous royal timetable can allow for everything, and there was an occasion when the Queen's schedule was thrown completely out of gear for some minutes by—of all things—an attack of hiccups. She was in the process of changing clothes for her next engagement when the attack seized her. In vain, Bobo MacDonald tried every conceivable cure she could think of, from getting the Queen to drink a glass of water to slamming a door suddenly behind her to make her jump with surprise. But the time for departure came with the Queen still hiccuping away like mad.

"Her Majesty can't possibly go like this," Bobo said to me. "You'd better tell the Equerry that there will be a delay."

"Has she tried drinking water with her thumbs in her ears?" I asked.

Bobo looked puzzled. I explained the old country cure to her in detail. You fill a glass with water. You then pick up the glass with your fingers in such a manner that you can seal the ears with the balls of your thumbs. With the ears sealed in this fashion, you drink the contents of the glass at a single draught without pausing to draw breath.

"Well, we might as well try it," said Bobo. "Nothing else works." And she disappeared into the Queen's bedroom.

It was a few minutes before the Queen finally emerged from her bedroom. She was no longer hiccuping.

"It worked," she said, delightedly. "Thank you very much." She gave an impish smile and added, "I suppose you'll want me to give you a royal warrant as Purveyor of a Cure for Hiccups."

10.

MONARCHY AND THE MODERN WORLD

I

SHORTLY before his own enforced abdication, the late King Farouk of Egypt made a curiously prophetic remark: "Soon there will be only five kings left ... the kings of diamonds, hearts, spades and clubs—and England."

In a century which has seen the eroding away of many thrones, with others so precariously perched they seem destined to topple, Britain's monarchy—in the person of a regally upright, always punctual, rather serious-looking wife and mother who dotes on dogs and horses, abhors smoking but enjoys barley sugar, prefers orange squash to champagne and tweeds to mink, and consistently declines to glamourise herself on the grounds that "I am not a film star"—continues to defy social change at home and political upheaval in the world at large.

True, the world estate over which Queen Elizabeth II now reigns—she can hardly be said to rule—has shrunk considerably and will doubtless go on shrinking. Grants of self-government to developing countries and the forced withdrawal from one-time outposts of empire have eliminated much of the power and grandeur which Britain forged for itself in the days of Elizabeth's great-great-grandmother. Victoria's long reign saw Britain complete the conquest of India, the settlement of Australia and New Zealand, and the acquisition—by conquest, diplomacy or purchase—of such additional territories as South Africa and Burma, Cyprus and the Gold Coast, Aden and Hong Kong.

Other times, other ways. Since Victoria's great-great-granddaughter celebrated her twenty-first birthday, the Union Jack has been hauled down in more than twenty territories. The inscription "Ind. Imp." (Emperor of India) no longer appears on the coins which bear her image, as it did on those minted at the outset of her father's reign. And much of Britain's one-time colonial empire in Africa and Asia has switched from royalism to republicanism.

Of the twenty-six countries of the Commonwealth (with two more scheduled for independence by the time this book is published), Elizabeth remains Queen of twelve, including Britain, Canada, Australia and New Zealand. The remaining fourteen acknowledge her as "Head of the Commonwealth." So, in one guise or the other, as Queen or Head of the Commonwealth, she is still the symbolic figurehead of some 750 million people occupying ten million square miles of the earth's surface.

But to the people of South Africa, where she made her historic declaration of dedication on her twenty-first birthday, she is neither Queen nor "Head." South Africa has not only gone republican, it has pulled out of the Commonwealth. And neighbouring Rhodesia, after its unilateral declaration of independence, found itself in the anomalous position of claiming still to recognise the Queen while boycotting the Governor appointed by her. Elizabeth showed what she thought of that curious state of affairs by making the Governor a Knight Commander of the Royal Victorian Order, significantly one of the few honours she can still bestow as a personal gift.

In Britain, it has been said, a single Beatle can today attract a bigger crowd than Queen Elizabeth II. Even if this is true—

which I doubt—it would be a juvenile crowd. Pop singers and girl models may rank as Britain's new nobility, but Elizabeth remains pre-eminent for the respect, esteem and affection in which she is held by the vast bulk of the population at all levels. There may be a small hard core who regard Queen and monarchy alike as expensive anachronisms, but opinion polls still show a three-to-one vote in favour of monarchy and have even revealed a three-in-ten minority of the population who still cling doggedly to the old belief in the Divine Right of Kings (and presumably Queens). Even among the younger generation, the voting is still two-to-one on the side of monarchy, while a recent canvas found teenagers nominating the Queen as the person they most admired (after their own parents).

The fact is that Britain's monarchy sits more four-square and rock-steady today than it did in Victorian and Edwardian times. There was a point in Queen Victoria's reign when it seemed briefly doubtful whether her playboy son, the Prince of Wales, would be permitted to succeed her. He did succeed her, as Edward VII, but held out little hope that the monarchy would long survive, even going so far as to say that his son would probably be England's last king.

Curiously, it was that same son, George V, who was to swing public opinion stolidly in favour of monarchy. It was during the reign of this bearded father-figure that people first began to think of the monarchy in terms of a royal *family*, a development Walter Bagehot, the eminent Victorian historian, had foreseen.

Bagehot wrote in his book, *The English Constitution*, "A family on the throne is an interesting idea also. It brings down the idea of sovereignty to the level of petty life. No feeling could seem more childish than the enthusiasm of the English at the marriage of the Prince of Wales. They treated as a great political event what, looked at as a matter of pure business, was very small indeed. But no feeling could be more like common human nature as it is and as it is likely to be. The women—one half of the human race at least—care fifty times more for a marriage than a ministry."

Bagehot, of course, was referring to the marriage of the Prince of Wales who ascended the throne as Edward VII. But when the time comes for the present Prince of Wales to marry, history will almost certainly repeat itself.

The interlude of the abdication, though it may have dented the family image a little, did not finally shatter it, and it was still there for George VI to pick up and enhance as a respectable, God-fearing family man with a winsome Scots wife and two quite adorable daughters.

The Queen, in her turn, projected the same warm image of family life when she succeeded to the throne. She had other advantages, too . . . youthfulness, a Greek god of a husband, two small children, and the national—indeed, worldwide—sympathy felt for her after the tragic death of her overworked father. The result was a wholesale and perhaps slightly unwholesome adulation which could not and did not last.

Adulation has today given way to esteem and affection. But it is affection from a distance. The idea that the monarchy has drawn closer to the people in recent times is a myth. The Queen and her family have become more widely publicised, but that is not the same thing.

Those who may have hoped that the dawning of a new Elizabethan era would also witness a considerable democratisation of the monarchy have been largely due for disappointment. Except in the finer details, it continues to rumble along much the same as ever . . . lofty, grand, remote . . . and most Britons prefer it that way.

There has been some slight streamlining of royal ceremonial, some slight widening in the variety of people the Queen gets to meet, though the resulting conversations are usually brief and superficial. In a day and age when the Queen can fly from London to Ottawa more quickly than she can chug north by train from Buckingham Palace to Balmoral, there has been much more travelling.

The Queen's remoteness stems not from the fact that people cannot get to see her—her world-wide travels and the spread of television have enabled millions more to see her than ever saw her father or grandfather—but from the fact that few people outside the immediate circle of her family and friends have the slightest idea of the sort of person she really is or what makes her tick. Philip's public image does give some sort of idea of the man within. In a television interview not long ago, for instance, he had this to say, "People say this is a permissive society, but we live in the most regimented society ever in this country. You have practically to have a licence to breathe." And when an orang-utan at London Zoo treated him in a considerably undignified fashion, Philip told the whole world about it in blunt words: "He widdled all over me." When Philip comes out with things like that, people feel they know him and identify with him.

The Queen has never been able to project herself in this fashion . . . nor, if the truth is known, has she any wish to do so. Over the years she has made some small concessions to her critics. While still clinging to her favourite tweeds in private, she is at some pains to dress more fashionably in public. With Philip's help—and that of a tape-recorder—she now manages to "deliver" her speeches rather than merely trot them out parrot-fashion. As opportunity has served, she has introduced a less blue-blooded, more professional type of adviser into the small team of top brass who stage-manage her public and private life.

Yet she remains as remote as ever, and perhaps the real reason for this lies in the unreal and isolated life she leads. Cut off from everyday life, her few contacts with it abundantly cushioned, she and her advisers are inclined to think that the world begins and ends at the palace railings. Even those who enter the royal circle from outside usually soon succumb to its cloying atmosphere and, to an extent, this has been true even of Prince Philip. He is no longer the royal rebel he seemed in earlier times. Then, it seemed possible that he might take the monarchy and mould it in his own contemporary image. But this he has done only in the occasional small detail. For the most part, he himself has been taken over by the monarchy and been moulded after its fashion.

Yet, in fairness, it is difficult to imagine what the Queen might do to render her life less remote and more democratic, even if she had the inclination to do so. Her uncle, the Duke of Windsor, during the brief period when he was King Edward VIII, once tried walking across the few yards of road which separate Buckingham Palace from the Duchy of Cornwall office. This simple act caused so much excitement and controversy that he never repeated the experiment. The Queen's car is sometimes so scratched and scarred after a comparatively short drive through milling crowds that it has to go back to the factory for an expensive repaint job.

At Balmoral, a few years back, the Queen and her mother organized a charity sale in aid of the local church, with members of the royal family helping out at the various stalls. So great was the resulting crush that children were knocked flat, women were hurt, and the rear of the Queen's tent was ripped apart by frustrated sensation-seekers unable to get in at the front. In all this chaos, the Queen, who had removed her tweed coat for greater comfort, intervened only just in the nick of time to prevent the coat being sold. She was concerned not so much with the coat as with the diamond love-knot brooch which was pinned to it. "Hi, my brooch," she cried, grabbing coat and brooch back.

With this in mind, it is not difficult to visualise what would happen if the Queen tried to make a casual stroll through Hyde Park or went window-shopping along Oxford Street. It is all very well to say, as I have heard it said, that the public would soon become accustomed to such behaviour and take it for granted. I doubt it. Long before the experiment could go that far, the police would have to be called out to rescue a harassed Queen from a throng of over-loyal Britons and over-excited tourists.

So the Queen wisely confines her walking to the lonely acres of Balmoral and the sanctity of the palace gardens. Her shopping is similarly restricted to one or two pre-Christmas jaunts to fashionable stores with the manager showing her round and her personal detective never very far away. Her public appearances, except that they are rather more frequent, remain as formal and ordained as her grandfather's were in his day.

Yet is this not perhaps as it should be? Even in the modern world, surely a monarch must remain entirely regal even if this involves being remote from those over whom she reigns. It was Walter Bagehot, again, who wrote, "Above all this our royalty is to be reverenced and if you begin to poke about it you cannot reverence it. When there is a select committee on the Queen, the charm of royalty will be gone. Its mystery is its life. We must not let daylight in upon magic." He was writing about Queen Victoria, of course. But what he wrote applies almost equally to her great-great-granddaughter.

Undoubtedly I am biased because of my years in the Queen's service, but the idea of what is commonly called a "Scandinavian-type" monarchy, with kings and queens shopping in supermarkets or riding about the streets on bicycles (if, indeed, that is how they go on), holds no appeal for me. I would far rather the Queen should glide by in a stately Rolls or a lumbering coach drawn by elegant greys than have her queue for buses and rub shoulders with those who shop in Oxford Street stores. Bicycle-riding and bus-queueing might result in a brief spate of greater popularity—and give the photographers a succession of field-days—but they are actions not calculated to enhance royal dignity and prestige. And without its dignity and prestige ... without its remoteness ... monarchy, as Bagehot said, becomes meaningless.

II

While the institution of monarchy has changed little in the years since Queen Elizabeth II succeeded to the throne, there have been considerable changes in the Royal Family's private life ... particularly concerning the upbringing of the children. These changes mark the beginning of a trend which will have a considerable effect upon the monarchy of the future and even, perhaps, on the very future of the monarchy in Britain.

History shows clearly that the relationships between earlier British monarchs and those destined to succeed them were not always of the happiest. George V may have emerged as a father-figure to the British nation, but he was hardly a good father to his own sons. It was he who blew the gaff on the relationship between royal parents and their offspring when he confided to a friend, "My father was frightened of his mother; I was frightened of my father; and I'm damned well going to see to it that my children are frightened of me."

He succeeded only too well, and the lifelong stutter from which George VI suffered has been attributed, in part at least, to the tension which seized him whenever he was summoned to his father's study.

Queen Victoria disapproved of her son, the Prince of Wales who became Edward VII, refused to let him play his proper part in royal life and neglected to train him for his role as future king. Edward, you would have thought, would have learned his lesson. He didn't, and his son, George V, never really understood him. George V, in turn, stands condemned as a parent out of his own mouth, and not until the advent of George VI do we find the doctrine that royal children should be frightened of their parents being finally discarded.

Both as Duke of York and, later, as King George VI, Elizabeth's father did all he could to ensure that his daughters enjoyed a warm, happy and secure upbringing. Indeed, one of his main worries when he became King was that it might make a difference to the family relationship. But because he was the type of man he was, it didn't. To the day he died the relationship between the King and his daughters was warm and close.

The Queen, in turn, has ensured the same sort of warm, happy, secure upbringing for her own children. She has done more. Under Philip's guidance, she is contriving that her children's upbringing should be as down-to-earth and "ordinary" as is humanly possible for royal youngsters.

It was Philip who suggested sending Prince Charles to a boys' boarding school where he would have to learn to live with other kids on their own terms. Left to her own devices, Elizabeth would hardly have thought of such a thing. The idea of "schooldays" is something outside the rather limited range of her own experience. Her own schooling consisted of easygoing lessons from a private governess, plus occasional outings to Eton College for constitutional-history classes in which she was the only pupil.

In many ways, the Queen's knowledge of ordinary everyday life is extremely limited. Except for two brief childhood trips, one on a London bus and the other on the subway, she has never in her life travelled as an ordinary ticket-holding passenger. Except for formal, official visits, she has never been in a chain store or supermarket. Except for specially-organised pre-Christmas excursions to select stores, with a detective at her heels and the store manager at her side to conduct her round, she has never been shopping. Until she was required to do so at the official opening of a new telephone exchange a few years ago, she had never dialled a telephone; her calls are normally either by direct line or dialled for her. Except for the one-pound note she puts into the collection bag when she goes to church, she never handles money. In consequence, though she may and can put an expert value on an old painting or a thoroughbred colt, she has no idea of the cost of living.

By contrast, she is bringing up her children to have a much broader knowledge of life as it is lived in the big world outside the palace railings. Charles has been to both boarding school and university. He has travelled as a fare-paying passenger by rail and plane. Anne, similarly, has spent four years at a girls' boarding school. When she first went there, faced with the task of making her own bed, she confessed that she had no idea how to go about it and was forced to look on helplessly while the other girls showed her how it was done. Charles, when he first went to school, had little or no idea what money was. Why should he have had? As a small boy, he seldom handled it. To-day, both Charles and Anne think nothing of doing their own shopping. Not long ago, a tall, fair-haired girl breezed into a chain store in Oxford Street, produced a blouse she had purchased at the store and asked them to change it for her. She had tried it on when she got home and found it too small, she said. The girl was Princess Anne and the "home" was Buckingham Palace. Similarly, Charles, shopping for some neckties, was shown a selection of hand-painted ones. He shook his head. They were "too expensive," he said. And purchasing an umbrella from a chain store in Cambridge, he was quick to spot that he had been given the wrong change and asked for the balance. His mother would not have paid cash in the first place and would certainly not have known whether the change she was given was right or wrong.

In many ways, their years at school have had a value for the royal youngsters far outweighing the actual academic learning involved. Schooldays have taught them how the rest of the world lives, have enabled them to experience something of the give and take of ordinary, everyday life. True, the schools selected for them were expensive ones and relatively exclusive on that account. But this has by no means rendered the ex-periment less valid or less successful. Youngsters from the middle and upper brackets can be just as rough, upon occasion, as those drawn from any other section of society, as Charles quickly discovered when he turned out to play rugby football at Gordonstoun. For him, there was no special protection such as was afforded his grandfather half a century earlier. When the Queen's father played football in boyhood, his tutor's whistle soon shrilled to halt the game if there seemed the slightest danger that he might sustain a hard knock or a sharp hack on the shin. No such molly-coddling was accorded Charles at Gordonstoun. On the contrary, he not infrequently found himself playing against boys only too eager to boast that they had rubbed the future king's face in the mud. The result was that he was tackled harder and more frequently than any other player on the field, and was brought down so heavily on one occasion that he sustained a broken nose. Not surprisingly, Charles did not really enjoy his games of football, and it says much for his strength of character that he continued to play ... perhaps as much as anything because he wanted to be the sort of youngster he thought his father wanted him to be.

Philip had several motives for winkling Charles out of the royal nursery and having him buzzed off to boarding school. As a parent, he wanted the boy to experience and enjoy some degree of ordinary schooling and ordinary boyhood before being finally subordinated to an endless round of royal chores. As the Queen's consort, he saw clearly that a broader outlook and wider experience were necessities for any future monarch if the monarchy was to fulfill a worthwhile function. As a man, he wanted his eldest son, for all that he bore his mother's name of Windsor, to be moulded in his own image, and how better to achieve that than by sending him to the selfsame schools he himself had attended in boyhood?

Charles, at the time he was first sent to school, was already showing signs of succumbing to the cloying, introverted atmosphere which pervades the palace. It could hardly have been otherwise. His upbringing and education, so far, had followed much the same pattern as his mother's before him. A sitting room on the nursery floor had been converted into a schoolroom by the simple introduction of a blackboard and easel, and a governess had been engaged to give him lessons. Initially, Charles had his lessons alone. Later the class doubled in size with the addition of Princess Anne.

As can be imagined, the boy, at this stage of his development, was the object of considerable petticoat influence. His small sister, Anne, was almost his only playmate. With his father so frequently away, he lived in an almost exclusively feminine world consisting of his mother, his nanny and his governess. Politeness was drilled into him to an almost excessive extent. Except on holidays at Sandringham and Balmoral, he scarcely knew what it was to run wild . . . and such running wild as he was permitted even there was of a relatively genteel nature. His natural boyishness was stifled. Even so small an adventure as scrambling out of bed early in the morning and slipping along to the footmen's room to help brew the morning pot of tea came to an end as soon as his nanny got wind of it. As a result of this, Charles was growing up to be shy and over-serious, spoilt and precocious. The shyness and seriousness were perhaps part of his natural inheritance. The rest was induced by his environment.

One incident illustrates both the precociousness and almost excessive politeness typical of his behaviour at this time. It was while the Royal Family were travelling north by train to Balmoral. Charles came into the compartment in which several of us, members of the Queen's staff, were relaxing. "Please," he said, "don't bother to stand up." A rather lofty remark from a youngster of seven or eight.

Prince Philip always speaks of his schooldays as being "among the happiest days of my life." For Charles, by contrast, they were never really enjoyable . . . seldom easy, sometimes boring, occasionally unhappy. Yet however little he may have enjoyed them, he certainly benefited from them . . . even if he did not appreciate the fact at the time. Arriving home at the palace for vacations he was noticeably less shy, more independent, less precocious, more self-reliant. He was physically hardier and less preoccupied, though still of an inherently serious nature.

Schooldays were undoubtedly tougher on him than on an ordinary youngster. However much his parents may have urged that he should be treated as an ordinary boy, the undeniable fact was that he was someone special and everyone with whom he came into contact was conscious of the fact. They could hardly have been otherwise with a royal detective moving into residence at the school to keep an eye on his charge. As a result, masters and boys varied between two extremes. Some regarded him with awe and kept their distance. Others—like the boys who went onto the rugby pitch with the vowed intention of "hammering" him, and the master at Gordonstoun who always addressed him either as "Windsor" or "Charlie-boy"—went out of their way to take him down a peg. Hardly anyone adopted a middle course. The few boys who did make friendly overtures were quickly labelled "suckers" and "crawlers" by their school-fellows, and perhaps in some cases the nickname was justified. As a result, during his years at school Charles made very few friends and none of them either quickly or easily.

Anne, by contrast, thoroughly enjoyed her years at Benenden. Partly this was due to the fact that the environment of a girls' school is essentially different from that of a boys'. No one tried to rub her nose in the mud during schoolgirl games of hockey. Mainly, however, it was due to the fact that Anne has inherited her father's open manner and complete lack of self-consciousness, rather than her mother's seriousness and reserve. More easily than Charles she could meet her schoolmates on level terms. She made friends easily and quickly. She skipped nimbly along the narrow tightrope which separates royal dignity from ordinary childhood. Charles found this more difficult—indeed, almost impossible. Just as his mother, on or off duty, is nearly always the Queen, so Charles, in or out of school, was nearly always the Prince of Wales. Anne, by contrast, finds no difficulty in acting sometimes as Princess Anne and sometimes simply as Anne Windsor. "Dance properly," she has been known to tell a boy with whom she was dancing. "Don't treat me as though I'm a piece of Dresden china."

However little Charles may have enjoyed his schooldays, they provided opportunities for him to find out about himself. He discovered, among other things, that he had a talent for singing and acting. As a result, he sang the part of the Pirate King in a school production of *The Pirates of Penzance*, and played the title role in *Macbeth*. Eminently fitting though such roles were for a future King, Charles himself had a hankering for something different . . . "a part in which I can make a legiti-mate fool of myself." His spell at Trinity College, Cambridge, which followed Gordonstoun, gave him the opportunity: the role of the vicar in the Joe Orton comedy, *Erpingham Camp*. Initially, at Trinity, Charles read archeology and anthropology, obtaining an upper second pass (60-66 percent) in Part 1 of his Tripos. Later, towards fitting himself for his future role in public life, he switched to reading social and political history. In several different ways, Cambridge broadened his horizons still further. He went on a "dig" with a mixed group of archeological students, sleeping in a puptent, living on a diet of stews and steamed puddings, and shaving in cold water. He took his cello along to Trinity College Chapel to play in a recital given by the college orchestra. He judged a beauty contest of mini-skirted students; he wrote an article for the university newspaper, *Varsity*.

In the article, recording his first impression of college life, he mentioned the fact that he found himself awakened at seven o'clock in the morning by the resounding clang of garbage cans being emptied and the lusty refrain of "Come All Ye Faithful" intoned by one of the garbage collectors. There were two interesting sequels. The time for collecting garbage was put back to nine o'clock to avoid disturbing him, and the singing garbage collector was promptly placed under contract by a leading recording company.

His grandfather, the late King George VI, when he was at Trinity, lived a segregated life in a specially rented house some distance from the college. Charles, by contrast, "lived in," occupying two rooms on a stair shared with about ten other students, most of whom he invited to his rooms at one time or another for student discussions. He ate his meals in hall with the other students. When he needed time off for royal duties, he asked permission like any other student—and made the time up later. About his only privilege of any consequence was a bathroom of his own instead of sharing.

Throughout childhood and into his teens, Charles hero-worshipped his tall, forthright, athletic father and did his best to model himself upon him. As a small boy, he would strut around with his hands clasped behind his back in imitation of a favourite stance of Prince Philip's. To some extent, he still copies his father, as witness his recently acquired trick of conversing with one hand stuffed deep in his coat pocket. He has inherited his father's habit of asking innumerable, and sometimes knotty, questions, but lightning quips come less easily and spontaneously to him than they do to Philip. On his first day at Trinity College someone in the watching crowd called out, "Good luck, Charles." For all his grin, there was perhaps a small, hard core of truth in Charles' retort. "I'll need it," he called back. Philip would have come up with something a good deal sharper and wittier. Indeed, in many ways, Charles is more his mother's son than his father's, a Coburg rather than a Mountbatten ... shy where Philip is thrusting, serious where his father is witty, ploddingly painstaking as against quick and clever.

While he still hero-worships his father to a more limited degree, he is completely devoted to his mother, and between them you will often see the same quick, affectionate exchange of glances, the same unspoken exchange of secret thoughts, that I remember so well between the Queen and her father.

Anne, by contrast, is more her father's daughter than her mother's. She has inherited his forthrightness, his ready wit and the occasional arrogance which sometimes shows through. "Are you referring to Her Majesty the Queen?" she asked pointedly of someone who had made a casual reference to "your mother." Charles, however, merely scowled and said nothing when a friend made a wisecrack about getting Charles "to invite you home, meet Anne and get her to marry you. Then you'll be all right."

Anne, when smaller, was quite possessive in her relationship with her father and capable of flying into a tantrum if he paid more attention to someone else than he did to her. The passage of the years has reduced her attitude to more reasonable proportions. Yet it is to her father rather than her mother that she goes with her teenage problems, and she is still capable of displaying all the signs of almost childish delight if he accords her a few words of praise. She is a tall, angular, tomboyish girl who loves horses and enjoys messing about with boats, looking more at home in a sweater and jeans than ever she does in a dress or suit. For public occasions she is still influenced by her mother in matters of dress, and the Queen makes the same mistake as her mother made before her. As a result, Anne in public often dresses older than her years, as the Queen so often did when she was Princess Elizabeth. But in private Anne has a casual wardrobe which includes most of the latest fads of London's swinging younger set . . . mini-skirts (though not too mini), hipster trousers, jazzy sweaters, trouser suits and ribbed stockings.

In the pony-jumping competitions which she enters from time to time, she puts her mount over the jumps with the same dash and daring, the same hell-for-leather verve, that her father displays on the polo field. "I don't know how she dare," gasped her mother, no mean shakes on a horse herself, on one occasion when she watched Anne going over the jumps.

In their relationships with the opposite sex, both Charles and Anne tend to be hamstrung by their birth and background. Anne has been permitted to go out with boys since she was about seventeen, but usually in groups of four or six young people. Her boy-friends, for the most part, are the sons of people who know her parents well or fairly well. Only rarely is she permitted to go out alone with a young man, and then the two of them are never completely alone. A royal detective rides in the back of the car in which the boy-friend collects Anne and takes her home again, and sits stolidly at an adjoining table as the two youngsters dine by candlelight at some discreet Chelsea restaurant. But Anne is her father's daughter, and the odds are that royal detectives will have as tricky a task keeping tabs on her in the future as they did with her aunt, Princess Margaret, when she was young and unmarried.

But with Charles there are unlikely to be any such problems. He is his mother's son and the chances of his doing anything which might reflect upon his royal position, however slightly, are extremely remote. Like Anne, he tends to go out socially with small mixed groups, fighting shy of a more romantic two-some which might serve as fodder for the gossip columnists. For the most part, the girls he goes out with are either friends of Anne's or daughters of his mother's friends, and very probably it is from this small, tight circle that Britain's next queen will come.

There is little or no chance of Charles marrying a girl from a European royal house, as his predecessors once did, if only because there are few European royalties still in existence, and none at all with a daughter in the right age-group. Theoretically, he could marry almost anyone he wished provided she was of good character. His bride need not be English. She could be Scottish (as the Queen Mother is) or Welsh. She could be European, American, or from one of the countries of the Commonwealth. But if she was a Catholic, then under ancient British law she could not reign as queen. And as both the Duke of Windsor and Princess Margaret found out, she could not be a divorcee, however innocent. If she were, history would assuredly repeat itself and his younger brother, Andrew, would step into the regal shoes. The British are still that hidebound by institution and convention.

If Charles was the son that the Queen had to ensure the succession to the throne, and Anne has turned out to be more her father's daughter than her mother's, then Andrew, the third of the royal children, was surely the child the Queen had for herself. As a young bride and mother, for various reasons, she missed out on many of the joys of motherhood. After Charles was born, she was torn between a desire to be with the baby and a conflicting desire to be with Philip, at that time a naval officer based in Malta. Malta won. Following Anne's birth, motherhood was frequently interrupted by the necessity for Elizabeth to make trips and tours on behalf of her sick father. Then came her own succession to the Throne, with all the new duties it entailed, something to absorb and consume her completely in the initial apprenticeship stage.

But by the time Andrew was born she was an experienced

monarch who could take royal duties in stride. The major foreign tours of the new reign were already behind her. She could afford time out to play mother to the full. She cut down on public appearances and similar engagements and concentrated on the new baby. With Charles and Anne already of an age for school, the births of Andrew and, later, Edward, were like having a family all over again.

While it is still too early to judge fully, Edward, like Charles, seems to have inherited the serious, conscientious Coburg royal strain from his mother. He is a quiet, reserved, placid child. But Andrew is more a mixture of the mercurial Hanoverians, who are also in his mother's family tree, and the extroverted, thrusting Mountbattens of his father's. In Andrew there is not an ounce of shyness. He is a determined, resilient youngster, tousle-haired, energetic and agile, with a ready grin and a quick trick of hunching his shoulders about his ears in moments of excitement or surprise. Like his father before him, he is a considerable practical joker and not long ago kept the duty footman at Windsor Castle dashing fruitlessly from room to room in answer to a succession of ringing bells.

Last fall (1968), in keeping with the new royal tradition, Andrew was buzzed off to boarding school. The chances are that he will enjoy his schooldays even more than Anne did and certainly more than his brother Charles. Charles was a bit of a loner at school. Anne was one of the crowd. But the indications are that Andrew will be a leader, bossing the other kids, organising the japes and occasionally running foul of authority.

III

All four royal youngsters, as they grow up, will have a part to play in the future pattern of monarchy. But Charles, as the firstborn, is the important one, and has been all his life. He was born next in line to the Throne after his mother. In this, he has a decided advantage over his recent predecessors. His great-grandfather, later King George V, was a naval officer in his twenties when the death of his elder brother made him the next heir to the throne. His grandfather was a man in his middle years, virtually untrained for kingship, when his brother abdicated and monarchy was thrust so suddenly upon him. His mother, the present Queen, though trained for possible future monarchy from an early age by her grandmother, that far-sighted old lady, Queen Mary, was a girl of ten when the abdication changed the pattern of her life and made future queenship virtually inevitable. Charles, by contrast, was only two steps away from the Throne at the very moment he was born and already, in a childish way, aware of his future destiny when he was taken to Westminster Abbey at the tender age of three to witness his mother's coronation.

The unforeseen apart, Britain's next coronation will be his. But the wait could be a long one. His mother's health is good. Her reign could be as long as that of her great-great-grandmother, Queen Victoria. She is unlikely to abdicate in favour of her son, as Prince Philip made clear at a press conference in New York. He was asked when the Queen was likely to retire. "Are you asking me when the Queen is likely to die?" was his curt rejoinder.

While she may not believe in the Divine Right of Kings, as some few of her subjects still do, Queen Elizabeth II certainly regards monarchy as a divine calling ... a high office handed down to her by her father and which she holds in trust for her eldest son and those who come after him. To abdicate, in her view, would be to sacrifice some at least of the remaining value of monarchy. The longer a monarch is on the Throne, the more valuable he or she becomes. As the Victorian statesman, Disraeli, put it, "The longer the reign, the influence of the Sovereign must proportionately increase. Then it is that the Sovereign can appeal to a similar state of affairs that occurred perhaps thirty years before. A Minister who could venture to treat such influence with indifference would not be a constitutional minister but an arrogant idiot."

Prime ministers, like presidents, come and go. Monarchs re-

[269]

main, furnishing a link between one government and the next, sometimes—like Queen Victoria—between one generation and the next. Her great-great-granddaughter, Elizabeth II, has already outlived two prime ministers—Winston Churchill and Clement Attlee. She will almost surely outlive still more, and the day may come when long years of monarchy will enable her to tell some future prime minister, as her great-great-grandmother once did, "Your idea is not new. It was put forward by one of your predecessors. It was wrong then."

Lut if the Queen is unlikely to abdicate, neither is she likely to keep Prince Charles in that state of unblissful ignorance in which Victoria kept her eldest son. Even as a grown man, the Prince of Wales who finally became King Edward VII was not permitted a glimpse of his mother's state papers. The present Queen, by contrast, was shown the contents of the almost legendary royal "Boxes" by her father while he was still alive. She will assuredly show them to Charles in the same way, if, indeed, she has not already done so.

Until recent times, Charles was screened from public gaze as much as possible. His parents wanted his boyhood to be as free and "ordinary" as possible. As his father told an inquirer who wanted to know why the young prince was not at one of the royal garden parties, "There'll be plenty of time for that later on."

There was one morning, soon after he started day school, when his mother refused to let him go until the crowd of photographers and sightseers hanging round the school entrance had largely dispersed. He arrived at school that morning forty-five minutes late. The decision to send him to Cheam and Gordonstoun, while mainly taken because they were his father's old schools, was also partly influenced by their relative seclusion. During his early days at school the Queen appealed more than once to Britain's newspaper proprietors not to let their reporters and photographers hound him. With rare exceptions, she declined to let him participate in public life during his educational years. As a result of all this, up to the time he went to university he could still get around, if not unrecognised, at least largely unnoticed.

But as he grows to manhood the situation will change drastically ... indeed, is already changing. In the fall of 1967, for the first time, he took his place beside his mother for the annual state opening of Parliament. That December he flew to Australia as her official representative at the memorial service to the late prime minister, Mr. Harold Holt. Last year (1968), during the summer vacation from university studies, he embarked upon a crash course specially designed by his father as an object-lesson in what lies ahead. He visited the docks at Tilbury, government departments in Wales, and a newspaper office in Edinburgh. He descended 70 feet below the streets of London to talk with mole-men tunnelling a new subway. At a Nottinghamshire colliery he went 2000 feet down the shaft to watch miners at work at the coal-face. He flew in a Royal Air Force training plane, getting the feel of the controls as a necessary prelude to learning to fly, something his father rightly considers a necessity for a twentieth-century Prince of Wales. Returning to Cambridge, he sandwiched further flying lessons at a convenient R.A.F. establishment into his student curriculum to such purpose that in January, after 14½ hours' tuition, he was able to fly solo for the first time.

A visit to Cardiff, the Welsh capital, designed as an appetiser to this year's ceremonial investiture as Prince of Wales, was not without incident. Smoke bombs were let off, an egg hit the accompanying police car as the royal party arrived at the civic centre, and shouting demonstrators flourished placards and banners adorned with such slogans as "No Foreign Prince," "Pretender Go Home" and "Charlie Windsor Shall Not Pass." Showing himself in some respects very much his father's son, Charles walked boldly away from his police bodyguard and towards the demonstrators.

"What does it say?" he asked one of them, pointing to a placard lettered in Welsh.

"You should learn to speak Welsh," came the retort. "It refers to Llewelyn, Prince of Wales, massacred by the English." (This piece of ancient history, incidentally, happened nearly 700 years ago, in 1282.)

"I am trying to learn Welsh," said Charles, who had, in fact, been practising the tongue-twisting language with the aid of a set of recordings. "And I am sorry I am not very well up in history."

"I can believe that," retorted the demonstrator, bluntly but rudely. "You got into university with two poor examination results. You are not very brilliant."

Prince Philip, looking on, saw and heard this exchange with a grin of parental pride on his lean features, and as Charles walked back to the rest of the party, a demonstrator called after him, "I admire your guts—but not your job."

The Queen, concerned for her son's safety, has asked for extra security precautions at his investiture in July and during the term previous which he was due to spend at the University College of Wales in Aberystwyth. The decision to send Charles to Aberystwyth for a term had already brought criticism from the Welsh Committee of the National Union of Students, in the form of a motion which stated, "This committee in no way feels privileged at welcoming this special student; the only person who can feel privileged is the said student."

A small but vociferous group of hotheaded Welsh Nationalists have gone further. "They will have to move in armed troops to invest Charles as Prince of Wales," they have threatened . . . and pointed their argument by exploding a time-bomb in Cardiff's Temple of Peace building, only a few hours before the council responsible for arranging the £200,000 investiture was due to meet there under the chairmanship of Lord Snowdon.

For Charles, the way ahead promises to be more stormy than it was for that previous Prince of Wales who became the Duke of Windsor. And as he graduates fully into public life, the pattern of monarchy may really begin to change.

Elizabeth II, though she is Queen of Canada, Australia and the rest of the Commonwealth every bit as much as she is Queen of the United Kingdom, is quite unable to pay her other realms and territories more than the occasional flying visit. Yet these other peoples would naturally like to see more of her. It was a former Australian ambassador to France, speaking in London, who told the British bluntly, "There is a very strong inclination here to regard the Queen as your private property. She is not. She is our Queen of Australia just as much as she is your Queen, and we rather resent the suggestion that her right place is at Buckingham Palace, Balmoral or Sandringham. Many of us would like to see the day when she can come out for two months a year to live in her residence in Canberra and carry on her duties there as Queen of Australia just as she carried them on here as Queen of the United Kingdom."

For several reasons, not the least of which are personal family reasons, it is clearly impracticable for the Queen to shift from London to Canberra, from Canberra to Ottawa, from Ottawa to one or other of the remaining several countries equally justified in demanding her presence. But there would seem to be fewer valid reasons why her son and heir, the Prince of Wales, a youthful bachelor with fewer personal ties to keep him in Britain, should not fill in the long years of waiting to step into his mother's shoes by living in Australia for a year or part of a year, in Canada similarly, and so on. Such periods of residence could be important in preserving the fabric of monarchy during the years ahead, strengthening what the late Sir Winston Churchill, a statesman with a gift for the right graphic phrase, once referred to as "the mystic circle of the Crown." Living on the spot, moving about with rather more freedom than his mother could ever hope for, Charles would be enabled to come to a proper understanding of each country in turn, its people and its problems.

To a very considerable extent, the future of the monarchy is in the youthful hands of the latest Prince of Wales. There is hardly the slightest doubt that the monarchy will last the lifetime of the present Queen. Between them, she and her husband, Prince Philip, provide exactly the right combination of rock-steady respectability and regal glamour to fit the pattern of a changing age. But in a country where hereditary peers have already had their wings sharply clipped, and are likely to have them clipped still further, it is doubtful if even Britain's monarchy, firm-rooted though it is in centuries of history and tradition, could easily survive another abdication or similar upheaval. Nor would a monarch of extremes long survive in today's Britain. While the government, on the one hand, would tolerate no interference from a politically minded monarch, the people, on the other hand, would certainly not be prepared to indulge the follies and extravagances of a playboy prince. Either would bring the monarchy into disrepute and almost certainly to an end.

Much therefore depends upon Charles, both as a person and as a prince, and it is fortunate perhaps that he has inherited so many of his mother's duller but more solid qualities ... reserve, seriousness, an undoubted regality, and a high sense of duty. To these inherited qualities, thanks to his father, can be added the fact that he has already seen and experienced more of life outside the high railings of Buckingham Palace than his mother has or ever will have. Thanks also to his father, he has developed rather than inherited a fairly forthright nature, which enables him to meet people like the hotheaded Welsh Nationalist demonstrators he encountered in Cardiff rather more than halfway.

It would be a bold man who would venture to prophesy how Charles will turn out—or, indeed, what Britain and the world will be like—on that (probably) distant day when he succeeds to the throne. But the odds—birth and breeding, background and upbringing—would seem to be very much in his favour.

And on that distant day when he succeeds to the throne, I wonder if memory will take him back through the years to a small incident of childhood. It was a few weeks before his mother's coronation. I had been given the task of brushing the Queen's coronation robe before it was taken to Westminster Abbey for the actual ceremony. It took two of us to carry the voluminous ermine-trimmed robe of rich royal purple, with the

Queen's EIIR cypher woven into it with gold thread, down from the third floor wardrobe room to the Queen's corridor and spread it carefully out along the red carpet. Kneeling, I set to work to impart a smooth, satiny flow to the rich velvet. I was busy in this fashion when Charles, then only four years old, came out of the elevator and began hop-skipping his way along the corridor towards his mother's sitting room. He stopped when he saw me, watching with interest. Boy-like, he wanted to know what I was doing.

"Brushing the Queen's robe ready for the coronation," I told him.

A small, childish frown etched itself across his brow. "Who is the Queen?" he asked.

I paused in my brushing and told him that the Queen was his mother. Briefly and simply, in words suitable for four-year-old understanding, I explained about the coronation. It was, I like to think, his first lesson in the meaning of monarchy.

Seemingly the lesson struck. Some weeks later, when the coronation had come and gone, I overheard him in childhood conversation with his small sister, Anne. "There won't be another coronation for years and years and years," he was telling her. "And when there is, it will be mine."